The Melodramatic Imagination

The Melodramatic Imagination

Balzac, Henry James, Melodrama, and the Mode of Excess

with a new Preface

Peter Brooks

Yale University Press
New Haven and London

Library of Congress catalog card number: 75-43305
International standard book number: 0-300-06553-1 (pbk.)
Set in Baskerville type.
Printed in the United States of America.

A catalogue record for this book is available from the British Library.
The paper in this book meets the guidelines for permanence and durabil-
ity of the Committee on Production Guidelines for Book Longevity of the
Council on Library Resources.

10 9 8 7 6 5 4 3 2

Contents

to Sophie Brooks Laing

this new edition for another

Preface 1995

The Melodramatic Imagination Twenty Years After

This book was written out of an attempt to clarify something I didn't quite grasp—an element that I felt to be part of our experience in reading great writers who could not be wholly constrained within a realist aesthetic. This experience appeared to be connected to our response to popular forms of representation that we held to be not quite respectable yet found animating and somehow necessary. Melodrama—less as a genre than as an imaginative mode—came to seem the key to understanding this elusive element. As I began unearthing stage melodramas from the library stacks, the term *melodrama* imposed itself more and more as the contours of a coherent mode of imagining and representing began to take shape.

Work with a neglected or disdained concept such as melodrama inevitably brings a kind of anxiety of solipsism. You find yourself wondering, Does anyone else see it this way? Does anyone else care? Most gratifying has been the gradual discovery that I was not alone in thinking about the role of the melodramatic imagination in modern literature and culture. The book got off to a slow start but has gained a readership that evidently felt, as I did, that melodrama as I've tried to describe it—with critiques and revisions—belongs in our cultural and critical repertory.

Since this book's publication in 1976, then, its argument has had a respectable afterlife in literary criticism. A renewed attention to popular cultural forms has brought a willingness to recognize the melodramatic element in the work of such authors as Balzac, James, Dostoevsky, and indeed a recognition that the melodramatic mode is an inescapable dimension of modern consciousness. Beyond the confines of literary criticism, one now finds the term melodrama much more frequently used in everyday discussion of literature and other forms of art—not solely through the influence of this book, of course, but because of a convergence of cultural interests. Melodrama has become an issue in modern painting—for instance, in the work of such artists as Robert Longo, whose grandiose canvases call on the imagery of popular entertainment. Most striking of all to me is my belated discovery that this book early on engaged a readership in a field I had merely alluded to, and of which I then knew practically nothing: film studies. Melodrama was becoming a key concept in the critical discussion of film—particularly Hollywood film of the 1940s and 1950s, and its later avatars, perhaps especially New German cinema—and *The Melodramatic Imagination* provided a historical and theoretical basis for a body of interesting work.

The timing of this convergence of interests is remarkable. I published a first sketch of the argument of this book in an essay, "The Melodramatic Imagination," that appeared in *Partisan Review* in 1972. In *Monogram*, journal of the British Film Institute, Thomas Elsaesser in 1972 published his seminal essay "Tales of Sound and Fury: Observations on the Family Melodrama," which provoked a reassessment of Hollywood melodrama, in the films of Douglas Sirk, especially, and Vincente Minnelli and Nicholas Ray, among others, and in the continuities between stage melodrama and silent cinema. Elsaesser's essay and my own, although addressing different bodies of material, crosscut in many ways: in our conception of melodrama as an expressionistic aesthetic, in our understanding of its affinity with certain psychoanalytic formulations, in our attention to the use of music and other nonverbal signs in melodrama's signifying practices, and in our histories of its origins in the bourgeois revolutions of the end of the eighteenth century. Elsaesser at one point even uses the phrase "melodramatic imagination," though so far as I know, neither of us had read the other at that time.

Such a convergence of interests suggests that by the early 1970s retrieving and discussing the concept of melodrama had taken on a certain cultural importance: workers in different (though not distant) fields who analyzed the imaginative modes in which cultural forms express dominant social and psychological concerns sensed that the category of the melodramatic needed revival because it pointed to—as no other term quite could—a certain complex of obsessions and aesthetic choices central to our modernity. In our efforts to characterize and describe certain kinds of fictions we confined ourselves to traditional categories— tragedy, comedy, romanticism, and realism. Sooner or later, melodrama—or some cognate thereof—was needed if we were to make sense of cultural forms that mattered to us.

Explaining why melodrama has proved so important for cultural critics and historians since the 1970s would be too large a discussion for a Preface, and it would repeat too much of what I tried to say in the Conclusion. I remain largely convinced by my own arguments: that melodrama is a form for a post-sacred era, in which polarization and hyperdramatization of forces in conflict represent a need to locate and make evident, legible, and operative those large choices of ways of being which we hold to be of overwhelming importance even though we cannot derive them from any transcendental system of belief. My thesis has been criticized for overemphasizing the ethical dimension of melodrama, its tendency to postulate a "moral occult": the hidden yet operative domain of values that the drama, through its heightening, attempts to make present within the ordinary. And I readily admit that heightening and sensation for their own sake, a dramaturgy of hyperbole, excess, excitement, and "acting out"—in the psychoanalytic sense— may be the essence of melodrama without any reference to ethical imperatives. I would still, however, contend that those melodramas that matter most to us convince us that the dramaturgy of excess and overstatement corresponds to and evokes confrontations and choices that are of heightened importance, because in them we put our lives—however trivial and constricted—on the line.

It is perhaps part of our postmodern sophistication that we don't quite take melodrama "straight" anymore—maybe no one ever did—but always with a certain ironic detachment. Yet, remarkably, as spectators we can demur from the melodramatic—find it a hoot, at times—and yet still be seriously thrilled by it. Excess can itself be thrilling, even when it is somewhat campy, even when—as in postmodern architecture—it is more a citation of past systems of meaning than a serious investment in present reality. Indeed, postmodernism has reveled in the revival of nineteenth-century melodramas—several have been restaged, especially in London, or reanimated in new versions, such as *Sweeney Todd* or the musical version of the epic melodramatic novel *Les Misérables*—as well as film and television transformations. However sophisticated we have become, the appeal of the melodramatic remains a central fact of our culture.

In addition to Elsaesser's essay, there have been a host of interesting discussions of film melodrama, especially women's melodrama—the melodramatization of the domestic sphere—in film and television serials. From *Stella Dallas* through the Hollywood films of Douglas Sirk (*Magnificent Obsession, All That Heaven Allows, Imitation of Life*) and the television series *Peyton Place* and *Dynasty*, a vast body of material that makes up our popular entertainment—our daily imaginative fare—has been retrieved for critical discussion through the perception that melodrama is a coherent aesthetic system, with a repertory of expressive features and devices that can be subjected to analysis—formal, sociological, and psychoanalytic.

The films of Sirk, for instance, have become a touchstone of popular domestic melodrama because they consistently offer a stylish refusal of the dailiness of the everyday. They insist that 1950s American reality be equal to the demands of the imagination for a heightening of existence, a more interesting psychic engagement of the ordinary transactions of urban and suburban life. The essential point may be that melodrama, even when it starts from the everyday—as it does in domestic and familial melodrama—refuses to content itself with the repressions, the tonings-down, the half-articulations, the accommodations, and the disappointments of the real. Melodrama's relation to realism is always oblique—it is tensed toward an exploitation of expression beyond. It insists that the ordinary may be the place for the instauration of significance. It tells us that in the right mirror, with the right degree of convexity, our lives matter.

Perhaps the most evident continuity between my discussions of nineteenth-century stage and novelistic melodrama and the studies of film melodrama lies in

early silent cinema, which almost inevitably, of necessity, looks to stage melodrama for its expressive effects. Because stage melodrama was born out of a wordless form, pantomime, and because it made its messages legible through a register
of nonverbal as well as verbal signs, it offered a repertory of gestures, facial
expressions, bodily postures and movements readily adapted to the silent cinema,
which could not help but be expressionistic in its acting and directorial styles.

A telling example here is D. W. Griffith. Especially pertinent is his *Orphans of the
Storm*, a film which, in its subject and setting, reaches back—with conscious intent
or not, I can't tell—to the French Revolution, the historical context in which melodrama (or proto-melodrama: it wasn't yet named) came into being. *Orphans of the
Storm* reworks a French melodrama of 1872, Adolphe Dennery's *Les deux orphelines*,
concerning two young women raised as sisters: Henriette, the daughter of peasants who almost disposed of her as an infant on the steps of Notre-Dame Cathe-
dral, and Louise, whom they rescued from those steps when they decided to keep
their own daughter, and who has gone blind. Henriette and Louise (played by Lil-
lian and Dorothy Gish) travel from the provinces to Paris in search of a medical
miracle, and instead encounter dark intrigue and nightmarish risk before Louise's
aristocratic birth is recognized and thereby produces the happy ending.

Griffith elaborates an expressionistic aesthetics of the body within a thematics
of the French Revolution—which was not part of Dennery's original—perhaps
from an intuitive understanding that here lies the inception of the imaginative
mode and its expressive repertory that he so successfully exploited. By setting
Orphans of the Storm during the Revolution, from its outbreak through the Terror,
Griffith pays tribute to the moment of origin of the imaginative mode—melodrama—making the "storm" a central metaphor not only of a crucible of modern history—and with repeated references, in the intertitles, to its unfortunate
replay, four years earlier, in the Bolshevik Revolution—but also of an enabling
condition of modern representation. Griffith's cinema is indeed technically similar to that bastard form that precedes and prepares melodrama, *pantomime dialoguée*,
in that the intertitles offer a skeletal structure of verbal meanings that the film
enacts and embodies. The intertitles are quite like those banners and placards that
are often presented in pantomime dialoguée, the display of the semantics of a situation, which often simply doubles the message the audience can deduce from the
action itself.

Henry James, reviewing the New York production of Dennery's play, singles out
for praise two *coups de théâtre* "as your French playwright who really knows his business manages them." Both are preserved in *Orphans of the Storm*. One is the
moment when the good brother, Pierre—thus far the ineffectual protector of
Louise, who has been kidnapped by his villainous mother, La Frochard—finally
revolts against the evil brother, Jacques, with the words: "As you say yourself, we

come of a race that kills!" This needs intertitling, since it cannot be communicated through gesture alone, though what is most memorable in the scene is Pierre's expression of manic joy and defiance, and his bodily movement of self-assertion, his casting off of years of subjection.

The other coup de théâtre noted by James needs no words at all. It is the moment when Henriette in her apartment recognizes the voice of Louise, singing in the street. In Griffith's film, this develops as a major sequence. As Henriette converses with the Countess (who will turn out to be Louise's mother, of course), Louise appears in a long view, at the very end of the street, groping her way forward, forcing herself to sing under La Frochard's command. Henriette's face meanwhile begins to register recognition, almost preconsciously. Then Henriette begins to tremble, her whole person seized with the drama of discovery. The scene then unfolds in the mode of panic action: Henriette leans from the window, with gestures of yearning, hope, desperate seeking. The spectator has the impression that she may throw herself into the street, while below, Louise casts about for the source of the voice calling to her.

It is a moment when the bodies behave nearly hysterically, if by hysteria we understand a condition of bodily writing, a condition in which the repressed affect is represented on the body. Indeed, Griffith's cinema is always on the verge of hysteria, and necessarily so, because hysteria gives us the maximal conversion of psychic affect into somatic meaning—meaning enacted on the body itself. The psychic overload, the hyperbole of the moment, is then confirmed by the arrival of the soldiers to arrest and imprison Henriette, by means of the *lettre de cachet* obtained by the father of her noble suitor, the Chevalier de Vaudrey. This crisis serves of course only to increase and justify an aesthetics of hysteria, because there can be no discharge of the overwhelming affect, as Henriette and Louise are again separated, and because the recognition between the Countess and Louise is again delayed.

I argue in this book that there is a convergence in the concerns of melodrama and of psychoanalysis—and indeed, that psychoanalysis is a kind of modern melodrama, conceiving psychic conflict in melodramatic terms and acting out the recognition of the repressed, often with and on the body. Now I have become convinced that the hystericized body offers a key emblem of that convergence, because it is a body preeminently invested with meaning—a body that has become the place for the inscription of highly emotional messages that cannot be written elsewhere, and cannot be articulated verbally. Hysteria offers a problem in representation: Freud's task, from the *Studies of Hysteria* onward, is learning to read the messages inscribed on the hysterical body—a reading that is inaugural of psychoanalysis as a discipline. Griffith appears to understand that whoever is denied the capacity to talk will convert affect into somatic form, and speak by way of the expressionist body.

The hysterical body is of course typically, from Hippocrates through Freud, a woman's body, and indeed a victimized woman's body, on which desire has inscribed an impossible history, a story of desire in an impasse. Such an impasse will be typical of Hollywood domestic melodrama. It is pertinent as well to Griffith's bodily enactments of moments of emotional crisis, and in general to the moments in which melodrama distorts the body to its most expressionistic ends. A notable example in *Orphans of the Storm* comes when Henriette is in the tumbrel, on the way to the guillotine, and makes her last farewell to Louise, who is in the street—the sequence formally intertitled, as a kind of set piece, "The Farewell." As she leans from the tumbrel for a last embrace from Louise, and their lips meet and are held long together, Henriette's body appears to be in an almost impossible position, tilted from the cart, rigid, already nearly inanimate, like a mummy or a puppet, a bleached image, *pallida morte futura*. It is a pure image of victimization, and of the body wholly seized by affective meaning, of message converted onto the body so forcefully and totally that the body has ceased to function in its normal postures and gestures, to become nothing but text, nothing but the place of representation.

May these cursory remarks on cinematic melodrama stand as tribute and thanks to a number of critics—Laura Mulvey, Tom Gunning, Christine Gledhill, David Rodowick, Charles Musser, Stephen Heath, Miriam Hansen, Ann Kaplan, Linda Williams, among others—who have opened new horizons for me and helped me think further about the implications of my study of melodrama. If literary criticism and theory have been useful to students of film, the debt now goes the other way as well: literary scholars have much to learn from the theoretical and critical work carried forward in film studies. One of the heartening characteristics of our moment in intellectual and scholarly life is that we are all reading one another—to the extent that we are able—across disciplinary boundaries, with a sense of recognition, and a sense that the aesthetic and cultural stakes are the same.

What we have learned, in the different spheres where melodrama has been studied, is that the melodramatic mode no longer needs to be approached in the mode of apology. We know about its limitations, its easier effects, and its more inauthentic thrills, but we have also learned that it is an exceptionally supple and adaptable mode that can do things for us that other genres and modes can't. Perhaps melodrama alone is adequate to contemporary psychic affect. It has the flexibility, the multifariousness, to dramatize and to explicate life in imaginative forms that transgress the traditional generic constraints, and the traditional demarcations of high culture from popular entertainment. The study of melodrama has come to be an engagement with an inescapable and central form of our cultural lives.

Preface to the original edition

This is a book about excess, about a mode of heightened dramatization inextricably bound up with the modern novel's effort to signify. My argument in the chapters that follow has its source in a movement—that of my own thinking—from adjective to substantive. In teaching and writing about a number of authors, particularly Balzac and Henry James, I found myself using the adjective *melodramatic*. It seemed to describe, as no other word quite did, the mode of their dramatizations, especially the extravagance of certain representations, and the intensity of moral claim impinging on their characters' consciousness. Within an apparent context of "realism" and the ordinary, they seemed in fact to be staging a heightened and hyperbolic drama, making reference to pure and polar concepts of darkness and light, salvation and damnation. They seemed to place their characters at the point of intersection of primal ethical forces and to confer on the characters' enactments a charge of meaning referred to the clash of these forces. Reading these novelists with a full awareness of their ambitions more and more appeared to me to pose problems and to demand understanding of the melodramatic mode: a certain theatrical substratum used and reworked in the novelistic representations.

If *melodramatic* seemed a necessary descriptive term (the question will be treated in more detail in the first chapter), I yet needed to know more accurately what the word meant. This implied (perhaps with naive realism) an attempt to find out what melodrama itself was. The end of this exploration might have been an impasse: the descriptive use of an adjective—especially when applied in such an extended manner—might have proved to have precious little to do with the noun from which it derived. Yet I found, to the contrary, that melodrama itself was of the utmost pertinence: to defining the adjective, to controlling and deepening its broader meaning, and to an understanding of such authors as Balzac, Dickens, Victor Hugo, Dostoevsky, Conrad, James—indeed, to an understanding of an important and abiding mode in the modern imagination. It is this process of reflection, leading from the use of melodramatic as a descriptive term and analytic perspective back to melodrama as a dramatic genre and an aesthetic, that has determined my choice of material and its organization.

My "discovery" of the pertinence and importance of melodrama no doubt has something to do with a recent renewal of critical interest in the forms of popular literature. The detective story, science fiction, children's literature, popular music, commercial art have all recently come to be seen as valid subjects of critical study. The renewed attention directed to them may derive in part from an increasing interest in the sociology of culture and in part from an implied lesson of structural anthropology and linguistics, that man's sense-making in sign-systems is omnipresent and that all its forms have functional similarities. Still more important may be the extent to which contemporary writers and artists have themselves turned to popular and even commercial forms and conventions to renew the vocabulary of their art in an age of what John Barth has called "the literature of exhaustion." [1] The most sophisticated art and literature, concerned with their own ontology, suspicious of their relationship to the tradition in which they stand, have sought to make use of structures and stereotypes from the most widely distributed and unselfconscious fictions and objects, which may furnish the contemporary literary equivalent of what Claude Lévi-Strauss, in his analyses of myths from "primitive" societies, calls "mythemes." The novel, born as a resolutely popular form, may in particular need to renew itself through contact with the most grossly popular forms, as Leslie Fiedler has recently argued. [2]

The novel clearly yearns after its nineteenth-century status as *summa*. The novel during the nineteenth century was of course, on the whole, far from playing the sophisticated endgames of contemporary fiction; it still maintained an unembarrassed relation to popular entertainment. Balzac began by writing penny dreadfuls and later conceived himself the rival of such successful serialists as Alexandre Dumas and Eugène Sue. Even Henry James felt himself to be working within an inherently popular medium, one that offered unexplored possibilities for craftsmanship and formal perfection, yet remained rooted in the desire for compelling, exciting fabulation. He accepted the constraints of serialization and liked to think of himself as competing for recognition in a literary marketplace. As he once said in criticism of Flaubert, even if we are so strangely constituted as to be nine-tenths purely literary, there must still be that one-tenth that makes us want to buy the book and sit down to read it. So that part of the "anxiety of influence," to adopt Harold Bloom's phrase, with which any nineteenth-century novelist contended derived from the popular, from the literature of the masses, the fictions that influence on a scale that higher literature must regard with envy.[3] And in the nineteenth century, among the most vital of these popular forms is melodrama.

Melodrama, as I have been using and shall use it, is a descriptive term. It has, of course, most often been used pejoratively, and its rehabilitation as a descriptive critical category requires some argument, which the following chapters will try to provide where it seems necessary. There are in fact some signs pointing to a revaluation of melodrama in theatrical criticism: the importance of the term and the concept has been argued in perceptive essays by Eric Bentley and James L. Rosenberg, in Robert B. Heilman's *Tragedy and Melodrama,* and in recent studies of the genre—Michael R. Booth's *English Melodrama,* David Grimsted's *Melodrama Unveiled,* James L. Smith's *Melodrama.*[4] Some of these authors suggest—Bentley most explicitly and persuasively—that melodrama at heart represents the theatrical impulse itself: the impulse toward dramatization, heightening, expression, acting out. Then to conceive melodrama as an eternal type of the theatre, stretching from Euripides to Edward Albee, is a logical step, and one that Rosenberg, Heilman, and Smith explicitly make and document. Yet here I think the term may become so extended in its meaning that it loses much of its usefulness, at least for our purposes. When Euripides, Shakespeare, and Molière all become melodramatists at least some of the time, and when tragedy becomes only a special subset of melodrama, we lose a sense of the cultural specificity of the genre. While recognizing that melodrama, like such other terms as *romanticism* and *baroque,* may be legitimately extended to represent constants in imaginative literature, it seems to me more interesting that melodrama (like romanticism and baroque, in fact) can also be located historically and culturally, that there is a form, calling itself melodrama, that comes into existence near the start of the nineteenth century, and that this form itself is vital to the modern imagination. The adjective *melodramatic* will take on greater critical force, greater definitional use, if we can refer back from it to a relatively well-characterized set of examples under the head of melodrama. In the "real" melodramatists of the nineteenth century, we find the structure of an aesthetic worth talking about because it shows in such clear outline what much nineteenth-century literature—that of what I

have called the melodramatic imagination—must take as its premises
and expressive techniques.

There is not in this study an attempt to "cover" the field of
melodrama even as so defined: no attempt to give a coherent history of
the genre or a full conspectus of its varieties. Since my primary interest
is in deriving the melodramatic from melodrama, in defining and
sharpening the adjective by the substantive, it seemed best to
concentrate on a body of material which, under scrutiny, would
permit me to disengage the typical structures and ambitions of the
genre. My point of reference in melodrama proper is almost exclusively "classic" French melodrama as it came to be established at the
dawn of the nineteenth century—in the aftermath of the Revolution—
and as it endured, with modifications and complications, into the
1860s, to be relayed, eventually, by the cinema and then by television.
This point of reference is not entirely arbitrary, since it includes the
original state of melodrama—Pixerécourt is regarded as the founder of
the genre—and the period of its greatest flourishing, when it
dominated the stages of Paris and included in its audiences the
greatest mixture of social classes. Here in particular must lie my
justification for neglecting British and American melodrama in favor
of French. Not only were the word and the genre of French invention
(and a clear instance of exportation from France to England and then
America), the classic examples of French melodrama were written for
a public that extended from the lower classes, especially artisans and
shopkeepers, through all sectors of the middle class, and even
embraced members of the aristocracy—including the Empress Jose-
phine herself at one moment. Whereas in England, melodrama seems
quickly to have become exclusively entertainment for the lower orders,
indeed, in the Surreyside houses, for the mob. Good society stayed
away from the theatre, until later in the century, when smaller, more
elite houses began providing "drawing-room melodrama."[5] In
France, where the theatre had long been and continued to be a
glorious tradition and a necessary social institution, melodrama, at
least during the first thirty years of the century (high and low culture
would tend to diverge further later on), was remarkably encompassing. This suggests why French melodrama, while radically democratic
in style, pitched to a popular audience, strove toward more coherence
as an entertainment, toward greater aesthetic self-consciousness in
regard to its effects and their means. While my choice of point of
reference excludes some of the amusing later exploitations and

transformations of the genre in late nineteenth-century England and America, it may have the merit of concentration and coherence.

I shall not, then, make much of an attempt to recount a linear history of melodrama; rather, I shall only make use of melodrama's history as it contributes to defining the melodramatic mode. In terms of my enterprise as I have defined it, I have been able to isolate and to talk about melodrama only as it becomes significant, by which I mean only as it becomes part of a larger sense-making enterprise that is touched upon by my own critical and interpretive gestures. Traditional literary history explicitly or implicitly claims the possibility of arranging literary events in a diachronic pattern that is itself the basis of explanation, and which has, whether the claim is voiced or not, almost of necessity the logic of the causal chain. Most often, such history has given what Geoffrey Hartman describes as "picaresque adventures in pseudo-causality." [6] It cannot be otherwise, for the very claim to causal explanation is undermined by the necessary failure in totality. Surreptitiously, it is more often teleology that takes over as the controlling principle: history becomes a *development*, heading toward realization in a genre, an author, a work. To the extent that literary history addresses itself to the dynamics of a particular genre—its metaphorically biological emergence, flourishing, and wane—it can illuminate, especially when it acts as a study in intertextuality, considering the interaction of the texts defining the space known as the genre. More often, however, generic literary history falls victim to its biological metaphor, or to arguments of source and influence, or else to a tracing of thematic constants and their variations.

None of these means of addressing the question seems appropriate to our concern, which is not melodrama as a theme or a set of themes, nor the life of the genre per se, but rather melodrama as a mode of conception and expression, as a certain fictional system for making sense of experience, as a semantic field of force. The only way in which I find myself able to make sense of melodrama as a sense-making system is through the act of interpretation itself, through the discovery of meaning and its particular coördinates, which means that melodrama is recaptured and understood only insofar as it can be touched by my own critical gesture. To the extent that this critical gesture is exercised within historical coördinates, we can say that literary history itself is a product of the act of interpretation. It is itself a form of interpretation, one that proceeds to plot, on the diachronic axis, points derived from analysis of the synchronic axis.

The organization of my study, then, follows as much as possible the path of my own interpretive thinking. It opens with a brief encounter with Balzac and James, in order to pose the problems of reading and interpretation that motivated an exploration of melodrama, and then moves back to suggest the relevance of melodrama itself to the melodramatic. The second chapter proceeds to explore the structure of stage melodrama as a system of meaning. Chapter 3 addresses a problem of representation and semantics posed with particular acuteness by melodrama and, at the same time, crucial in the enterprise of the nineteenth-century novel. It is only in chapter 4 that the questions of the "origins" and evolution of melodrama are addressed, and the points of tangency between melodrama and more respectable, "higher" literary forms discussed; this gives an opportunity to direct suspicion toward traditional versions of the literary history of French Romanticism. Then in chapters 5 and 6, Balzac and Henry James, who throughout have been the major figures of reference, are more intensively explored within the interpretive field provided by melodrama.

This organization inevitably results in lacunae. If there is a certain amount of attention given to the birth of melodrama, its constitution as a new genre at the moment of decadence of the old and at the moment of social and ethical upheaval, there is only the briefest mention of its transformations and the modes of its survival into our time—for melodrama is by no means finished, either as outlook or as aesthetic genre. The concluding chapter briefly notes the contemporary persistence of melodrama as a pervasive if unrecognized cultural form, but the question clearly deserves more extended treatment. Nor is there any orderly survey of those other novelists who most significantly belong to the melodramatic mode, whose work is most illuminated by reference to melodrama. The figure whose absence may most be felt is Dostoevsky, a direct heir of Balzacian melodrama and one of the novelists who puts melodramatic representations to most effective use. My study makes no claim to be complete; I hope that it may have value as a beginning.

Writing of this book was made possible by the award of a Guggenheim Fellowship in 1973-74, and it is a pleasure to express publicly my gratitude to the John Solomon Guggenheim Memorial Foundation for its generous support. Previously, some preliminary research in France had been facilitated by a Grant-in-Aid from the

American Council of Learned Societies. My research in France was aided by many kindnesses from librarians, particularly at the Bibliothèque de l'Arsenal, and from friends. I owe a special debt of thanks to Mme Chemin of the Bibliothèque André Monglond (directed by Pierre Viallaneix), at the University of Clermont-Ferrand, and to Mlle Ducoing of the Bibliothèque Historique de la Ville de Paris.

Some parts of the book originally appeared, usually in very different form, in periodicals, and some were first presented as lectures. A version of part of chapter 1 was first a lecture under the auspices of the Yale English Department, at the kind instigation of Harold Bloom and David Thorburn; it was first published in *Partisan Review* (vol. 39, no. 2, 1972), then reprinted in *Romanticism: Vistas, Instances, Perspectives*, edited by David Thorburn and Geoffrey Hartman (Ithaca, N.Y.: Cornell University Press, 1973). A French translation of an earlier version of part of chapter 2 was published in *Poétique* (no. 19, 1974) as "Une esthétique de l'étonnement: le mélodrame." I take this opportunity to acknowledge all that I owe to the precept and conversation of two of the editors of *Poétique*, Tzvetan Todorov and Gérard Genette. Part of this chapter has also been published as "The Aesthetics of Astonishment" in *The Georgia Review* (vol. 30, no. 2, 1976). A preliminary version of chapter 3 was first presented as a lecture to the Comparative Literature Colloquium at Yale, at the invitation of Thomas M. Greene, and then published in *New Literary History* (vol. 5, no. 3, 1974), under the editorship of Ralph Cohen. A very early version of the mid-section of chapter 5 first appeared under the title "Balzac: Melodrama and Metaphor," in *Hudson Review* (vol. 22, no. 2, 1969).

The other debts of gratitude, less specific but utterly real, are to the friends and colleagues who, through their willingness to engage in discussion of these and related problems, fed my own thinking: Richard Poirier, Michael Holquist, David Thorburn, Geoffrey Hartman, Paul de Man, Victor Brombert, Robert Lifton, Richard Sennett, Alvin Kernan. They have all, at one point or another in the process of writing, been in my mind as ideal readers and critics. The manuscript was read and criticized with generous acuity by Philip Lewis. The need to plumb the depth of popular literature of the romantic period was first suggested to me, years ago, by Harry Levin, a teacher whose high example remains before me. Among the students on whom I first tried out some of these ideas, two deserve special thanks for the

intensity and quality of their response: David A. Miller and Susan
Goode Crulli. Typing of the final manuscript was performed with
admirable patience and care by Sheila Brewer. And Ellen Graham of
Yale University Press was a most helpful and genial editor.

1

The Melodramatic Imagination

> Qu'on n'aille pas s'y tromper, ce n'était pas peu de chose que le mélodrame; c'était la moralité de la Révolution!
>
> —Charles Nodier

OVERTURE

There is at the start of Balzac's first major novel, *La Peau de chagrin*, a passage that indicates how we should read Balzac, how he locates and creates his drama, and, more generally, how the melodramatic imagination conceives its representations. When Raphaël de Valentin enters a gambling house to play roulette with his last franc, a shadowy figure crouched behind a counter rises up to ask for the young man's hat. The gesture of surrendering one's hat forthwith elicits a series of questions from the narrator:

> Is this some scriptural and providential parable? Isn't it rather a way of concluding a diabolical contract by exacting from you a sort of security? Or may it be to oblige you to maintain a respectful demeanour toward those who are about to win your money? Is it the police, lurking in the sewers of society, trying to find out your hatter's name, or your own, if you've inscribed it on the headband? Or is it, finally, to measure your skull in order to compile an instructive statistic on the cranial capacity of gamblers? [1]

The gestures of life call forth a series of interrogations aimed at discovering the meanings implicit in them. The narrative voice is not content to describe and record gesture, to see it simply as a figure in the interplay of persons one with another. Rather, the narrator applies pressure to the gesture, pressure through interrogation, through the evocation of more and more fantastic possibilities, to make it yield meaning, to make it give up to consciousness its full potential as "parable."

Throughout these opening pages of *La Peau de chagrin*, we can observe the narrator pressuring the surface of reality (the surface of his text) in order to make it yield the full, true terms of his story. In the face of the old man who takes the hat, we are told we can read "the wretchedness of hospital wards, aimless wanderings of ruined men, inquests on countless suicides, life sentences at hard labor, exiles to penal colonies." The gambling house itself elicits a contrast between the "vulgar poetry" of its evening denizens and the "quivering passion" of daytime gamblers. The crowd of spectators is like the populace awaiting an execution at the Place de Grève. Finally we reach this judgment: "Each of the spectators looked for a *drama* in the fate of this single gold piece, perhaps the final scene of a noble life" (9:17).

Use of the word *drama* is authorized here precisely by the kind of pressure which the narrator has exerted upon the surface of things. We have in fact been witnesses to the creation of drama—an exciting, excessive, parabolic story—from the banal stuff of reality. States of being beyond the immediate context of the narrative, and in excess of it, have been brought to bear on it, to charge it with intenser significances. The narrative voice, with its grandiose questions and hypotheses, leads us in a movement through and beyond the surface of things to what lies behind, to the spiritual reality which is the true scene of the highly colored drama to be played out in the novel. We have entered into the drama of Raphaël's last gold piece; that coin has become the token of a superdrama involving life and death, perdition and redemption, heaven and hell, the force of desire caught in a death struggle with the life force. The novel is constantly tensed to catch this essential drama, to go beyond the surface of the real to the truer, hidden reality, to open up the world of spirit.

One could adduce a multitude of other examples. There is always a moment in Balzac's descriptions of the world where the eye's photographic registration of objects yields to the mind's effort to pierce surface, to interrogate appearances. In *Le Père Goriot*, after a few initial lines of description of Mlle Michonneau, the narrator shifts into the interrogatory: "What acid had stripped this creature of her female forms? She must once have been pretty and well-built: was it vice, sorrow, greed? Had she loved too much, been a go-between, or simply a courtesan? Was she expiating the triumphs of an insolent youth?" (2:855). Reality is for Balzac both the scene of drama and mask of the true drama that lies behind, is mysterious, and can only be alluded to, questioned, then gradually elucidated. His drama is of the true, wrested from the real; the streets and walls of Paris, under pressure of the narrator's insistence, become the elements of a Dantesque vision, leading the reader into infernal circles: "as, step by step, daylight fades, and the song of the guide goes hollow when the visitor descends into the catacombs." (2:848).

The same process may be observed in Balzac's dramatizations of human encounters. They tend toward intense, excessive representations of life which strip the facade of manners to reveal the essential conflicts at work—moments of symbolic confrontation which fully articulate the terms of the drama. In *Gobseck*, for instance, the sinning Comtesse de Restaud, struggling to preserve an inheritance for her two illegitimate children, is caught in the act of trying to extort her husband's secrets from the oldest son (the legitimate child) when the comte rises from his deathbed:

> "Ah!" cried the comte, who had opened the door and appeared suddenly, almost naked, already as dried and shriveled as a skeleton. . . . "You watered my life with sorrows, and now you would trouble my death, pervert the mind of my own son, turn him into a vicious person," he cried in a rasping voice.
>
> The comtesse threw herself at the feet of this dying man, whom the last emotions of life made almost hideous, and poured out her tears. "Pardon, pardon!" she cried.
>
> "Had you any pity for me?" he asked. "I let you devour your fortune, now you want to devour mine and ruin my son."
>
> "All right, yes, no pity for me, be inflexible," she said. "But the children! Condemn your wife to live in a convent, I will obey; to expiate my faults toward you I will do all you command; but let the children live happily! Oh, the children, the children!"
>
> "I have only one child," answered the comte, stretching his shriveled arm toward his son in a gesture of despair. [2:665]

I have deliberately chosen an extreme example here, and in quoting it out of its context, I run the risk of simply confirming the view, popularized by Martin Turnell and others, that Balzac is a vulgar melodramatist whose versions of life are cheap, overwrought, and hollow. Balzac's use of hyperbolic figures, lurid and grandiose events, masked relationships and disguised identities, abductions, slow-acting poisons, secret societies, mysterious parentage, and other elements from the melodramatic repertory has repeatedly been the object of critical attack, as have, still more, his forcing of narrative voice to the breathless pitch of melodrama, his insistence that life be seen always through highly colored lenses. "His melodrama," Turnell comments, "reminds us not so much of Simenon or even Mrs. Christie as of the daily serial in the BBC's Light Programme." In his most waspish *Scrutiny* manner, Turnell adds, "It must be confessed that our experience in reading Balzac is not always very elevated and that his interests are by no means those of the adult." [2]

To the extent that the "interests of the adult" imply repression, sacrifice of the pleasure principle, and a refusal to live beyond the ordinary, Turnell is right, but his terms of judgment blind him to Balzac's characteristic drive to push *through* manners to deeper sources of being. Such representations as the scene I quoted from *Gobseck* are necessary culminations to the kind of drama Balzac is trying to evoke. The progress of the narrative elicits and authorizes such terminal articulations. The scene represents a victory over repression, a climactic moment at which the characters are able to confront one another with full expressivity, to fix in large gestures the meaning of their relations and existence. As in the interrogations of *La Peau de chagrin* we saw a desire to push through surface to a "drama" in the realm of emotional and spiritual reality, so in the scene from *Gobseck* we find a desire to make starkly articulate all that this family conflict has come to be about.

The desire to express all seems a fundamental characteristic of the melodramatic mode. Nothing is spared because nothing is left unsaid; the characters stand on stage and utter the unspeakable, give voice to their deepest feelings, dramatize through their heightened and polarized words and gestures the whole lesson of their relationship. They assume primary psychic roles, father, mother, child, and express basic psychic conditions. Life tends, in this fiction, toward ever more concentrated and totally expressive gestures and statements. Raphaël de Valentin is given a lesson by the old antiques dealer: "*Desire* sets us afire, and *power* destroys us"—terms which reveal the true locus and the stakes of his drama. Eugène de Rastignac, in *Le Père Goriot*, is summoned to choose between Obedience, represented by the family, and Revolt, represented by the outlaw Vautrin. The metaphoric texture of the prose itself suggests polarization into moral absolutes: Rastignac's "last tear of youth," shed over Goriot's grave, from the earth where it falls "rebounds into heaven." The world is subsumed by an underlying manichaeism, and the narrative creates the excitement of its drama by putting us in touch with the conflict of good and evil played out under the surface of things—just as description of the surfaces of the modern metropolis pierces through to a mythological realm where the imagination can find a habitat for its play with large moral entities. If we consider the prevalence of hidden relationships and masked personages and occult powers in Balzac, we find that they derive from a sense that the novelist's true subject is hidden and masked. The site of his drama, the ontology of his true subject, is not easily established: the narrative must push toward it, the pressure of the prose must uncover it. We might say that the center of interest and the scene of the underlying drama reside within what we could call the "moral occult," the domain of operative spiritual values which is both indicated within and masked by the surface of reality. The moral occult is not a metaphysical system; it is rather the repository of the fragmentary and desacralized remnants of sacred myth. It bears comparison to unconscious mind, for it is a sphere of being where our most basic desires and interdictions lie, a realm which in quotidian existence may appear closed off from us, but which we must accede to since it is the realm of meaning and value. The melodramatic mode in large measure exists to locate and to articulate the moral occult.

We shall return to these summary formulations. It is important first to extend our understanding of the kind of representation of social life offered by melodrama of manners, and to extend the demonstration beyond Balzac by calling upon his greatest admirer among subsequent novelists, Henry James. The melodramatic tenor of James's imagination was beautifully caught by his secretary, Theodora Bosanquet:

> When he walked out of the refuge of his study into the world and looked about him, he saw a place of torment, where creatures of prey perpetually thrust their claws into the quivering flesh of the doomed, defenseless children of light.[3]

James's moral manichaeism is the basis of a vision of the social world as the scene of dramatic choice between heightened moral alternatives, where every gesture, however frivolous or insignificant it may seem, is charged with the conflict between light and darkness, salvation and damnation, and where people's destinies and choices of life seem finally to have little to do with the surface realities of a situation, and much more to do with an intense inner drama in which consciousness must purge itself and assume the burden of moral sainthood. The theme of renunciation which sounds through James's novels—Isabel Archer's return to Gilbert Osmond, Strether's return to Woollett, Densher's rejection of Kate Croy—is incomprehensible and unjustifiable except as a victory within the realm of a moral occult which may be so inward and personal that it appears restricted to the individual's consciousness, predicated on the individual's "sacrifice to the ideal."

As Jacques Barzun has emphasized, James always creates a high degree of excitement from his dramatized moral dilemmas, partly because of his preoccupation with evil as a positive force ever menacing violent conflict and outburst.[4] Balzac did an apprenticeship in the *roman noir,* nourished himself with Gothic novel, melodrama, and frenetic adventure story, and invented cops-and-robbers fiction. These are modes which insist that reality can be exciting, can be equal to the demands of the imagination, which in Balzac's case means primarily the moral imagination, at play with large and basic ethical conflicts. With James, the same insistence has been further transposed into the drama of moral consciousness, so that excitement derives from the characters' own dramatized apprehension of clashing moral forces. A famous sentence from the preface to *The Portrait of a Lady* suggests James's intent. He is describing Isabel's vigil of discovery, the night she sits up and makes her mind move from discovery to discovery about Gilbert Osmond. "It is," says James, "a representation simply of her motionlessly *seeing,* and an attempt withal to make the mere still lucidity of her act as 'interesting' as the surprise of a caravan or the identification of a pirate." [5] The terms of reference in the adventure story are mocked; yet they remain the terms of reference: moral consciousness must be an adventure, its recognition must be the stuff of a heightened drama.

The excitement and violence of the melodrama of consciousness are obviously and derivatively Balzacian in such an early novel as *The American.* Christopher Newman's initiation into the epistemology of good and evil is represented through a dark ancestral crime hidden beneath, and suggested by, the gilded surface of Faubourg Saint-Germain society: depths open beneath the well-guarded social image of the Bellegarde family; crisis is revelation of sin, and Newman's consciousness must open to receive the lurid, flashing lights of melodrama. But even in James's latest and most subtle fiction—probably most of all in this fiction—the excitement of plot is generated almost exclusively from melodramatic conflict within the realm of the moral occult. There is a pressure similar to Balzac's on the textual surface, to make reality yield the terms of the drama of this moral occult. To take this time deliberately a low-keyed example—standing in apparent opposition to the quotation from *Gobseck* and thereby suggesting the range of the mode—from *The Ambassadors*: following the revelation of Mme de Vionnet's relationship with Chad, Strether goes to pay her a final visit. He stands for the last time in her noble apartment:

> From beyond this, and as from a great distance—beyond the court, beyond the *corps de logis* forming the front—came, as if excited and exciting, the vague voice of Paris. Strether had all along been subject to sudden gusts of fancy in connexion with such matters as these—odd starts of the historic sense, suppositions and divinations with no warrant but their intensity. Thus and so, on the eve of the great recorded dates, the days and nights of revolution, the sounds had come in, the omens, the beginnings broken out. They were the smell of revolution, the smell of the public temper—or perhaps simply the smell of blood.[6]

That this vision is ascribed to Strether's "gusts of fancy" does not really hedge the bet. James makes the "unwarranted" vision exist, wrests forth from "beyond" the facades of Paris sinister implications of impending disaster and chaos, and pervades the final encounter of Strether and Mme de Vionnet with "the smell of blood." Their relation has all along been based on Strether's "exorbitant" commitment to "save her" if he could. Here, the evocation of bloody sacrifice, eliciting a state of moral exorbitance, authorizes the intensity of the encounter, where Strether sees Mme de Vionnet as resembling Mme Roland on the scaffold, and where he moves to his most penetrating vision of the realm of moral forces in which she struggles. "With this sharpest perception yet, it was like a chill in the air to him, it was almost appalling, that a creature so fine could be, by mysterious forces, a creature so exploited" (2:284). Strether, and James, have pierced through to a medium in which Mme de Vionnet can be seen as a child of light caught in the claws of the mysterious birds of prey. After this perception, when Strether speaks it is to say, "You're afraid for your life!"—an articulation that strikes home, makes Mme de Vionnet give up "all attempt at a manner," and break down in tears. This stark articulation, which clarifies and simplifies Mme de Vionnet's position and passion, which puts her in touch with elemental humanity ("as a maidservant crying for her young man," thinks Strether) and with the ravages of time, finally differs little from the exchanges of the Comte and Comtesse de Restaud in *Gobseck*. The Jamesian mode is subtler, more refined, but it aims at the same thing: a total articulation of the grandiose moral terms of the drama, an assertion that what is being played out on the plane of manners is charged from the realm of the moral occult, that gestures within the world constantly refer us to another, hyperbolic set of gestures where life and death are at stake.

There is a passage from James's 1902 essay on Balzac (he wrote five in all) that touches closely on the problem of melodramatic representation. A notable point about the passage is that it constitutes a reparation, for in his 1875 essay, in *French Poets and Novelists,* James had singled out, as an example of Balzac's ineptitude in portrayal of the aristocracy, the episode in *Illusions perdues* where Mme de Bargeton, under the influence of her Parisian relation the Marquise d'Espard, drops her young provincial attachment, Lucien de Rubempré. The two women desert Lucien, whose dress is ridiculous and whose plebeian parentage has become public knowledge, in the middle of the opera and sneak out of the loge. Aristocratic ladies would not so violate manners, James argues in the earlier essay, would not behave in so flustered and overly dramatic a fashion. His view in 1902 is more nuanced and marks an effort to come to terms with those features of Balzacian representation that he had previously criticized:

> The whole episode, in "Les Illusions perdues," of Madame de Bargeton's "chucking" Lucien de Rubempré, on reaching Paris with him, under pressure of Madame d'Espard's shockability as to his coat and trousers and other such matters, is either a magnificent lurid document or the baseless fabric of a vision. The great wonder is that, as I rejoice to put it, we can never really discover which, and that we feel as we read that we can't, and that we suffer at the hands of no other author this particular helplessness of immersion. It is *done*—we are always thrown back on that; we can't get out of it; all we can do is to say that the true itself can't be more than done and that if the false in this way equals it we must give up looking for the difference. Alone among novelists Balzac has the secret of an insistence that somehow makes the difference nought. He warms his facts into life—as witness the certainty that the episode I just cited has absolutely as much of that property as if perfect matching had been achieved. If the great ladies in question *didn't* behave, wouldn't, couldn't have behaved, like a pair of nervous snobs, why so much the worse, we say to ourselves, for the great ladies in question. We

know them so—they owe their being to our so seeing them; whereas we never can tell ourselves how we should otherwise have known them or what quantity of being they would on a different footing have been able to put forth.[7]

James's somewhat baffled admiration here seems to arise from a perception of "surreality" in Balzac's representation of the episode: the fact that its hyperbolic mode and intensity make it figure more perfectly than would an accurate portrayal of manners what is really at stake for the characters and in their relationships. If reality does not permit of such self-representations, he seems to say, then so much the worse for reality. By the manner in which the thing is "done"—by the quality of the narrative performance—we know the characters essentially; we are, if not in the domain of reality, in that of truth.

James poses the alternative of judging Balzac's episode to be "either a magnificent lurid document or the baseless fabric of a vision," only to conclude that we cannot tell which it is. This alternative, and the admission of defeat in the attempt to choose, strikes close to the center of the problem of melodrama. The melodramatic imagination needs both document and vision, and it is centrally concerned with the extrapolation from one to another. When the Balzacian narrator pressures the details of reality to make them yield the terms of his drama, when he insists that Raphaël's gestures refer to a parabolic story, or when he creates a hyperbolic scene of Lucien de Rubempré's social defeat, he is using the things and gestures of the real world, of social life, as kinds of metaphors that refer us to the realm of spiritual reality and latent moral meanings. Things cease to be merely themselves, gestures cease to be merely tokens of social intercourse whose meaning is assigned by a social code; they become the vehicles of metaphors whose tenor suggests another kind of reality. In *The Ambassadors*, Strether's discovery of Mme de Vionnet's affair with Chad is essentially a vehicle for discovery of her entrapment and exploitation by "mysterious forces."

I. A. Richards has given an encompassing definition of metaphor as a "transaction between contexts," and in all these cases there is such a transaction: pressure on the primary context is such that things and gestures are made to release occult meanings, to transfer significance into another context.[8] Both Balzac and James weave a rich texture of metaphor in their prose, and the metaphors most often create an expanded moral context for the narrative. But it is not a question of metaphoric texture alone; it is rather that, to the melodramatic imagination, significant things and gestures are necessarily metaphoric in nature because they must refer to and speak of something else. Everything appears to bear the stamp of meaning, which can be expressed, pressed out, from it. The dandy de Marsay, refusing to recognize Lucien de Rubempré in *Illusions perdues*, lets his lorgnon fall "so singularly it seemed the blade of the guillotine" (4:624). In *Le Lys dans la vallée*, the narrator reads in the "forced smile" of the dying Mme de Mortsauf "the irony of vengeance, the anticipation of pleasure, the intoxication of the soul and the rage of disappointment" (8:1003). If with James we are tempted to believe that gestures receive their charge from social manners—this is after all the classic view of James—we find that, on the contrary, social signification is only the merest starting point for an immense construction of connotation. One could adduce this moment in *The Wings of the Dove* when Merton Densher learns from Milly Theale's servant that Milly can't receive him—his, and our, first indication that crisis is at hand:

> [Eugenio] now, as usual, slightly smiled at him in the process— but ever so slightly, this time, his manner also being attuned, our young man made out, to the thing, whatever it was, that constituted the rupture of peace.
>
> This manner, while they stood for a long minute facing each other over all they didn't say, played a part as well in the sudden jar to Densher's protected state. It was a Venice all of evil that had broken out for them alike, so that they were together in their anxiety, if they really could have met on it; a Venice of cold, lashing rain from a low black sky, of wicked wind raging through narrow passes, of general arrest and interruption, with the people engaged in all the water-life huddled, stranded and wageless, bored and cynical, under archways and bridges.[9]

The Jamesian prestidigitation is in full evidence here. Eugenio's slight, *too* slight smile is the detailed token which indicates a larger manner which in turn indicates a "rupture of peace"—already the vocabulary is taking on strong coloration—and this rupture then becomes the passageway for a flood of evil, conjuring into existence a new Venice of storm, darkness, and suppressed violence.

We will later pursue in more detail the questions posed by this metaphoricity of gesture that evokes meanings beyond its literal configuration. We may already be struck by the seeming paradox that

the total expressivity assigned to gesture is related to the ineffability of
what is to be expressed. Gesture is read as containing such meanings
because it is postulated as the metaphorical approach to what cannot
be said. If we often come perilously close, in reading these novelists, to
a feeling that the represented world won't bear the weight of the
significances placed on it, this is because the represented world is so
often being used metaphorically, as sign of something else. If we
consider in this light the implications of works like *The Beast in the
Jungle* and *The Sacred Fount*, we find that the more elusive the tenor of
the metaphor becomes—the more difficult it becomes to put one's
finger on the nature of the spiritual reality alluded to—the more
highly charged is the vehicle, the more strained with pressure to
suggest a meaning beyond. The violence and extremism of emotional
reaction and moral implication that we find in the prose of both James
and Balzac may in part derive from their lack of clear foundation,
their location in an ethical consciousness that cannot be shown to
correspond evidently and necessarily to the way life is lived by most
people. To the uncertainty of the tenor corresponds the exaggeration,
the heightening of the vehicle. The heightening and hyperbole, the
polarized conflict, the menace and suspense of the representations may
be made necessary by the effort to perceive and image the spiritual in
a world voided of its traditional Sacred, where the body of the ethical
has become a sort of *deus absconditus* which must be sought for,
postulated, brought into man's existence through the play of the
spiritualist imagination. We cannot, however, go farther without
saying more about melodrama, our understanding of the concept and
use of the word, its historical and ideological situation, and its nature.

The Uses of Melodrama

I have tried, in the opening pages, to suggest the pervasive
melodramatism of two such important novelists as Balzac and
James—the very consubstantiality of melodrama with the mode and
vision of their fiction. But I have not yet said anything in explication
or justification of the word melodrama, its appropriateness as a critical
term, the reasons for choosing a label that has a bad reputation and
has usually been used pejoratively. The connotations of the word are
probably similar for us all. They include: the indulgence of strong
emotionalism; moral polarization and schematization; extreme states
of being, situations, actions; overt villainy, persecution of the good,

and final reward of virtue; inflated and extravagant expression; dark plottings, suspense, breathtaking peripety. The few critics who have given serious attention to melodrama have noted its psychological function in allowing us the pleasures of self-pity and the experience of wholeness brought by the identification with "monopathic" emotion, in Robert Heilman's phrase.[10] Eric Bentley in particular has argued the importance of melodrama as a concept opposed to naturalism, its expression of emotion in the pure histrionic form of dreams, its representation of the quintessentially dramatic.[11] In his discussion of four dramatic types (melodrama, farce, tragedy, comedy), Bentley sets melodrama first, because it embodies the root impulse of drama—the need for dramatization, we might say, for acting out. The term seems useful, even necessary, because it points, as no other word quite does, to a mode of high emotionalism and stark ethical conflict that is neither comic nor tragic in persons, structure, intent, effect. That the term covers and, in common usage, most often refers to a cheap and banal melodrama—to soap opera—need not decrease its usefulness: there is a range from high to low examples in any literary field, and the most successful melodrama belongs to a coherent mode that rewards attention, in its literal as well as in its "extrapolated" forms. What I will say about melodrama in general will, I think, be relevant to the low examples as well as the high, with the difference that, as in all art, the low is attempting less, risking less, is more conventional and less self-conscious. At its most ambitious, the melodramatic mode of conception and representation may appear to be the very process of reaching a fundamental drama of the moral life and finding the terms to express it.

It might be idle to use the term melodrama were not the literal reference of the word also relevant to our critical perspective. Working back from the adjective *melodramatic*, used to describe such novelists as Balzac and James, one finds that melodrama proper, stage melodrama, constitutes a viable and important context. Considering mainly the "classical" melodrama as it was first established in France at the dawn of the nineteenth century, we find a fully realized, coherent theatrical mode whose structures and characteristics, in their very purity and even crudity, can teach us to read a whole body of modern literature with a finer perception of its project. Without now entering into the characteristics of stage melodrama (the subject of the next chapter) we can note that we find there an intense emotional and ethical drama based on the manichaeistic struggle of good and evil, a world where what one lives for and by is seen in terms of, and as determined by, the most fundamental psychic relations and cosmic ethical forces. The polarization of good and evil works toward revealing their presence and operation as real forces in the world. Their conflict suggests the need to recognize and confront evil, to combat and expel it, to purge the social order. Man is seen to be, and must recognize himself to be, playing on a theatre that is the point of juncture, and of clash, of imperatives beyond himself that are non-mediated and irreducible. This is what is most real in the universe. The spectacular enactments of melodrama seek constantly to express these forces and imperatives, to bring them to striking revelation, to impose their evidence.

In considering melodrama, we are in a sense talking about a form of theatricality which will underlie novelistic efforts at representation— which will provide a model for the making of meaning in fictional dramatizations of existence. The nineteenth-century novel needs such a theatricality, as we shall see, to get its meaning across, to invest in its renderings of life a sense of memorability and significance. With the rise of the novel and of melodrama, we find the entry into literature of a new moral and aesthetic category, that of the "interesting." Its first theoretician may be Diderot, in his effort to establish the new genre of *drame*, which owes much to the novels of Richardson and in some ways prefigures melodrama. Diderot's definition of *le genre sérieux*, intermediate between tragedy and comedy—but explicitly not a mixture of the two—addresses itself to the "interesting" in life. What he proposes is a serious attention to the *drama* of the *ordinary:* the "picture of the misfortunes that surround us," the representation of "dangers concerning which you must have trembled for your parents, your friends, yourselves." [12] This should not be read as a recommendation of naturalistic "realism." On the contrary, Diderot wants to exploit the dramatics and excitement discoverable within the real, to heighten in dramatic gesture the moral crises and peripeties of life. The *drame* is characterized by its specific form of the sublime, which Diderot defines through examples of hypothetical speeches: the father who has been nursed by his son in old age pronounces, "My son, we are even. I gave you life, and you have restored it to me"; or again, "Always tell the truth. . . . I so beg you by these feet that I warmed in my hands when you were in the cradle." [13] These enunciations, like the situations that frame them, possess the precise "sublimity" of melodramatic rhetoric: the emphatic articulation of simple truths and relationships, the clarification of the cosmic moral sense of everyday gestures. We are near the beginnings of a modern aesthetic in which Balzac and James will fully participate: the effort to make the "real" and the "ordinary" and the "private life" interesting through heightened dramatic utterance and gesture that lay bare the true stakes.

The word melodrama means, originally, a drama accompanied by music. It appears to have first been used in this sense by Rousseau, to describe a play in which he sought a new emotional expressivity through the mixture of spoken soliloquy, pantomime, and orchestral accompaniment.[14] The word then came to characterize a popular drama derived from pantomime (itself accompanied by music) that did not fit within any of the accepted genres. Music was an important element in Diderot's aesthetics; it was given a durable role in nineteenth-century theatre and then became a staple in the contemporary form that most relayed and supplanted melodrama, the cinema. Jean-Paul Sartre has well described the effect of musical accompaniment in the silent film, the kind of clear identity it provided for character and incident, the rigorous necessity it conferred on plot;[15] and we are aware of how in the speaking film it still determines mode and meaning. Even though the novel has no literal music, this connotation of the term melodrama remains relevant. The emotional drama needs the desemanticized language of music, its evocation of the "ineffable," its tones and registers. Style, thematic structuring, modulations of tone and rhythm and voice—musical patterning in a metaphorical sense—are called upon to invest plot with some of the inexorability and necessity that in pre-modern literature derived from the substratum of myth.

One might be tempted to consider melodrama as a constant of the imagination and a constant among literary modes: it could be (as some critics have proposed for the terms *baroque* and *romanticism*) one typological pole, detectable at all epochs, as Heilman suggests in his discussions of Elizabethan and Jacobean dramatists. Such a conception of the term is no doubt valid; one could reasonably, for instance, talk of the melodramatic in Euripides in distinction to the tragic in Sophocles.[16] But melodrama as we need the term—as it demonstrates its usefulness—appears to be a peculiarly modern form, and there is a specific relevance in the genre labeled melodrama as it comes into being in an historical context. The origins of melodrama can be accurately located within the context of the French Revolution and its aftermath. This is the epistemological moment which it illustrates and to which it contributes: the moment that symbolically, and really, marks the final liquidation of the traditional Sacred and its representative institutions (Church and Monarch), the shattering of the myth of Christendom, the dissolution of an organic and hierarchically cohesive society, and the invalidation of the literary forms—tragedy, comedy of manners—that depended on such a society. Melodrama does not simply represent a "fall" from tragedy, but a response to the loss of the tragic vision. It comes into being in a world where the traditional imperatives of truth and ethics have been violently thrown into question, yet where the promulgation of truth and ethics, their instauration as a way of life, is of immediate, daily, political concern. When the revolutionary Saint-Just exclaims, "Republican government has as its principle virtue; or if not, terror," [17] he is using the manichaeistic terms of melodrama, arguing its logic of the excluded middle, and imaging a situation—the moment of revolutionary suspension—where the word is called upon to make present and to impose a new society, to legislate the regime of virtue. A new world, a new chronology, a new religion, a new morality lay within the grasp of the revolutionary legislator and, particularly, in the power of his verbal representations. The Revolution attempts to sacralize law itself, the Republic as the institution of morality. Yet it necessarily produces melodrama instead, incessant struggle against enemies, without and within, branded as villains, suborners of morality, who must be confronted and expunged, over and over, to assure the triumph of virtue. Like the oratory of the Revolution, melodrama from its inception takes as its concern and raison d'être the location, expression, and imposition of basic ethical and psychic truths. It says them over and over in clear language, it rehearses their conflicts and combats, it reënacts the menace of evil and the eventual triumph of morality made operative and evident. While its social implications may be variously revolutionary or conservative, it is in all cases radically democratic, striving to make its representations clear and legible to everyone. We may legitimately claim that melodrama becomes the principal mode for uncovering, demonstrating, and making operative the essential moral universe in a post-sacred era.

This claim needs further attention. The Revolution can be seen as the convulsive last act in a process of desacralization that was set in motion at the Renaissance, passed through the momentary compromise of Christian humanism, and gathered momentum during the Enlightenment—a process in which the explanatory and cohesive force of sacred myth lost its power, and its political and social representations lost their legitimacy. In the course of this process, tragedy, which depends on the communal partaking of the sacred body—as in the mass—became impossible.[18] The crucial moment of passage could no doubt be located somewhere in the seventeenth century. Racine stands emblematically as the last tragic playwright (Milton as the last epic poet) and his career has much to tell us about the increasing difficulties encountered in the apprehension and representation of communal sacred imperatives. The Quarrel of the Ancients and the Moderns, at the close of the seventeenth century, was the symbolic annunciation of literature's divorce from the mythic substratum that had sustained it, its incipient privatization and desacralization.

Yet by the end of the Enlightenment, there was clearly a renewed thirst for the Sacred, a reaction to desacralization expressed in the vast movement we think of as Romanticism. The reaction both reasserted the need for some version of the Sacred and offered further proof of the irremediable loss of the Sacred in its traditional, categorical, unifying form. Mythmaking could now only be individual, personal; and the promulgation of ethical imperatives had to depend on an individual act of self-understanding that would then—by an imaginative or even a terroristic leap—be offered as the foundation of a general ethics. In fact, the entity making the strongest claim to sacred status tends more and more to be personality itself. From amid the collapse of other principles and criteria, the individual ego declares its central and overriding value, its demand to be the measure of all things. The *incipit* of modernity is the first page of Rousseau's *Confessions*, with its insistence on the uniqueness of his individual inner being, his difference from all other men, and on the necessity of expressing that being in its totality. The importance attached by Rousseau to his decision to "say all," *tout dire,* is a measure of the personalization and inwardness of post-sacred ethics, the difficulty of their location and expression.[19] A manic analogue can be found in Sade's effort to "say all" the possible crimes that are permitted in nature, in order to prove that the only principle to be observed is that of the individual's totalistic pleasure. Melodrama represents both the urge toward resacralization and the impossibility of conceiving sacralization other than in personal terms. Melodramatic good and evil are highly personalized: they are assigned to, they inhabit persons who indeed have no psychological complexity but who are strongly characterized.

Most notably, evil is villainy; it is a swarthy, cape-enveloped man with a deep voice. Good and evil can be named as persons are named—and melodramas tend in fact to move toward a clear nomination of the moral universe. The ritual of melodrama involves the confrontation of clearly identified antagonists and the expulsion of one of them. It can offer no terminal reconciliation, for there is no longer a clear transcendent value to be reconciled to. There is, rather, a social order to be purged, a set of ethical imperatives to be made clear.

Of particular pertinence in any discussion of desacralization and the response to it are two early Romantic ("pre-Romantic") forms that in fact nourish one another, melodrama and the Gothic novel. The Gothic novel stands most clearly in reaction to desacralization and the pretensions of rationalism; it represents, in D. P. Varma's phrase, a "quest for the numinous." [20] It reasserts the presence, in the world, of forces that cannot be accounted for by the daylight self and the self-sufficient mind. Yet the Gothicists typically discover that this reassertion of spiritual forces and occult issues hidden in the phenomenal world cannot lead to the resacralization of experience. The status of the Sacred as "wholly other"—in Rudolf Otto's phrase—as a realm of being and value recognized to be apart from and superior to man, is gone and is irrecoverable. Of the *mysterium tremendum*, which Otto defines as the essence of the Holy, only the *tremendum* can be convincingly revived.[21] This issue, in fact, is given a dramatization in M. G. Lewis' *The Monk* (along with Mary Shelley's *Frankenstein* the most interesting and intelligent of the Gothic novels) in relation to the problem of guilt and its definition. The monk's temptress, Matilda, proposes to call upon diabolical aid in the seduction of the virginal Antonia; and Ambrosio, who still retains vestigial belief in the Christian paradox of salvation, resists: "No, no, Matilda, I will not ally myself with God's enemy." In reply, Matilda is fiercely logical in her description of the changed ontology of the supernatural and Ambrosio's altered relationship to it:

> Are you then God's friend at present? . . . Are you not planning the destruction of innocence, the ruin of a creature whom he formed in the mould of angels? If not of daemons, whose aid would you invoke to forward this laudable design? Will the seraphims protect it, conduct Antonia to your arms, and sanction with their ministry your illicit pleasures? Absurd! But I am not deceived, Ambrosio! It is not virtue which makes you reject my

offer; you *would* accept it, but you *dare* not. 'Tis not the crime
which holds your hand, but the punishment; 'tis not respect for
God which restrains you, but the terror of his vengeance! [22]

In her logic of the excluded middle (the very logic of melodrama),
Matilda demonstrates that Ambrosio has moved out from under the
mantle of the Sacred, and that ethics are now determined, not by
virtue, but by terror. Her argument images a world in which God
exists still, but no longer as holy mystery and as moral principle
eliciting love, worship, and respect. No longer the source and
guarantor of ethics, "God" has become an interdiction, a primitive
force within nature that strikes fear in men's hearts but does not move
them to allegiance and worship. Guilt, in the largest sense, may itself
derive from an anxiety produced by man's failure to have maintained
a relation to the Sacred; it must now be redefined in terms of
self-punishment, which requires terror, interdiction of transgression,
retribution. As with the revolutionary legislator Saint-Just, we have a
new alternative basis for the ethical community: a sentimental virtue
(of the type often urged in Diderot's aesthetics) or else a retributive,
purgative terror.

The nature of the traditional idea of the Sacred is clarified in
Clifford Geertz' definition of the status it maintains in "primitive"
cultures: "The holy bears within it everywhere a sense of intrinsic
obligation: it not only encourages devotion, it demands it; it not only
induces intellectual assent, it enforces emotional commitment." [23] A
true Sacred is evident, persuasive, and compelling, a system both of
mythic explanation and implicit ethics. The traditional conception of
the *mysterium tremendum* requires man's sense of dependence in relation
to a "wholly other," and his feeling of being covered by it. The origin
of religious feeling, according to Otto, lies in the "primal numinous
awe," in a religious dread that may have at its root "demonic dread."
The radical emotion is a feeling of the "eerie" and "uncanny," then
elaborated into a concept in which the idea of awfulness and majesty
exists in relation to the numen. Matilda's theology starts from the
same point, but then evolves toward what a Christian theologian
would see as a perversion, the belief in spooks and spirits, where
"God" is merely one figure in a manichaeistic demonology. It is as if,
coming out of the Enlightenment, man had to reinvent the sense of the
Sacred from its source—but discovered it now skewed and narcissisti-
cally fascinated by its point of origin. There is a reassertion of magic

and taboo, a recognition of the diabolical forces which inhabit our world and our inner being. Since these forces achieve no sacred status as wholly other, they appear, rather, to abide within nature and, particularly, within nature's creature, man. If the *tremendum* has reasserted its presence and force against the reductions of rationalism, the *mysterium* that it should modify has been displaced from without to within. We are led back to the sources of the "uncanny" in the processes of desire and repression analyzed by Freud.[24] The desacralization and sentimentalization of ethics leads us—as Diderot discovered in reading Richardson—into "the recesses of the cavern," there to discover "the hideous Moor" hidden in our motives and desires.[25]

The Gothic castle, with its pinnacles and dungeons, crenellations, moats, drawbridges, spiraling staircases and concealed doors, realizes an architectural approximation of the Freudian model of the mind, particularly the traps laid for the conscious by the unconscious and the repressed. The Gothic novel seeks an epistemology of the depths; it is fascinated by what lies hidden in the dungeon and the sepulcher. It sounds the depths, bringing to violent light and enactment the forces hidden and entrapped there. *The Monk*—in which all the major characters are finally compelled to descend into the sepulcher of St. Clare, there to perform their most extreme acts—belongs to a moment of "claustral" literature, fascinated by the constrained and hidden, determined to release its energies.[26] The content of the depths is one version of the "moral occult," the realm of inner imperatives and demons, and the Gothic novel dramatizes again and again the importance of bringing this occult into man's waking, social existence, of saying its meaning and acting out its force. The frenzy of the Gothic, the thunder of its rhetoric, and the excess of its situations image both the difficulty and the importance of the breaking through of repression, where victory is achieved, as in melodrama, by finding the true stakes of the drama.

The Monk, this exemplary Gothic novel written at the dead end of the Age of Reason, at the intersection of revolution and reaction, offers a particularly forceful dramatization of passage into an anxious new world where the Sacred is no longer viable, yet rediscovery of the ethical imperatives that traditionally depended on it is vital. Rediscovery would then be the task of the individual ethical consciousness in struggle with an occult domain. Melodrama shares many characteristics with the Gothic novel, and not simply in the subjects that were traded back and forth between the two genres. It is equally preoccupied with nightmare states, with claustration and thwarted escape, with innocence buried alive and unable to voice its claim to recognition. Particularly, it shares the preoccupation with evil as a real, irreducible force in the world, constantly menacing outburst. Melodrama is less directly interested in the reassertion of the numinous for its own sake than in its ethical corollaries. Melodrama starts from and expresses the anxiety brought by a frightening new world in which the traditional patterns of moral order no longer provide the necessary social glue. It plays out the force of that anxiety with the apparent triumph of villainy, and it dissipates it with the eventual victory of virtue. It demonstrates over and over that the signs of ethical forces can be discovered and can be made legible. It tends to diverge from the Gothic novel in its optimism, its claim that the moral imagination can open up the angelic spheres as well as the demonic depths and can allay the threat of moral chaos. Melodrama is indeed, typically, not only a moralistic drama but the drama of morality: it strives to find, to articulate, to demonstrate, to "prove" the existence of a moral universe which, though put into question, masked by villainy and perversions of judgment, does exist and can be made to assert its presence and its categorical force among men.

I am not making an argument for the direct influence of melodrama proper on novelists like Balzac and James (though this influence is in fact discernible), I am rather suggesting that perception of the melodramatic in their work can usefully be grounded and extended through reference to melodrama. Melodrama is the reductive, literalistic version of the mode to which they belong. The world of melodrama constitutes a temptation for such as Balzac and James because it offers a complete set of attitudes, phrases, gestures coherently conceived toward dramatization of essential spiritual conflict. It provides the expressive premises and the clear set of metaphors that they will exploit in extrapolated form, with a more problematical sense of the relation between vehicle and tenor.

Such writers as Balzac and James need melodrama because their deep subject, the locus of their true drama, has come to be what we have called the "moral occult": the domain of spiritual forces and imperatives that is not clearly visible within reality, but which they believe to be operative there, and which demands to be uncovered, registered, articulated. In the absence of a true Sacred (and in the absence indeed of any specific religious belief of their own) they continue to believe that what is most important in a man's life is his ethical drama and the ethical implications of his psychic drama. Yet here they are dealing in quantities and entities that have only an uncertain ontology and, especially, an uncertain visibility: they are not necessarily seen in the same manner, if perceived at all, by an audience, since the social cohesion of an earlier society with a greater community of belief no longer obtains. In the manner of the melodramatist, such writers must locate, express, demonstrate, prove the very terms in which they are dealing. They must wrest them forth from behind the facades of life, show their meaning and their operation. Precisely to the extent that they feel themselves dealing in concepts and issues that have no certain status or justification, they have recourse to the demonstrative, heightened representations of melodrama.

We might, finally, do well to recognize the melodramatic mode as a central fact of the modern sensibility (I take Romanticism to be the genesis of the modern, of the sensibility within which we are still living), in that modern art has typically felt itself to be constructed on, and over, the void, postulating meanings and symbolic systems which have no certain justification because they are backed by no theology and no universally accepted social code. The mad quest of Mallarmé for a Book that would be "the Orphic explication of the earth," of Yeats for a synthetic mythology which would enable him to hold "in a single thought reality and justice," of Norman Mailer for dreams adequate to the moon—these are all versions of a reaction to the vertiginous feeling of standing over the abyss created when the necessary center of things has been evacuated and dispersed. Starting perhaps from Rousseau's decision that he must "say all" in his "enterprise without example," there is a desperate effort to renew contact with the scattered ethical and psychic fragments of the Sacred through the representation of fallen reality, insisting that behind reality, hidden by it yet indicated within it, there is a realm where large moral forces are operative, where large choices of ways of being must be made. The Promethean search to illuminate man's quotidian existence by the reflected flame of the higher cosmic drama constitutes one of the principal quests of the modern imagination. The melodramatic mode can be seen as an intensified, primary, and exemplary version of what the most ambitious art, since the beginnings of Romanticism, has been about.

What seems particularly important in the enterprise of the social melodramatists—and here one should include, beyond Balzac and James, Dickens, Gogol, Dostoevsky, Proust, Lawrence, to name only the most important—is their dual engagement with the representation of man's social existence, the way he lives in the ordinary, and with the moral drama implicated by and in his existence. They write a melodrama *of* manners. On the one hand, they refuse any metaphysical reduction of experience and refuse to reduce their metaphorical enterprise to the cold symbolism of allegory. They recognize, with Isabel Archer during her intense vigil, that "this base, ignoble world, it appeared, was after all what one was to live for" (2:197). On the other hand, they insist that life does make reference to a moral occult that is the realm of eventual value, and this insistence makes them more interesting and ambitious than more "behavioristic" novelists who, from Flaubert onwards, have suggested that there are not more things on earth than can be represented exclusively in terms of the material world. The melodramatists refuse to allow that the world has been completely drained of transcendence; and they locate that transcendence in the struggle of the children of light with the children of darkness, in the play of ethical mind.

It comes back, once again, to that alternative posed by James in reading Balzac, between the "magnificent lurid document" and the "baseless fabric of a vision." To make the fabric of vision into a document, to make the document lurid enough so that it releases the vision, to make vision document and document vision, and to persuade us that they cannot be distinguished, that they are necessarily interconnected through the chain of spiritual metaphor, that resonances are set up, electrical connections established whenever we touch any link of the chain, is to make the world we inhabit one charged with meaning, one in which interpersonal relations are not merely contacts of the flesh but encounters that must be carefully nurtured, judged, handled as if they mattered. It is a question, finally, of that attention to the significant in life that James captured in a famous line of advice to young novelists: "Try to be one of the people on whom nothing is lost." [27] To be so sensitized an instrument, one upon whom everything leaves a mark, with whom everything sets up a correspondence, is not simply to be an observer of life's surface, but someone who must bring into evidence, even into being, life's moral substance. So that the task of the writer is like that assigned by Balzac to the exiled Dante, in his tale *Les Proscrits*: "He closed himself in his room, lit his lamp of inspiration, and surrendered himself to the terrible demon of work, calling forth words from silence, and ideas from the night." (10:344).

2

The Aesthetics of Astonishment

> Je défie qu'on me montre *ici* un spectacle valable, et valable dans le sens suprême du théâtre, depuis les derniers grands mélodrames romantiques.
>
> —Antonin Artaud, *Le Théâtre et son double*

THE SIGN OF VIRTUE

To illuminate the aesthetics and ethics of melodrama, to suggest the raison d'être of the form and its expressive means, we might at once go to a characteristic instance, one that demonstrates the kind of concern that necessitates and "legitimizes" the mode. My example comes, inevitably, from Guilbert de Pixerécourt—the "Corneille of the Boulevards," as he was called—author of some hundred and twenty plays, the better half of them melodramas, who reigned as France's most popular dramatist from about 1800 to 1830, and who did more than anyone else to establish, codify, and illustrate the form. His "historical melodrama" of 1819, *La Fille de l'exilé*, recounts the perilous journey of Elizabeth, sixteen-year-old daughter of the exiled Stanislas Potoski, from Siberia to Moscow to seek the czar's pardon for her unjustly persecuted father. Along the way (in act II), she seeks shelter with a humble boatman who turns out to be none other than Ivan, the author of her family's disgrace, formerly a rich Boyard, now himself ruined, repentant, and punished by the death of his own daughter, Lizinska, whose tomb stands beside his rude cabin on the riverbank. A Tartar attack ensues, and Ivan's life is threatened. Elizabeth rushes forth from the cabin, takes the cross from her neck—the cross solemnly bestowed on her, in act I, by her blind mother (whose own mother's it was)—and suspends it above Ivan's head, saying: "Wretches! bow down before this revered sign, and do not forget that in this vast Empire any being placed under its protection is inviolable" (II,v). The Tartars are taken aback and let fall their arms. Ivan, who understands the deeper heroism of the gesture, turns to Elizabeth: "Angel from heaven! It is you, my victim, who protect my life!"

The emphatic phrase expresses the hyperbolic terms of the situation—a hyperbole resulting from the absolute purity and polarization

24

of the concepts in play: the victim saving the life of her persecutor, placing him under the protection of the sacred emblem which represents her mother's virtue and suffering (she has gone blind from the hardships of exile). The Tartars are grudgingly respectful, but they don't yet understand the full dimensions of the gesture, and Ivan must explicate to them Elizabeth's situation, show them why she is worthy not only of their "respect" but also of their "admiration." He tells first of her journey across four thousand versts of desolate landscape to intercede with the czar, an act of "sublime devotion, without parallel." To this the Tartars respond with what the stage direction calls "a cold admiration." Ivan has not finished: "But what will perhaps seem to you more astonishing, what appears to me the highest degree of heroism, is the generous movement that made her fly to my defense. Learn that it is I who have caused her misfortunes, and those of her family." He goes on to reiterate and underline the unique, remarkable, and impressive situation: that she who most should despise him, and who is worn down by months of journey through the wilderness, should come to his rescue and possess the force to save him. "Ah! such generosity overwhelms me! I lack the words to express... Elizabeth, all I can do is admire you and bow my head before you!" Which doing, he calls upon the Tartars to follow suit, to "render to virtue the homage that it merits." And by a "spontaneous movement," the Tartars close into a semi-circle around Elizabeth and fall on their knees. Their leader, Alterkan, offers his purse and speaks in their name: "Astonishing woman, take this gold." The gold is refused; the Tartars depart after Alterkan's benediction: "Go, follow out your generous design, and may you succeed."

This scene of dramatic confrontation and peripety takes us to the core of melodrama's premises and design. The spectacular excitement, the hyperbolic situation, and the grandiose phraseology that this situation elicits are in full evidence; and virtue, triumphant, sets off a movement of conversion that brings barbarian tribesmen to their knees. This may be easily identified as the stuff of melodrama. What needs greater attention is what dramaturgy, situation, and language exist for. Their focal point can perhaps best be characterized as the admiration of virtue. Confrontation and peripety are managed so as to make possible a remarkable, public, spectacular homage to virtue, a demonstration of its power and effect; and the language has continual recourse to hyperbole and grandiose antithesis to explicate and clarify the admirableness of this virtue. We must know unambiguously that

Elizabeth is a remarkable example of filial piety; we must know, further, that it is the man whom she has the right most to loathe that she is protecting; we must see that this makes its effect, that Tartars are brought to their knees and virtue goes forth, unscathed, with the blessings of the unvirtuous, who recognize its superior power. Virtue is publicly recognized and admired in a movement of astonishment: Elizabeth is "femme étonnante" (a phrase which echoes her father's exclamation in act I upon hearing of her project: "fille étonnante!") because her demonstration, her representation, of virtue strikes with almost physical force, astounding and convincing. The melodramatic moment of astonishment is a moment of ethical evidence and recognition.

Pixerécourt's identification as the "Corneille of the Boulevards" implies a contemporary recognition of his dramaturgy of heroic admiration, for this lies at the heart of Corneille's universe. Corneille's tragedies, indeed, cannot be understood in the context of "pity and terror," but must rather be seen as dramas of a heroism constantly tensed to surpass itself, to reach a point of self-mastery and self-renunciation which is truly *exemplary*, and which elicits the wonderment and applause, the *admiratio*, of characters and spectators alike.[1] The moral character trait that permits such exemplary behavior is heroic *générosité:* that nobility of soul, self-knowledge and self-fulfillment, that allows a moral triumph over the pettiness of ambition, calculation, worldly victories. When a contemporary *Traité du mélodrame* characterizes Pixerécourt's manner as "ce grandiose cornélien qui étonne" ("this Cornelian grandiosity that astonishes"), it accurately suggests the kind of heroics that constitute this new version of admiration and of *générosité*.[2] Both his effects and the moral conditions that they signify are more exteriorized than Corneille's, more simplified and hyperbolic. He presents, and his plays work toward, the *éclat* of virtue, its dramatic representation and enunciation as a real and invincible force in a universe beset with forces working toward its undoing.

That this, and all of Pixerécourt's plays, and melodrama in general, should employ a dramaturgy which tends toward such spectacular moments of public homage to virtue and its effects is our clearest indication of the issues at stake in melodrama. If the term *melodrama* most readily suggests an exciting and spectacular drama of persecuted innocence and virtue triumphant, it is important to see that this conflict and this structure do not, in the "classical" examples of the genre, exist merely for the sake of pathos and thrills, and that the peripeties and *coups de théâtre* are not extrinsic to the moral issues as melodrama conceives them. On the contrary, this play, and melodrama typically, not only employs virtue persecuted as a source of its dramaturgy, but also tends to become the dramaturgy of virtue misprized and eventually recognized. It is about virtue made visible and acknowledged, the drama of a recognition. Through her long struggle to bring recognition and vindication to her father—the struggle represented by the four thousand versts of desolation between Siberia and Moscow, by storm and flood, and, in the last act, by the walls and guards of the Kremlin masking approach to the czar—Elizabeth, herself virtue and innocence, is the bearer of the sign and proof of virtue and innocence, which have concrete analogues in the written confession given her by Ivan and in the "revered sign" of her mother's cross. Her task is to overcome all that would deny or submerge this sign and to bring it to a moment of total visibility and acknowledgment. This moment is solemnized by the czar's pardon of her father, and his acclaim of Elizabeth: "Placed above her sex by her sublime action, she has become at once its glory and its model" (III,xxiii). This is the final act of admiration, rendered publicly before the Imperial Court. The *reward* of virtue—whether it be Alterkan's "Take this gold" or the czar's restitution of Stanislas Potoski's title and lands—is only a secondary manifestation of the *recognition* of virtue.

The distinction is important for an understanding of what melodrama is really about. To see the struggle as one for virtue's salvation from persecution and its reward for misfortune is to misread the trials of virtue beleaguered. To remain with the example of *La Fille de l'exilé*, it is worth considering what happens in the remainder of act II. Ivan's resolution to ferry Elizabeth to Sarapul, whence she will find passage to Kazan, is thwarted by the arrival of a fearful storm which quickly becomes a flood, faithfully reproduced on stage. Lightning strikes and fires Ivan's cabin; he is carried off by the flood and rescued by villagers on the other shore. The waves begin to engulf the island where Elizabeth remains alone. At this point she goes on the grave of Lizinska, Ivan's daughter, to address a last prayer for salvation. And—"ô prodige!"—the rude board marking the tomb floats to the surface to provide a raft for Elizabeth, who then, cross in hand, floats down the river to safety, as Ivan and the villagers on the mountainside, upstage, fall on their knees to thank God for "this kind of miracle." The action is silly enough but appropriate, precisely, as a visual representation of the recognition of virtue and its signs. The emblem of the persecutor's celestial punishment—the grave marker of his daughter—is employed to save the innocent and virtuous from the malignant forces of nature, and to present her to the admiring eyes of all as the very type and symbol of invincible innocence.

The message could not be clearer. What makes it worth attending to at all is the process of its articulation. The scene is essentially a play of signs—the cross, the grave marker, the lightning bolt, the flood itself, Elizabeth's very posture—all of which have a high emotional and ethical charge: the cross is not only a religious symbol, but also a sign of a family's misfortune and fortitude; the grave marker represents Ivan's punishment by way of one innocent and his salvation by way of another; the flood condenses and projects onto nature all of the evil that Elizabeth must struggle against. All these signs hence have a depth of symbolic meaning. We are not, however, asked to meditate upon their connotations, to plumb their depths. On the stage they are used virtually as pure signifiers, in that it is their spectacular, their visual, interaction that counts. Their very simplicity and exaggeration permits such a use: they can be deployed in interplay and clash in such a manner that the struggle of moral entities is visible to the spectator.

The articulation of melodrama's messages in this kind of sign language—and in verbal language which strives toward the status of sign language in its use of a vocabulary of clear, simple, moral and psychological absolutes—suggests the extent to which melodrama not only employs but is centrally about repeated obfuscations and refusals of the message and about the need for repeated clarifications and acknowledgments of the message. The expressive means of melodrama are all predicated on this subject: they correspond to the struggle toward recognition of the sign of virtue and innocence. The repertory of dramaturgic and rhetorical devices, the stage settings and acting style, all concur in a dramatization of the trials and eventual victory of this sign. This demands further explication, but it might be premature without some preliminary attention to the structure of melodrama, a question implicated by what we have said about the misprision and recognition of virtue.

Structures of the Manichaean

Melodrama does, I think, have a structure distinct from that of either tragedy or comedy. In "classical" melodrama (my remarks here will be largely based on Pixerécourt and his principal rivals and emulators, particularly Louis-Charles Caigniez, himself dubbed "the Racine of the Boulevards," and Victor Ducange,[3] in the period extending roughly from 1800 to 1830), the play typically opens with a presentation of virtue and innocence, or perhaps more accurately, virtue *as* innocence. We see this virtue, momentarily, in a state of taking pleasure in itself, aided by those who recognize and support it. (As a father says in the first act of *La Fille de l'hospice*, by Cammaille Saint-Aubin: "Rejoice, Abel, they are talking of the virtues of your daughter!") So that, in distinction to tragedy, we do not begin at the point of crisis, the moment at which—the apparition of Hamlet's father's ghost, Hippolyte's decision to leave Troezene—the tragic mechanism ineluctably goes into action. Yet, typically, the first exchanges of the play, or even the title (*Coelina, or the Child of Mystery, The Woman with Two Husbands, The Man with Three Faces,* all by Pixerécourt; *Thérèse, or the Orphan of Geneva,* by Ducange; *The Madwoman of Wolfenstein,* by Caigniez), suggest mysteries or ambiguities hovering over the world, enigmas unresolved. And there swiftly supervenes a threat to virtue, a situation—and most often a person— to cast its very survival into question, obscure its identity, and elicit the process of its fight for recognition.

Certain *topoi* belong to this structure. Remarkably prevalent is the setting of the enclosed garden, the space of innocence, surrounded by walls, very often presenting at stage rear a locked grille looking out on the surrounding countryside or onto the highroad leading from the city. Down this road, into this space, a villain, the troubler of innocence, will come to insinuate himself, either under the mask of friendship (or courtship) or simply as intruder. The intruder may be driven out temporarily, but only to return triumphant since virtue has not yet established the full proof of its sign, the resolution of the liminary enigmas. The villain's return produces the topos of the interrupted fête, the violated banquet which, most often toward the end of act I or in act II, represents the triumph of villainy, the fall, eclipse, and even expulsion of virtue. In Pixerécourt's *Coelina, ou l'Enfant du mystère,* the villain, Truguelin, who has insinuated himself into the household to make propositions of marriage to Coelina in behalf of his nephew, but has been rejected, sends his messenger in act II—during the preparations for the wedding feast of Coelina and her chosen fiancé, Stéphany, in the garden—with "proof" that Coelina is not what she appears but "the child of crime and adultery." This leads to her being driven from the garden by her virtuous but choleric and credulous protector. In *La Femme à deux maris*, the fête organized for the return of Count Edouard de Fersen to his estate is interrupted by his wife's seducer and former husband—a wretched criminal long believed dead—slipping through the gates of the garden and coming to present his claim that Eliza is a conscious bigamist. The same setting, with the same movement of fall, requiring later exoneration and redemption, returns in Ducange, Caigniez, and other melodramatists. The violation and spoliation of the space of innocence stands as a recurrent representation of the dilemma confronting innocence. Expulsed from its natural terrain, its identity put into question through deceiving signs, it must wander afflicted until it can find and establish the true signs in proof of its nature.

An important alternative to this structure, one almost as prevalent —and bearing close affinities to its probable source, the Gothic novel—is that of the thwarted escape. We begin in a Gothic chamber, for instance that of *Les Mines de Pologne* (in the Castle of Minski, somewhere "in the Krapack Mountains"), and within a few scenes the path of escape for the virtuous prisoner appears open, only to be discovered by the villain-tyrant, and to lead, in act II, to a more frightful and subterranean dungeon, or even to the death sentence. *Le Château des Appenins* (Pixerécourt's version of *The Mysteries of Udolpho*), *La Forteresse du Danube*, and *Latude, ou Trente-cinq ans de captivité* present similar structures, but they by no means exhaust the register of prisons, dungeons, and oubliettes in Pixerécourt and his contemporaries. *La Fille de l'exilé* in fact presents a variant form of this second structure: the journey of quest from Siberia to Moscow is analogous to the movement toward escape, and the impediments brought by Tartars, tempestuous nature, and by the lord marshall of the Kremlin retard the accomplishment of the mission into the czar's presence. The "quest" structure seems particularly appropriate to those melodramas qualified as "historiques," of which *La Fille de l'exilé* and *Tékéli, ou le Siège de Montgatz* are Pixerécourt's outstanding examples. Quest, escape, and fall-expulsion-redemption are in fact all structures that can be classed in the general category of romance (in Northrop Frye's terms); and melodrama—which often takes its subjects from the novel—generally operates in the mode of romance, though with its own specific structures and characters.[4]

In the typical case, then, melodramatic structure moves from the presentation of virtue-as-innocence to the introduction of menace or obstacle, which places virtue in a situation of extreme peril. For the greater part of the play, evil appears to reign triumphant, controlling the structure of events, dictating the moral coördinates of reality. Virtue, expulsed, eclipsed, apparently fallen, cannot effectively articulate the cause of the right. Its tongue is in fact often tied by the structure of familial relationships: virtue cannot call into question the judgments and the actions of a father or an uncle or a guardian, for to do so would be to violate its nature as innocence. This imposed silence and passivity may be represented by a vow, usually in the name of the father, which cannot be violated. In *La Pie voleuse* (by Caigniez and d'Aubigny), Annette is ready to go to the scaffold rather than betray her father; and in Hubert's *Clara, ou le Malheur et la conscience*, the heroine cannot disculpate herself from a charge of infanticide because she has promised silence to the true criminal, her ostensible father—who will, to solve the problem, turn out not to be so. In the more complex case of Anicet-Bourgeois' *La Vénitienne*, the Bravo is bound to his repugnant role as masked executioner for the Republic of Venice by a contract that preserves his father's life as long as he continues his occupation. These melodramatic vows and pacts are always absolutes; there is never a thought of violating them. The same is true of the inexorable deadlines that force a race against the clock. Vow and deadline provide an iron and ineluctable structure of plotting, a version of ancient tragedy's *moira*. We are not encouraged to investigate the psychology of the vow or the logic of the deadline but, rather, to submit to their dramaturgy, their functioning as mechanism.

Virtue fallen and eclipsed will, then, not so much struggle as simply resist. Its recovery will depend most often upon recognition of error by those set in the position of judges (Coelina's protector, her "uncle" Dufour; the czar; the Chevalier Gontran and the Sénéchal in Pixerécourt's *Le Chien de Montargis*; Clara's true father; Clémentine's duped husband, in *La Folle de Wolfenstein*), which itself depends on the recognition of evil: an acknowledgment of the presence of deceitful signs and the willful misprision of virtue. In a striking number of cases, this recognition requires a full-fledged trial, the public hearing and judgment of right against wrong, where virtue's advocates deploy all arms to win the victory of truth over appearance and to explain the deep meaning of enigmatic and misleading signs. This clarification of signs—first of evil, then of virtue—is the necessary precondition for the reëstablishment of the heroine. But correct recognition by the judges does not always bring immediate resolution: the bearer of the sign of innocence may still be lost, pursued, disguised, and must be brought into the sphere of public recognition and celebration. The third act, then, most often includes duels, chases, explosions, battles—a full panoply of violent action which offers a highly physical "acting out" of virtue's liberation from the oppressive efforts of evil. This violent action of the last act is possibly melodrama's version of the tragic catharsis, the ritual by which virtue is freed from what blocked the realization of its desire, and evil is expelled from the universe. The stage set of the third act will usually be designed to permit a truly spectacular enactment of the ritual.

The play ends with public recognition of where virtue and evil reside, and the eradication of one as the reward of the other. The reward, I suggested, is ancillary to the recognition, just as the threat to virtue (as to female chastity) is basically the refusal to allow its claim, to recognize its nature. As in comedy, then, there is blockage and a victory over blockage. Yet what is being blocked in melodrama is very seldom the drive toward erotic union—so typically the case in comedy—which, if sometimes present, is no more than another indicator of virtue's right to reward. What is blocked, submerged, endungeoned is much more virtue's claim to exist qua virtue. Thus with the triumph of virtue at the end, there is not, as in comedy, the emergence of a new society formed around the united young couple, ridded of the impediment represented by the blocking figure from the older generation, but rather a reforming of the old society of innocence, which has now driven out the threat to its existence and reaffirmed its values. Nor is there, as in tragedy, a reconciliation to a sacred order larger than man. The expulsion of evil entails no sacrifice, and there is no communal partaking of the sacred body. There is rather confirmation and restoration.

These questions of plot structure imply in turn the structure of opposing forces in melodrama and their embodiment in the characters. Virtue is almost inevitably represented by a young heroine, though in classical French melodrama (unlike later American melodrama) she need not be a virgin, for it is moral sentiment more than technical chastity that is at issue.[5] She may be threatened by natural cataclysm (storm, flood, fire, shipwreck, avalanche, volcanic eruption, savage attack, to name only some of those favored by Pixerécourt), but it is the rare melodrama that does not have a villain. Coelina's persecutions depend directly on Truguelin, Floreska's (in *Les Mines de*

Pologne) on Zamoski; Thérèse is unremittingly pursued by Valther, Clémentine (in *La Folle de Wolfenstein*) is locked up by Usbald, and so on. Opposed to virtue and innocence stands the active, concerted denial of them in the person of evil, known traditionally as *le traître*, no doubt because he dissimulates, but also because he betrays and undoes the moral order. Betrayal is a personal version of evil. Indeed, evil must be fully personalized, the villain highly characterized, in the post-sacred universe, where personality alone is the effective vehicle of transindividual messages. This does not mean that the villain is complex or nuanced as a psychological character. On the contrary, he is reduced to a few summary traits that signal his position, just as, physically, do his swarthy complexion, moustache, cape, and concealed dagger. But he is strongly characterized, a forceful representation of villainy.

The villainy at issue may be more or less motivated: Truguelin operates out of the fear of discovery, Fritz and Usbald from the common motive of greed, Zamoski and Valther are the frustrated lovers of their victims, Macaire (in *Le Chien de Montargis*) is jealous of honors bestowed on Aubri. The motivation is in fact often summary and benefits from the briefest of explanations. And in almost every case it appears somewhat inadequate to the quantity of villainy unleashed. The villain is simply the conveyor of evil, he is inhabited by evil. If there is a typical discrepancy between motive and villainy, it is no doubt because evil in the world of melodrama does not need justification: it exists, simply. As Voltaire was forced to conclude in his poem on the Lisbon earthquake, "Le mal est sur la terre." [6] And the less it is adequately motivated, the more this evil appears simply volitional, the product of pure will. Like the Gothic novel, melodrama discovers evil as a component of mankind which cannot be denied or ignored but must be recognized, combated, driven out.

We have, then, an underlying structure in which virtue stands opposed to what will seek to discredit it, misrepresent, silence, imprison, or bury it alive. If the villain has a number of traditional acolytes and lieutenants, damned souls bound to his service, his success depends largely on the errors of perception and judgment committed by those who should rightfully be the protectors of virtue, especially the older generation of uncles, guardians, and sovereigns. The heroine is herself supported by a handmaiden, a fiancé, a faithful (often comic) peasant, or very often by a child. Especially when the heroine is herself beyond adolescence, a child may be introduced as the bearer of the sign of innocence. Thus in *Les Mines de Pologne*, the child of Floreska and Edwinski, whose name happens to be Angéla, performs all the ruses (stealing the jailer's keys, intercepting the password) that will allow her parents to escape; and in *La Forteresse du Danube*, the daughter, Célestine, disguises herself and enters the fortress to effect her father's escape. Other plays (Pixerécourt's *Le Pèlerin blanc* and *Les Ruines de Babylone*, Caigniez' *Le Jugement de Salomon*) put children at center stage as tests of other characters' reactions to patent virtue. For children, as living representations of innocence and purity, serve as catalysts for virtuous or vicious actions. Through their very definition as unfallen humanity, they can guide virtue through perils and upset the machinations of evil, in ways denied to the more worldly. Their actions, as their very existence, take on an aura of the providential: they suggest the workings of a higher, more enlightened design. Functionally analogous to the child, in the older generation, stands the figure of the *généreux*: a man, such as Edouard de Fersen in *La Femme à deux maris* or the Pastor Egerthon in *Thérèse*, who refuses to accept the discredit thrown on virtue and patiently guides it to rehabilitation.

In the clash of virtue and villainy, it is the latter that constitutes the active force and the motor of plot. If to what we have said about dramatic structures we add a consideration of affective structure, our starting point must be in evil. When contemporary audiences baptized the boulevard du Temple, site of the principal houses of melodrama, as the "Boulevard du Crime," they gave evidence of a recognition that, despite the ultimate triumph of virtue, it was the moment of evil triumphant that fascinated.[7] The villain had the *beau rôle*, the one played by the famous actors. The force of evil in melodrama derives from its personalized menace, its swift execution of its declarations of intent, its reduction of innocence to powerlessness. Evil is treachery in that it appears to unleash a cosmic betrayal of the moral order and puts all appearances into question.

In the manner of virtue, evil astonishes, and it disarms. "Tremble, all of you!" cries Truguelin at the end of act I, and we prepare to enter a period of nightmare in which innocence cannot speak its name, where we are the paralyzed spectators of all possible threats to the self. Evil's moment of spectacular power—when it imposes its rule and drives out innocence—provides a simulacrum of the "primal scene." It is a moment of intense, originary trauma that leaves virtue stunned and humiliated. In fact the true primal scene may be in the past (such as Truguelin's mutilation of Francisque, or Fritz's seduction of Eliza), and the breakthrough of evil in the play connects to it, offering a present horror fully explicable only in terms of a past horror, faithful in this to Freud's structure of pathogenetic trauma. Subjected to horror, virtue must undergo an experience of the unbearable. Melodrama is similar to tragedy in asking us to endure the extremes of pain and anguish. It differs in constantly reaching toward the "too much," and in the passivity of response to anguish, so that we accede to the experience of nightmare: Thérèse accused of murdering the mother of her beloved fiancé, Clara forced into the role of an infanticide to protect her father. The familial structure that melodrama (like Greek tragedy) so often exploits contributes to the experience of excruciation: the most basic loyalties and relationships become a source of torture. Like the characters, the audience experiences basic emotions in their primal, integral, unrepressed condition. From their full acting out, the "cure" can be effected. Virtue can finally break through its helplessness, find its name, liberate itself from primal horror, fulfill its desires. We awake from the nightmare.

It is clear that the affective structure of melodrama brings us close to the experience of dreams, a characteristic noted by Michael Booth and considered in detail by Eric Bentley, who calls melodrama "the Naturalism of the dream life" and notes its affinities with infantile narcissism, its indulgence in self-pity and grandiose emotional states, its exploitation of a childhood condition "when thoughts seem omnipotent, when the distinction between *I want to* and *I can* is not clearly made." [8] Bentley is surely right that the force of melodrama derives from the very origins of theatricality, of self-dramatization, in the infantile dream world. But it is important that, in talking of affective structure (which has most caught the attention of the best critics of melodrama), we not be deluded into thinking we are referring to the psychological structures of melodrama's characters. There is no "psychology" in melodrama in this sense; the characters have no interior depth, there is no psychological conflict. It is delusive to seek an interior conflict, the "psychology of melodrama," because melodrama exteriorizes conflict and psychic structure, producing instead what we might call the "melodrama of psychology." What we have is a drama of pure psychic signs—called Father, Daughter, Protector, Persecutor, Judge, Duty, Obedience, Justice—that interest us through their clash, by the dramatic space created through their interplay, providing the means for their resolution. This space can resemble the structure of mind, nearly in a Freudian sense, or a medium comparable to the dream text, but only because it works through the play of pure, exteriorized signs.

What we most retain from any consideration of melodramatic structures is the sense of fundamental bipolar contrast and clash. The world according to melodrama is built on an irreducible manichaeism, the conflict of good and evil as opposites not subject to compromise.[9] Melodramatic dilemmas and choices are constructed on the either/or in its extreme form as the all-or-nothing. Polarization is both horizontal and vertical: characters represent extremes, and they undergo extremes, passing from heights to depths, or the reverse, almost instantaneously. The middle ground and the middle condition are excluded. Melodrama proposes the total enjoyment of excruciating situations in their unadulterated or, in Robert B. Heilman's phrase, "monopathic" state.[10] Good or bad, characters are notable for their integrity, their thorough exploitation of a way of being or of a critical conjuncture. They exist at a moment of crisis as exemplary destinies. The peripeties through which they pass must be as absolute as they are frequent, bringing alternatively the victory of blackness and whiteness, and in each instance giving a full enunciation of the condition experienced. Polarization is not only a dramatic principle but the very means by which integral ethical conditions are identified and shaped, made clear and operative.

The fundamental manichaeism of melodrama, sensible in all its registers, should alert us that further analysis must be directed to the bipolar relation of its signs and their presentation, and must particularly be pursued on the plane of expression and representation. We must attend to melodramatic rhetoric. This will have the advantage of permitting us to confront what much criticism has simply dismissed from embarrassment: the overstatement and overemphasis of melodrama, its rhetorical excess. These are not accidental but intrinsic to the form.

The Rhetorical Drama

One of the most immediately striking features of melodrama is the extent to which characters tend to say, directly and explicitly, their moral judgments of the world. From the start, they launch into a vocabulary of psychological and moral abstractions to characterize themselves and others. Thus in act I, scene one, Coelina's maid and confidante says of Truguelin and his nephew, "I believe them to be envious, false, and wicked"; while in scene three Coelina will say of Francisque—the unfortunate mute who will turn out to be her father—that he "has an honest appearance." In *Le Pèlerin blanc*, the peasants Marceline and Gervais quickly inform us of correct valuations: "Let's not talk of that wicked woman. She is unworthy of the respectable name of Castelli" (I,ii). Moral epithets are strikingly frequent from the outset: people are "honest," "virtuous," "respectable," "interesting" (i.e., appealing to one's moral sympathies);[11] or else they are "false," "terrible," "wretched," "cruel," "tyrannical." Epithets can be almost as formulaic in melodrama as they are in the epic. Pixerécourt's biographer compiled from one play, *La Femme à deux maris*, a list which includes: "femme admirable," "femme vertueuse," "monstre inhumain," "respectable vieillard," "vil séducteur," "homme adroit," "bon jeune homme."[12] The epithet, a shorthand characterization—a sign for character—testifies to a concern to be clear and unambiguous, related of course to an audience unused to subtleties, but also constitutive of the play's structure and subject. Saying one's own and one another's moral nature is an important part of melodrama's action and substance.

This is particularly notable in the role of the villain, who at some point always bursts forth in a statement of his evil nature and intentions. Thus Truguelin's "tremble, all of you!"; or Valther's menace to Thérèse: "Yes! I will always pursue you! Everywhere! You will see me ceaselessly, a shadow following your footsteps! You will no longer have a single day of rest" (*Thérèse*, II,v); or Orsano, in soliloquy, in *L'Homme à trois visages*: "Courage, Orsano! the decisive moment approaches, and everything seems to promise success. Ungrateful Rosemonde! You will soon know the consequences of outraged love! For eight years my heart, wrung by your cruel disdain, has known only one feeling: revenge! It is not enough for me to have struck you in the object of your love: only your death and that of your father can quench my hatred, and both of you shall die" (I,viii). Such overt statement and celebration of evil may lead, later in the play, to another soliloquy, in which the villain recognizes his damnation, his entrapment in his integral identification with evil, and even expresses the pangs of belated remorse. Act III, scene one of *Coelina* is given over to Truguelin's monologue, in a "savage place" during a thunderstorm, and includes:

It seems to me that everything in nature unites to accuse me. These terrible words reverberate ceaselessly in my ears: no rest for the murderer! Vengeance! Vengeance! ... (*The words are repeated by the echo. Truguelin turns round in fright.*) Where am I? What menacing voice? Heaven! What do I see? This bridge, those rocks, this torrent, here, here it is that my criminal hand shed the blood of an unfortunate. O Lord! thou that I have so long neglected, see my remorse, my sincere repentance. Stop, wretch, cease to outrage Heaven! . . . Ah! if everyone knew what it costs to cease being virtuous, we would see few villains on earth.

We can judge from these examples the distance separating the melodramatic soliloquy from the soliloquy of tragedy, which, particularly in the theatre of Corneille and Racine, exteriorized a mind divided against itself, the dilemma of a situation where choice is both impossible and necessary, an anguished introspection. Here soliloquy has become pure self-expression, the venting of what one is and how it feels to be that way, the saying of self through its moral and emotional integers.[13]

If it is the villain who most fully articulates the stark monochrome of his moral character, his polarized position in the scheme of things, the heroine must express her continued identification with purity, despite contrary appearances. Thus Eliza in *La Femme à deux maris*: "I may be overwhelmed by misfortune, calumny may pour on me all its poisons; but heaven is witness that my soul remains pure" (II,xi). Or, in a striking example—since it constitutes act I, scene one in its entirety—from Hubert's *Clara*: "There are then creatures whose innocence does not preserve them from the persecution of men! Unfortunate Clara, for three months fugitive, wandering under a false name, charged with the weight of a crime of which your father is guilty... Your father! ah! what a painful thought! What torture not to be able to recall the image of a father without seeing the features of a villain, of a cowardly murderer! Such, however, is my destiny." When the opposing forces and allegiances confront each other, we have duels in the saying of self, bravura combats expressed in the tight exchange of *stichomythia*.

A specific and very significant version of self-expression is the act of self-nomination which echoes throughout melodrama, breaking through disguises and enigmas to establish true identities. Thus in *La Fille de l'exilé*, Ivan, meeting Elizabeth and discovering that she is the daughter of Stanislas Potoski ("Heaven. . . . Here then is one of my victims!"), elaborates his identity:

> *Ivan.* You see before you the artisan of your family's prolonged misfortunes.
> *Elizabeth.* You! Heaven! (*She steps back.*). . . .
> *Ivan.* You must be acquainted with my name. I am that man whom your father's curse must have followed relentlessly.
> *Elizabeth.* Who then are you?
> *Ivan.* Ivan.
> *Elizabeth.* Ivan!
> *Ivan.* Himself. Eighteen years ago, I was . . . [*etc.*].
>
>   [II,ii]

In varying forms, the statement "I am the man . . ." returns again and again. Both heroines and villains announce their moral identity, present their name and the qualifications attached to it, in the form of revelation. To take a particularly flowery example from Ducange's *Elodie, ou la Vièrge du monastère*: "Curse me then, daughter of Saint-Maur; the man of exile and misfortune, the man who dares adore the daughter of heaven, the hermit, finally, is Charles the Bold" (III,ii). The periphrastic epithets lead through the roles he and she have played into the name itself. Pixerécourt's *Le Belvéder* turns on its hero's three names, each of which represents a different layer of "truth." It should not surprise us that the *extrait de baptême*, the birth certificate, is regularly called upon to play an important dramatic role. It is the most important of those numerous melodramatic papers and parchments, forged or authentic, that are produced to establish true or seeming proof of moral identity. It is the sign which, almost in the etymological sense of "symbol," provides the missing half of the token, permitting identification and recognition.

The peripeties and coups de théâtre so characteristic of melodrama frequently turn on the act of nomination or its equivalent, for the moment in which moral identity is established is most often one of dramatic intensity or reversal. Such is the case both with Ivan's confession to Elizabeth and with Elizabeth's presentation of herself to the Tartars. In *Coelina*, the moment of sensation is created by the reading of the birth certificate, which gives on the one hand: [*Dufour*] "No, she is not my niece. She is the child of crime and adultery!"; and on the other: [*Coelina*] "You, my father! (*Francisque opens his arms and she throws herself into his embrace.*)" (II,vi). Or again, in *Tékéli*, we have the hyper-dramatic appearance of the hero through the windows at stage rear to confound the enemy messenger who is at that moment announcing his death. Or, finally, in Ducange's somber *Sept Heures!*, the striking of the clock, indicating her family's escape, allows Mlle d'Argens to turn the tables on her seducer and proclaim aloud her uncompromised allegiance to purity. These are all moments of clarification, of expressive victory, whose dramatic effect depends on the acting-out of moral identifications. Melodrama needs a repeated use of peripety and coups de théâtre because it is here that characters are best in a position to name the absolute moral attributes of the universe, to say its nature as they proclaim their own.

Melodramatic rhetoric, as our accumulating examples sufficiently suggest, tends toward the inflated and the sententious. Its typical figures are hyperbole, antithesis, and oxymoron: those figures, precisely, that evidence a refusal of nuance and the insistence on dealing in pure, integral concepts. The *Traité du mélodrame* claims that if in a traditional theatre one could distinguish among simple, ornate, and sublime styles, in melodrama "everything should be sublime, including the style of the simpleton." [14] The forcing of tone, the constant reaching toward sublimity of expression, is indeed characteristic. The search for a dramaturgy of admiration and astonishment needs a rhetoric that can infuse the banal and the ordinary with the excitement of grandiose conflict. Melodramatic rhetoric implicitly insists that the world can be equal to our most feverish expectations about it, that reality properly represented will never fail to live up to our phantasmatic demands upon it. The universe must always show itself as inhabited by cosmic ethical forces ready to say their name and reveal their operation at the correct gesture or word. To figure such a world, rhetoric must maintain a state of exaltation, a state where hyperbole is a "natural" form of expression because anything less would convey only the apparent (naturalistic, banal) drama, not the true (moral, cosmic) drama. Consider two examples from the first act of *La Fille de l'exilé*. When Elizabeth offers her mother a rose: "I thank you my daughter . . . Ah! I can best compare its sweet perfume to the innocence, to the purity of your soul" (I,ix); when Elizabeth has told her father of her project: "Elizabeth, this sublime conception is worthy of the blood that flows in your veins" (I,xii). Such bombastic sublimity forcibly removes us—and no doubt is intended to remove us—from the plane of actuality, to place us in a more rarefied atmosphere where

each statement is a total and coherent gesture toward the representation of the cosmic moral drama.

This rhetoric, supported by a diction and an acting style equally
inflated and unreal, forced toward the grandiose, postulates a very
different attitude toward the emotions and toward moral sentiments
from what we are used to. Melodrama handles its feelings and ideas
virtually as plastic entities, visual and tactile models held out for all to
see and to handle. Emotions are given a full acting-out, a full
representation before our eyes. We come to expect and to await the
moment at which characters will name the wellsprings of their being,
their motives and relations, the moment when a daughter cries out,
"O my father!" or a villain, "Yes, it is I who sought the ruin of
innocence!" They proffer to one another, and to us, a clear figuration
of their souls, they name without embarrassment eternal verities.
Nothing is *understood*, all is *overstated*. Such moments provide us with
the joy of a full emotional indulgence, the pleasures of an unadulterated exploitation of what we recognize from our psychic lives as one
possible way to be, the victory of one integral inner force.[15]

We may now advance the hypothesis that melodramatic rhetoric,
and the whole expressive enterprise of the genre, represents a victory
over repression. We could conceive this repression as simultaneously
social, psychological, historical, and conventional: what could not be
said on an earlier stage, nor still on a "nobler" stage, nor within the
codes of society. The melodramatic utterance breaks through everything that constitutes the "reality principle," all its censorships,
accommodations, tonings-down. Desire cries aloud its language in
identification with full states of being. Melodrama partakes of the
dream world, as Bentley and Booth suggested, and this is in no wise
more true than in the possibility it provides of saying what is in "real
life" unsayable. To stand on the stage and utter phrases such as
"Heaven is witness to my innocence" or "I am that miserable wretch
who has ruined your family" or "I will pursue you to the grave" is to
achieve the full expression of psychological condition and moral
feeling in the most transparent, unmodified, infantile form. Desire
triumphs over the world of substitute-formations and detours, it
achieves plenitude of meaning.

The critical resistance and embarrassment that melodrama may
elicit could derive from its refusal of censorship and repression—the
accommodations to the reality principle that the critical witness

himself then supplies, from his discomfort before a drama in which people confront him with identifications judged too extravagant, too stark, too unmediated to be allowed utterance. There is indeed a certain scandal in melodrama, most sensible at the moments of ringing identification, perhaps especially apparent when the villain lets loose in nomination of his villainy. That such pure destructive sentiment should exist, and should so acknowledge its existence, disturbs us, and the case is not substantially different where pure filial or maternal sentiments are expressed. The expressive language acts as carrier or conduit for the return of something repressed, articulating those very terms that cannot be used in normal, repressed psychic circumstances. When we say "father" and "daughter" in real life, it is in a lower key, with an accommodation to convention and the complication of experience. When we utter the same terms in melodrama, it is to name the plenitude of the pure, and excessive, feeling. The emotions and conditions expressed are almost overwhelming in their instinctual purity; they taste too strong. Yet here, surely, is a profound source of melodrama's appeal and persistence. The genre's very existence is bound to this possibility, and necessity, of saying everything. If we can sense its appeal (as well as its evident limitations), it must be because we are attracted to (though perhaps simultaneously repulsed by) the imaginary possibility of a world where we are solicited to say everything, where manners, the fear of self-betrayal, and accommodations to the Other no longer exert a controlling force.

The rhetorical breaking-through of repression is closely linked to melodrama's central effort to locate and articulate the moral problems in which it deals. Ethical imperatives in the post-sacred universe have been sentimentalized, have come to be identified with emotional states and psychic relationships, so that the expression of emotional and moral integers is indistinguishable. Both are perhaps best characterized as moral sentiments. Each play, we saw, is not only the drama of a moral dilemma, but the drama of the dilemma of the moral sentiment itself, seeking to say its name. The play's outcome turns less on the triumph of virtue than on making the world morally legible, spelling out its ethical forces and imperatives in large and bold characters. In the drama of the recognition of the sign of virtue, virtue achieves an expressive liberation from the "primal scene" that repressed, expulsed, silenced it, to assert its wholeness and vindicate its right to existence. As the persecuted victim confronts her oppressor with the claims of virtue to respect and recognition, so the sign of virtue eventually confronts all witnesses, on stage and in the audience, with its liberation from oppression and misprision. We noted that melodramas often contain liminary mysteries and enigmas: what cloud envelopes Coelina's birth? why has Francisque lost the power of speech? how has Eliza been led into bigamy? why has Thérèse changed her name? These apparent moral ambiguities turn out to be the result of plotting, evil, conscious obfuscation; they are not inherent to morality itself, which can and will be shown to be unambiguous. Evil will first be articulated and recognized, then the sign of virtue will begin to overcome its repression. By the end of the play, desire has achieved its satisfaction. No shadow dwells, and the universe bathes in the full, bright lighting of moral manichaeism. Hence the psychic bravado of virtue, its expressive breakthrough, serves to assure us, again and again, that the universe is in fact morally legible, that it possesses an ethical identity and significance. This assurance must be a central function of melodrama in the post-sacred universe: it relocates and rearticulates the most basic moral sentiments and celebrates the sign of the right. From its very inception during the Revolution—the moment when ethical symbols were patently, convulsively thrown into question—melodrama addressed itself to this relocation and rearticulation of an occulted morality.

This indicates the sense in which we can best speak of melodrama as a "democratic" art, or, as Charles Nodier wrote of Pixerécourt's theatre in 1835, "the only popular tragedy befitting our age." Nodier—a perceptive critic and a seminal figure in French Romantic letters, whose continued attention to Pixerécourt and to melodrama is significant in itself—is highly conscious of the special role of melodrama in the context of a post-sacred universe, specifically in the post-Revolutionary landscape. "I have seen them," he writes of Pixerécourt's plays, "in the absence of religious worship, take the place of the silent pulpit." For "in this difficult period, when the people could begin anew its religious education only at the theatre, there was in the application of melodrama to the fundamental principles of any sort of civilization a providential aspect." [16] If we go beyond Nodier's moralizing solemnity, his perception remains just: Pixerécourt's is a theatre of grandiose and absolute moral entities put within the reach of the people, a moral universe made available. That melodrama should have been born during the Revolution, and come of age with

Coelina in 1800, is far from an accident: in both its audience and its profound subject, it is essentially democratic. It represents a democratization of morality and its signs.

There are other elements as well that define the form's democracy. Villains are remarkably often tyrants and oppressors, those that have power and use it to hurt. Whereas the victims, the innocent and virtuous, most often belong to a democratic universe: whatever their specific class origin, they believe in merit rather than privilege, and in the fraternity of the good. Among the repressions broken through by melodramatic rhetoric is that of class domination, suggesting that a poor persecuted girl can confront her powerful oppressor with the truth about their moral conditions. If the social structure of melodramas often appears inherently feudal—landed gentry or bourgeoisie and their faithful yeomanry—it is also remarkably egalitarian, and anyone who insists upon feudal privileges is bound to be a villain. Melodrama is another episode in Nietzsche's "slave revolution" in morals, remarkably consistent in its insistence that the democracy of ethical relationships passes through the sentimentalization of morality, the identification of ethics with basic, familial psychic patternings.[17]

REGISTERS OF THE SIGN

Returning to the plane of expression and representation, we are prepared to recognize the full extension of the repertory of signs which render the world expressive of moral sentiments. Not only is the rhetorical mode based on verbal signs that provide a full enunciation of how and what one is, there is also a realm of physical signs that make one legible to others. When Edouard de Fersen confronts Fritz in *La Femme à deux maris,* he claims to have "irrecusable proof" of Fritz's guilt. Fritz asks what this could possibly be, and Edouard replies, "that your face has gone pale" (II,xi). In *Le Jugement de Salomon,* Lélia, the true mother, claims to have recognized her child "by sure signs." The false mother, startled, exclaims, "Sure signs!"; to which comes the reply, "Yes, madam, and I see another on your face" (II,vi). And at the end of *La Folle de Wolfenstein*:

> *Adolphe.* Arrest Usbald.
> *Usbald (angrily).* How now, Baron! It is on the testimony of this wretch that you dare ...
> *Adolphe.* On your own testimony, villain; your countenance has betrayed you.

[III,xiii]

Virtue also has its revealing signs for those who are alert observers. As the faithful fiancé says of the falsely accused Annette, in *La Pie voleuse*, "No, no, this cannot be; one cannot simulate this accent of the truth, this candor, sure signs of an honest soul" (III,iv); or, in *Clara*, "Crime has not this energetic accent, nor this eloquence of pain that only the soul can express (I,xii). Such signs, testifying to the ultimate moral transparency of even false faces, are comparable to the scar on Truguelin's hand, which he tries in vain to hide when pursued by justice, or indeed to Elizabeth's cross. They exceed in their significance the traditional birthmark of comedy, which permits the final recognition and untying of knots. In melodrama, these signs bear the message of the action and decipher the moral text of the world.

The conflict of signs, we noted, is often such that it must be resolved in public trial: the tribunal scene is a recurrent motif which we find in many of the proto-melodramas of the Revolutionary period, and in Pixerécourt, Caigniez, and Ducange. It represents a final public reading and judgment of signs which brings immanent justice into the open, into operative relation with men's lives. The most impressive example occurs in the last act of *Thérèse*, where the heroine is put on trial for murdering her mother-in-law-to-be, Madame de Sénange, who has in fact been the victim of Valther, who thought (in the dark) that he was striking Thérèse. Human justice is heading toward error; Pastor Egerthon, who has never ceased to believe Thérèse innocent, then obtains permission from the magistrate to try a ruse. This involves the simulation of extraterrestrial justice: Valther is presented with the "spectre" of Thérèse, done up in a white sheet. The result is all that could be desired: Valther falls to his knees: "Ah! ... Divine justice! ... stop ... terrible ghost! ... yes, yes, I am your murderer, I confess my crime ... spare me. I will publish your innocence, my crimes.... Here are the proofs." (III,xiv). Signs will out; evil declares itself and provides the symbols necessary to establish the recognition of virtue. After this, Egerthon can produce the final coup de théâtre: "Gentlemen, recognize in Thérèse the Countess of Volmar, and may the esteem of her suitor become the price of her tears and the recompense of her virtue."

The celebrated topos of the *voix du sang*—the secret impulse by which parents and children and siblings are irresistibly drawn to one another despite mistaken and lost identities—belongs to this realm of signs that organize and decipher the world. There is here a substratum of irreducible moral sentiment that can be called upon to act toward recognition or self-betrayal. Another dimension of signs appears in the choice of extreme physical conditions to represent moral states: the halt, the blind, and the mute people the world of melodrama, striking examples of past misfortunes and mysteries—Francisque, whose muteness conceals Truguelin's past villainies; Werner, whose blindness prevents him from recognizing his lost and maligned daughter, Eliza; the deranged Dalègre in *Latude*; the amnesiac Clémentine in *La Folle de Wolfenstein*; Caigniez's *Illustre Aveugle*. The moral drama has physical repercussions which stand before us as its living symbols. A further step brings us to the use of non-human actors—the dog of *Le Chien de Montargis*, the magpie of *La Pie voleuse*—which perform as clear indicators of the significant message to those who can read their non-verbal signs. But the whole question of mute action and sign needs larger development, in the context of gesture and action, to be pursued in the next chapter.

We should at present recognize that the drama of the sign is played out across a whole scale, or staff, of codes—or perhaps more accurately, a set of different registers of the sign, which can reinforce and also relay one another. Melodrama tends toward total theatre, its signs projected, sequentially or simultaneously, on several planes. One of the most important of these planes or registers is that of stage setting, conceived to support the rhetoric of moral recognition. Scenery, like all other elements of the genre, had to be expressive, and melodrama was in fact the form that had the most to do with transforming the traditions of stage decoration, moving toward a spectacular illusionism impossible earlier. Melodramatic playwrights were very often men of the theatre, with a hand in the staging of their plays; Pixerécourt was at once author, director, stage manager, and designer. His indications of decor and machinery, as of stage action, are elaborate and precise; and he was seconded by stage design workshops of great inventiveness. Cicéri, Charles Séchan, Daguerre, and others created both backdrops and *praticables* that could be used for spectacular actings-out of melodrama's emotions and issues.[18] *La Fille de l'exilé*, we saw, called for a flood in act II, complete with the grave-marker raft; and Pixerécourt's instructions to the *machiniste* give a sense of the admirable effect achieved. Act III of *Coelina* employs a mill by a millrace and an elevated bridge, on which the final sensational combats unfurl. *Christophe Colomb* includes a shipwreck of grandiose proportions. Ducange in both *Thérèse* and *Trente ans, ou la Vie d'un joueur* stages fires set by lightning. The last act of *Les Mines de*

Pologne, which presents the final barriers to escape from the Castle of Minski, shows us the outer gates of the castle, complete with moat, working drawbridge, operating rowboat on the moat, and snow storm. Audience satisfaction seems to have reached an apogee with *Le Belvéder*, which includes an eruption of Mount Etna, followed by a serene and magnificent sunset, the masterpiece of Daguerre. Melodrama—in ways that we shall have to explore further—is the main laboratory for the decisive break with the French classical theatre, a theatre of the word where visual representation and action were of minimal importance, and it brings a transformation of the stage into plastic tableau, the arena for represented, visual meanings.

Here actors could exercise a histrionic style of emphatic and striking proportions. Melodramatic acting is almost inconceivable to us today, though we detect many of its elements in the silent cinema, an equally expressionistic medium. The relation of actor to emotion rested on postulates very different from those we accept; emotion, as we noted, was held to be susceptible of complete externalization in legible integral postures. Acting style was predicated on the plastic figurability of emotion, its shaping as a visible and almost tactile entity. We know something of the repertory of devices called upon to this end: the striking of dramatic postures, the exaggeration of facial grimace (including eye rolling and teeth gnashing), the use of an artificial diction to support a bombastic rhetoric. Diction was conceived as a heightening of language, another trope of hyperbole. Soliloquies were punctuated by heavy sighs, and strong points were underlined by striking the boards with one's heels, known in the trade as "faire feu." [19] Gautier has left us a memorable account of a sonorous verbal duel between two actors—one famous for his rolled r's, the other for his hissed s's—a set piece that brought enthusiastic audience response.[20] Such a non-naturalistic, irreal style of acting allowed the actor to call upon moments of direct communication with the audience, face to face confidences and asides: not only does the heroine confide her inner virtue, appearances to the contrary, directly to the audience, in what it knows must be the very message of truth, the villain tends to call the audience to witness with the aside "Dissimulons," the announcement of his assumption of the false face.[21] The style is of course conceived to assure the legibility of signs, and there are many testimonies to remarkable expressive transparency achieved by the finest melodramatic actors. They were capable of holding a house in a charged emotional medium that could seem—

even to such a detached observer as Charles Dickens—the very essence
of the art of the drama and the drama of life.[22] If many later actors
have looked back on melodrama with nostalgia, it is because they
recognized that, within the genre, "life" has become wholly "drama,"
and that this offers the actor an unrivaled opportunity for the
uninhibited play with style.

To the specific and important question of gesture and mute action
we shall need to return. We should, however, note here that there
tends throughout melodramas, and most especially at the end of scenes
and acts, to be a resolution of meaning in *tableau,* where the characters'
attitudes and gestures, compositionally arranged and frozen for a
moment, give, like an illustrative painting, a visual summary of the
emotional situation. When Dufour announces that Coelina is not his
niece but the child of crime and adultery, we have a tableau of
"stupéfaction générale." At the end of act II of *La Fille de l'exilé,* the
final play of signs takes place during what is a spectacular silent
tableau as, in the midst of the storm, Ivan and the villagers, kneeling
on the mountainside, watch Elizabeth, herself on her knees and
holding aloft her cross, exit stage right on her floating plank. In the
tableau more than in any other single device of dramaturgy, we grasp
melodrama's primordial concern to make its signs clear, unambiguous,
and impressive.

Finally, there is the additional legibility conferred by music. Not
only is the very existence of melodrama as a distinct genre originally
linked to its use of music, music is inherent to its representations, as to
those of the cinema, its inheritor in this convention. Through the film
and the pervasive exploitation of background music, we have become
so accustomed to music used toward the dramatization of life that it is
difficult for us to recapture its radical effect, to measure its determination of our reading of the representations before us. Music in
melodrama first of all marks entrances, announcing by its theme what
character is coming onstage and what emotional tone he brings to the
situation. Then there is in every classic melodrama a ballet (often part
of the fête that will be interrupted, then sometimes resumed at the
end) and frequently a song or two. Later, Adolfe Dennery's *La Grâce de
Dieu* (1841) develops the technique of the "theme song," played on the
hurdy-gurdy, passed on from mother to daughter as a talisman.
Further recourse to music is most evident at climactic moments and in
scenes of rapid physical action, particularly mute action, which
receive orchestral underlining.[23] Music seems to have been called

upon whenever the dramatist wanted to strike a particular emotional pitch or coloring and lead the audience into a change or heightening of mood. We find, for instance, this stage direction in Joseph Bouchardy's *Les Enfants trouvés*: the Maréchal "enters slowly on the last measures of the orchestra and stops at center stage." Then the soliloquy, punctuated: "O terrors! ... hope, remorse, mortal suspicion! ... Why do you fight ceaselessly for mastery of my soul? ..." (II,i). The monologue, we detect, is on its way to becoming operatic aria—and melodrama finds one possible logical outcome in grand opera (which did in fact use many libretti from melodrama), where melody and harmony, as much as the words, are charged with conveying meaning.

Though incomplete, this rapid survey of the different registers of the sign reinforces our conviction that what we think of as melodramatic, even in the common and pejorative use of the term, is motivated by a totally coherent ambition to stage a drama of articulation, a drama that has as its true stakes the recognition and triumph of the sign of virtue. There is a victory wrought both within the conflictual system of the play and within the medium of communication encompassing play and spectator, since the play strives toward making evident the very problematic that it takes as its subject. The structural, thematic, and expressive elements that we have noted belong to a dramaturgy conceived to prove the existence and validity of basic moral sentiments and their incidence on men's lives, to establish the field of force of the ethical universe. We might now reassemble the component elements that we have considered in a final discussion of their dramatic coherence.

"Latude"   Reformulation   Conclusion

It is worth dwelling for a moment on Pixerécourt's last melodrama at the Gaîté, staged in 1834, when he was past the prime of his popularity, and structured, exceptionally, in five acts, as if to rival the burgeoning Romantic theatre and its pretentions to tragic structure. *Latude, ou Trente-cinq ans de captivité* is based on an incident from the reign of Louis XV when an artillery officer, Masers Latude, spent thirty-five years in prison for having importuned Madame de Pompadour with a somewhat maniac passion. In the play, he is instead locked up because he is found to possess some satirical verses about the *maîtresse en titre*, in fact written by one Dalègre, onto whom the trait of incipient madness will be transferred. The first act of the play, set in the gardens of the Trianon with Mme de Pompadour and her courtiers, rehearses the "violated garden" and "interrupted fête" structure, with Mme de Pompadour giving a perverted version of the young heroine role. The rest of the play elaborates the full possibilities of the "thwarted escape" structure.

The play is most basically about virtue and innocence held prisoner—virtue *as* innocence, as guiltlessness, in its purest melodramatic form, unable to assert its nature as innocence. The dreamworld is specifically nightmare and frustration. It in fact represents the ultimate (Gothic) nightmare of burial alive, loss of mobility and of identity, apparent in other Pixerécourt plays and particularly prominent in Caigniez. *Latude* sums up the whole space of claustration, which is so important in melodrama from its beginnings. Boutet de Monvel's *Les Victimes cloîtrées* (1791)—a play that Matthew Gregory Lewis saw and translated, and which was a stimulus to his writing *The Monk*—is considered by some historians to be the first melodrama (though not yet so labeled). It concerns the sequestration of hero and heroine in the dungeon of a monastery and a convent (respectively) by evil monks and nuns working at the behest of a guilty aristocrat, and it ends with a republican mayor, draped in the tricolor, leading a descent into the subterranean depths to free the victims. The play suggests the connection of the claustral space to the Gothic on the one hand, to the Revolution on the other: the Revolution as an opening up of and liberation from the claustral, the victory of democracy as virtue and innocence. This liberation will be rehearsed over and over: the dungeon is rebuilt and torn down in hundreds of melodramas. In Pixerécourt alone, *Le Château des Appenins, Les Mines de Pologne, La Forteresse du Danube, La Citerne* all have literal prisons; and *Latude* has two, the Bastille and Bicêtre. What is of particular interest in *Latude* is the use of this claustral space as the setting for the denial and eventual assertion of the sign of innocence, the central drama of the play, which makes it, despite some external variants, an appropriate summation of Pixerécourt's career.

The word *liberty* echoes throughout the play, the leitmotif of aspiration, unquenchable through refused appeals, two foiled escapes, solitary confinement, and persecution by jailers. Liberty is in chains, and they clank about on the stage. The evil behind the chains appears so arbitrary it is almost capricious: not only is Latude innocent, the crime of which he is accused is a peccadillo and his punishment

grotesquely disproportionate. It is evil as pure tyranny—the whim of
the king's favorite, which is perpetuated even after both king and
favorite are dead and a successor has ascended the throne. Latude is a
kind of parapolitical prisoner. The arbitrariness of his imprisonment is
matched by his jailers' conviction that he is especially dangerous. In
order to block any attempts at communication with him from the
outside, to incarceration is added a disguise of names, so that the sign
of innocence is completely obscured even from those who might have
the good faith to recognize it. The final scene of the play, when the
enlightened minister, Malesherbes, comes to free Latude, turns
dramatically on nomination: this man who has reiterated his nomination through thirty-five years in an attempt at vindication has now
fallen into such lassitude, and such fear of additional oppression, that
when he is dragged from his solitary confinement he cannot at first
bring himself to break through his forced disguise and give his true
name. It is only upon reflecting that his self-nomination may assure
his more rapid execution that he does finally speak: "If I speak, (*with
joy*) ah! if I speak, perhaps they will kill me . . . but at least I won't
return to that horrible cell. . . . Yes, to you, sir; to all of you, I will say
my name; I am not Daury, nor Jédor, I am Latude; and here are my
torturers" (V,xvi).

This final act of nomination as liberation has its earlier counterparts
in Latude's two attempted escapes. That from the Bastille, at the end
of act III, is particularly dramatic. The stage set shows us both the
interior of his cell and the outside of the Bastille, rising above the roofs
of Paris. We see Latude and Dalègre climb up the chimney, appear on
the parapet, hang their ladder (manufactured from sheets and
firewood) on a cannon, and begin the descent. The scene is a silent
one, except for the sentinel's cry:

> The two friends embrace once more. Latude lets himself first down the ladder,
> which is supposed to descend into the moat. Dalègre, on his knees on the edge
> of the parapet, holds the ladder; his face expresses the greatest anxiety. Snow
> has fallen during this mute scene, broken two or three times by the cry of the
> guards in the distance: "Sentinels! On the alert!"

If we can take imaginative possession of the scene, we can grasp its
plastic effect as a representation of the struggle of the sign of innocence
toward liberty.

Latude is a rich and effective play that helps us to read many
elements latent throughout Pixérécourt's theatre. An example is the

way in which he has developed the role of the physically deprived and maimed in the person of Dalègre, the man who originally is the unwitting cause of Latude's imprisonment, who breaks from the Bastille with him, and who eventually goes mad in prison, hallucinating himself in the role of the jailer, and foiling Latude's second escape attempt. The very end of the play has him grabbing the lieutenant of police by the collar and shouting: "In the name of the king! you are under arrest." The crazed victim who imagines himself as the torturer, and imagines the torturer as his victim, at times creates an atmosphere strikingly close to the theatre of Genet, or to Weiss's *Marat/Sade*. Dalègre's role points to the implicit paradox that the torturers are more thoroughly damned—because morally damned—than their victims, and it suggests the full range of horrors resulting from ethical perversion. The other remarkable role is that of Henriette Legros, who is a child in act I when she meets Latude in the Trianon gardens, and then later, as a woman, remains faithful to the child's perception of innocence and virtue and dedicates her life to Latude's exoneration, inventing a system of pigeon post (eventually discovered by the jailer, and the pigeons strangled on stage), soliciting ministers, discovering Latude's letter of appeal—proof that after thirty years he is still alive and still in prison—and forcing it upon Malesherbes, insisting that the prison be searched for a man whose name does not figure in its registry. Henriette, like the child Angéla in *Les Mines de Pologne*, like the virtuous young mute, Eloi, in *Le Chien de Montargis*, bears the message of innocence, searching for someone who will not refuse to receive it.

The whole of the play, then, dramatizes a nightmare struggle for recognition of the sign of innocence, which is also the struggle for the assertion of selfhood: the second depends on the first, the sole token permitting eventual escape from primal horror and reintegration of self and society. These in turn constitute the struggle for recognition of the very terms of melodrama, the effort to articulate the moral universe—a universe finally recognized on the stage with the arrival of Malesherbes, reformist minister, precursor of Revolution, "democratic" reader capable of deciphering the sign of innocence. The movement toward human dignity, self-assertion, and self-nomination perfectly coincides with the movement toward enunciation of ethical truth. *Latude* suggests decisively how the repertory of expressive signs exploited by melodrama takes on its full significance and motivation through the thematization of these signs within the drama. Their interplay constitutes its fundamental theme, and the final victory of the sign of virtue stands as a palpable demonstration that the terms in which melodrama traffics have a real existence, that its premises are vindicated. The temporary suppression of virtue's sign further indicates that these ethical absolutes are by no means visible to all men: they must be asserted and imposed in the face of willful erasure. Recognition of true moral identities "here below" is never finally assured; that is why it must be repeatedly dramatized.

Its dramatization works from bipolarization, as a system of competitive signs. Our analytic attention to signs is elicited by their very obviousness and exaggeration. It is their dramatic interplay, rather than psychological conflict or the clash of "character," that arrests our attention and bears the weight of represented meanings. "Character" is itself generated as a simple sign from a set of bipolar oppositions and cannot arrest our attention by any illusion of "depth" or "innerness." If in a novel by Dickens or a play by Ibsen we may be tempted to talk about "identity," the movement of the plot toward discovery of identity, and the moral anagnorisis that accompanies it, such terminology appears inappropriate in a theatre where persons are so very typological, and where structure is so highly conventional. Anagnorisis in melodrama thus has little to do with the achievement of psychological identity and is much more a matter of the recognition, the liberation from misprision, of a pure signifier, the token for an assigned identity. In a universe of such pure signs, we are freed of a concern with their reference—conventional and typical, this is immediately established—and enabled to attend to their interrelationship and hierarchy. To the extent that we have been educated by a contemporary theatre (Artaud) and a contemporary novel (Robbe-Grillet) that also refuse depth psychology in order to stage a drama of emblems, to construct an architecture of pure signifiers, we should be able to see the validity and the force of melodrama's sign languages.

What we might have tended to consider a most crude, transparent, and utilitarianly referential sign-system proves upon inspection to be inhabited, as much as any highly structured text is, by its own coherent interreferentiality. What counts is less reading through the signs than finding the right signs in relation to others, making the correct gestures, recognizing the important emblems. Near the start of *La Femme à deux maris*, Eliza cries out, "Ah! . . . I understand; there is no peace given to the child who has merited the hatred of her father" (I,iii). In act II, when she almost reveals herself prematurely to that father—before he has been convinced of her essential virtue—he begins to raise his hands in a gesture of malediction, and she says, aside, "Heaven! what a threatening attitude! ... He is ready to curse me again! Imprudent woman!" (II,vi). By the end of act III, Edouard has recovered, from Fritz's wallet, "irrecusable proofs" of Eliza's innocence. Werner, persuaded by these documentary signs, finally takes her in his arms, and Edouard concludes: "A wronged father who grants pardon is the most perfect image of the divinity" (III,xvi). The way in which these statements, gestures, and postures reticulate suggests the interplay of emblems, the textual logic of the play of signs.

Creating situations of astonishment, melodrama realizes, in heightened form, the aesthetics of the "interesting" proposed by Diderot. It always makes an implicit claim that the world of reference—"real life"—will, if properly considered, live up to the expectations of the moral imagination: that the ordinary and humble and quotidian will reveal itself full of excitement, suspense, and peripety, conferred by the play of cosmic moral relations and forces. If to its audience melodrama's sublime emotion and moral claim were in the realm of evidences—were precisely made evident by the play—to critical retrospect they may appear unfounded, in excess of what the play has demonstrated. This excess is in fact inherent to the form and its conception of its mission, for the action played out on the stage is ever implicitly an emblem of the cosmic ethical drama, which by reflection illuminates life here below, makes it exciting, raises its stakes. Hence melodrama's mode must be centrally, radically hyperbolic, the mode of the bigger-than-life, reaching in grandiose reference to a noumenal realm.

The domain of moral imperatives is, on another model, that of basic psychic modes and relations. The familial structure of melodrama's persons and problems persistently suggests this, and the use of a rhetoric that names pure states of being and relationships can legitimately be read as a breaking-through of repression, reaching toward a drama of pure psychic signs. Melodrama regularly rehearses the effects of a menacing "primal scene," and the liberation from it, achieved through articulation and a final acting-out of conflicts. Desire achieves full satisfaction in enunciation of the integral psychic condition. Morality is ultimately in the nature of affect, and strong emotion is in the realm of morality: for good and evil are moral feelings.

Melodrama cries them aloud. In psychic, in ethical, in formal terms, it may best be characterized as an expressionistic genre. If we began with the aesthetics of astonishment, it has been to work from the impressive to the expressive, to suggest that the impressive, the striking dramaturgical moment of admiration, is a particularly significant version of a pervasive concern with expression. Melodrama, one might say at this point in definition, is the expressionism of the moral imagination. Such a formulation may begin to say why the melodramatic mode is so important a part of Romantic and post-Romantic literature, and why the failure to attend to it, or its dismissal in merely pejorative terms, leads one to neglect or misread not only melodrama itself but also the Romantic theatre and even the novel of "Romantic realism." [24] The sentiment that melodrama is only vulgar and degraded near-tragedy, that the Romantic theatre is warmed-over Renaissance bombast and failed tragedy, that such novelists as Balzac, Dickens, Dostoevsky, even Henry James have more or less frequent lapses from "serious (social) realism" into lurid romance, remains prevalent and blocks an understanding of the very premises of all this literature. Melodrama is a necessary mode of ethical and emotional conceptualization and dramatization in these forms and for these writers, and only in direct, unembarrassed confrontation of the melodramatic element do they yield their full ambition and meaning.

3

The Text of Muteness

I know not how it is that we need an interpreter, but the great majority of men seem to be minors, who have not yet come into possession of their own, or mutes, who cannot report the conversation they have had with nature.

—R. W. Emerson, "The Poet"

THE TEXT

Melodrama, we saw, is an expressionistic form. Its characters repeatedly say their moral and emotional states and conditions, their intentions and motives, their badness and goodness. The play typically seeks total articulation of the moral problems with which it is dealing; it is indeed about making the terms of these problems clear and stark. Melodrama appears as a medium in which repression has been pierced to allow thorough articulation, to make available the expression of pure moral and psychological integers. Yet here we encounter the apparent paradox that melodrama so often, particularly in climactic moments and in extreme situations, has recourse to non-verbal means of expressing its meanings. Words, however unrepressed and pure, however transparent as vehicles for the expression of basic relations and verities, appear to be not wholly adequate to the representation of meanings, and the melodramatic message must be formulated through other registers of the sign.

The "text of muteness" can be considered to include mute tableau and gesture—alluded to in the preceding chapter, but requiring further analysis—and the mute role. This last category is striking and unexpected, and by addressing ourselves to it first of all, we may be able to accede most directly to the reasons for the text. The mute role is remarkably prevalent in melodrama. Mutes correspond first of all to a repeated use of extreme physical conditions to represent extreme moral and emotional conditions: as well as mutes, there are blind men, paralytics, invalids of various sorts whose very physical presence evokes the extremism and hyperbole of ethical conflict and manichaeistic struggle. In the gallery of mutilations and deprivations, however, the mutes have a special place. One is tempted to speculate that the different kinds of drama have their corresponding sense deprivations: for tragedy, blindness, since tragedy is about insight and illumination; for comedy, deafness, since comedy is concerned with problems in communication, misunderstandings and their consequences; and for melodrama, muteness, since melodrama is about expression. There are enough famous examples to suggest the pertinence of blindness to the tragic universe; and it is easy to judge that deafness—real, assumed, figurative—can be used only to comic ends. The uses of muteness are perhaps more problematical, its symbolic value more difficult to establish. Yet it appears pervasive enough to warrant a place in a typology and to call for semantic analysis.

We can again start with an example, and choose it again from the work of Pixerécourt, from one of his most enduringly popular melodramas, Le Chien de Montargis, which packed the Théâtre de la Gaîté in 1814, then had several hundred performances in the provinces. Its title role is in fact played by a dog (a trained dog—not an actor in dog disguise) who has a couple of key scenes: he has been the sole witness to the murder, and he alerts the innkeeper to the crime; then, in act III, he indicates that justice has chosen the wrong man, by licking the hand of the falsely accused Eloi, and ferociously pursuing the true assassin, Macaire—which leads to the faithful animal's being done to death by Macaire's accomplice. This dramaturgy of the non-human already suggests the importance of unspoken, non-verbal indicators of plot and meaning in the play: as with the magpie of La Pie voleuse (by Caigniez and d'Aubigny), in the dog we find the indication of the proper direction of plot, its deeper intentionality.[1] But more important than the dog is the mute person, young Eloi, who in act I is entrusted by the gallant Aubri de Mont-Didier with his wallet and other personal effects before Aubri sets out across the forest, where lurks his enemy, on a mission to Paris. When Aubri is assassinated by his jealous rival, Macaire, several details seem to incriminate Eloi, and he is put on trial in act II, scenes ten and eleven. The trial brings to a high point the dramaturgy of muteness that has been building with each appearance of Eloi. The Sénéchal and the Chevalier Gontran, acting as examining magistrates, appoint the innkeeper, Dame Gertrude, as the court's interpreter: since she has long known Eloi, she is familiar with his "language" and can offer verbal equivalents where the court fails to understand.

One has, then, this impressive piece of highly emotional dramaturgy: a sympathetic and innocent young man facing a charge of
murder before an imposing court, and unable to speak in his defense.
Once again, we are dealing with the material of nightmare. Eloi's
situation is critical, because, as the Sénéchal puts it, "tears and denials
are not enough": the circumstantial evidence is all against him, and
he must furnish counterproofs of his innocence. This he cannot do, not
only because he doesn't himself know the true author of the crime, but
because the circumstances of his last interview with Aubri, and the
reasons for Aubri having entrusted Eloi with his effects, are of a nature
to make their expression in gesture nearly impossible, and gesture—
rather than any deaf-mute alphabet—is all that he has at his
command. To the court's demand for proof, the text—which here
means the stage direction indicating Eloi's act—tells us: "Eloi
responds that he cannot furnish any. He trusts only in Providence and
the equity of his judge." If this is not adequate, at least the sense of his
gestures here is clear enough to Dame Gertrude, who immediately
verbalizes their message for the court. But as we move on, even she
begins to have trouble in interpreting and crediting what his gestures
seem to express. When he is asked to justify his possession of Aubri's
effects, "Eloi employs all the art of pantomime to make it understood
that the unfortunate Aubri, who is now dead and can't bear witness to
the truth, gave him these things in order for him to take them to
Paris." If the destination, Paris, is finally established through Eloi's
gesturing, and the intended recipient, Aubri's mother, is identified
through a process of elimination, the logic and motivation of the
commission escape the court, and the dumb show seems only to point
to the incoherence of Eloi's self-justifications. As the scene proceeds,
Eloi's gestures in fact become less legible and less plausible.

At the end of scene ten, Dame Gertrude, in despair at the turn of
events, yet still convinced of Eloi's innocence—his serene countenance
betrays no sign of falsehood—leaves to search for further clues in the
world offstage. Eloi remains alone before the court. Judgment quickly
closes in on him. But—and here we approach the major semantic
problem—as his gestures become less and less legible and plausible as
explanations of his behavior, they become more and more charged
with spiritual meanings. When he pronounces Eloi's sentence, the
Sénéchal admonishes him to fall on his knees and pray for pardon
from heaven and men. Here we have this stage direction: "Eloi refuses
to kneel. He is condemned by men, but his conscience absolves him."

The Sénéchal interprets this refusal as a sign of an obdurate criminal soul. His formulation of this accusation leads to the stage direction that closes the scene:

> Eloi might perhaps accuse Providence, which lets him be condemned for a crime he hasn't committed, but he respects its decrees and awaits his fate with resignation. Without kneeling, he joins his hands and lifts his eyes to heaven with a noble assurance. He seems to launch himself into the bosom of the divinity. All the spectators burst into tears. The Sénéchal and the Chevalier themselves are moved: such steadfastness astonishes them. But the crime appears evident, they impose silence on pity. The guards lead Eloi away. Ursule falls in a faint at the feet of the Sénéchal. The curtain falls.

The scene, and the act, thus end in a full-scale tableau, where not only Eloi but all the characters express their emotions in posture and gesture. We shall return to this typical use of tableau. It is important first to note how much Eloi's gestures are conceived as expressing: Providence, false condemnation, the distinction between judgment by men and judgment by conscience, even the attempt to "s'élancer dans le sein de la divinité." The stage directions—and we know that they are the work of a professional man of the theatre who directed his own plays—give us in part an indication of the gestures to be performed by the actor, but much more a statement of the expressive effect, the meaning to be achieved by the gestures. The text of the play provides us with verbal equivalents of the gestures, and these verbal equivalents name grandiose spiritual concepts and entities. Gesture seems to be receiving a charge of meaning that we might suspect to be in excess of what it can literally support. This suggests a problem in reading the text of muteness.

Before facing that problem, we need to explore the dimensions of the text. Eloi, we briefly learn, lost his tongue in falling out of a tree as a child. In *Coelina*, we remember, Francisque has had his tongue cut out, and the act of violence in which this occurred, before the play began, is a true primal scene, the moment that holds the key to all the play's conflicts and motives, which must eventually explicate its blood relationships and moral dilemmas. The hidden truth that must by the end of the play be revealed, articulated, is both concealed and suggested by his muteness. Pixerécourt in this manner makes the fact of muteness a motivation of his dramaturgy; he thematizes it, here as in the trial of Eloi, where muteness becomes symbolic of the defenselessness of innocence. *Les Ruines de Babylone* quite naturally introduces mutes in the context of the sultanic palace and harem and even makes use of the *selam*, the bouquet whose symbolic arrangement of elements makes it the medium for transmitting mute messages.[2] In *Christophe Colomb*, it is the representatives of another culture, the American Indians, who must have recourse to dumb show. We find in *La Citerne* a character who must pretend to be dumb and communicate through gestural signs. In some other cases, scenes of dumb show are introduced with little thematic motivation: the intervention of the band of peacemaking children in *Les Maures d'Espagne* is a pantomimic interlude, comparable to a ballet. Finally there is a one-act melodrama, *La Muette de la forêt* (written in collaboration with Benjamin Antier), which is evidently nothing more than a vehicle for silent stage play, the invention of ingenious forms of communication, on the part of the heroine.

One begins to perceive that the mute role and act, whether dramatically motivated or else simply offered as a given, are of considerable importance in melodrama, and indeed that playwrights seek their introduction. When we look beyond the sole example of Pixerécourt, this impression is confirmed. We have such simple solutions as that in Franconi's *Robert le diable*, where the hero is vowed to silence during the course of a "penance"—which lasts the length of the play. Or there is the elaborate plotting of Dumanoir and Dennery's *Le Vieux Caporal*, the story of an old soldier long believed dead who returns to reëstablish himself and his family, elucidate mistaken identities, and untangle misalliances, but at the moment when he is arrested under a false charge of theft and finds that his own identity papers have been stolen, he is struck, on stage, with an apoplexy that renders him mute. For the succeeding acts, he must try to convey his message through dumb show, a task increasingly excruciating and doomed, especially since the key articulation must be a name (that of the heroine's true mother). At the moment of final crisis—as the heroine is about to sign a wedding contract with the villain, and her adorer has cocked his pistol to end his days—the Caporal leaps to prevent the suicide, the pistol goes off next his ear, and the shock restores his power of speech in time for the proper recognitions to be effected and for a satisfactory denouement to be achieved. *Le Vieux Caporal* was written for Frédérick Lemaître, and we can sense from its stage directions how much it is conceived as a vehicle for that actor's celebrated talents as mime, his expressive gestures and facial grimaces.

The mute role is in fact a virtuoso role, not only here but elsewhere, a role that demands of the actor a deployment of all his dramatic powers to convey meaning.[3] As such, it is a special case, a hyperbolic instance, of a more extensive recourse to muteness in melodrama. This is most sensible in scenes of climax, which often become mute scenes (between actors who otherwise speak) where moral allegiances are played out as acts of villainy or heroism, and conflict resolves itself into physical combat. These are often mysterious scenes, on a half-darkened stage, to the accompaniment of music. The escape of Latude and Dalègre from the Bastille, at the end of act III of *Latude*, gives a sense of the impression that can be created when symbolic action entirely replaces words. If what Charles Dickens most retained from seeing Frédérick Lemaître play in *Trente ans, ou la Vie d'un joueur* was a series of gestures which produced a "great cry of horror" from the audience, it is because in those gestures more than in the words were represented and made present the purest conflicts and issues of the play.[4]

Even the scenes constructed of words tend toward a terminal wordlessness in the fixed gestures of the tableau. We noted examples of the procedure at the end of the second act of *La Fille de l'exilé* and in *Coelina*, when Dufour's reading of the birth certificate gives a tableau of "general stupefaction." These instances are typical of the recourse to tableau at moments of climax and crisis, where speech is silenced and narrative arrested in order to offer a fixed and visual representation of reactions to peripety. Thus in Hubert's *Clara*, at the moment where Euphémie energetically proclaims Clara's innocence, the stage direction indicates: "*Tableau.* Each character should look at Euphémie expressing the sensation that he feels" (II,xii). Or to conclude the second act of Cammaille Saint-Aubin's *La Fille de l'hospice*, we have a "tableau of fear and sensibility." Occasionally the tableau will strive toward the memorability of a well-known painting, as when in *La Fausse Mère* (by Cammaille and Destival) the swearing of a pact at the end of act I is explicitly supposed to mime David's canvas of *Le Serment des Horaces*.[5] The *Traité du mélodrame* describes the uses of the device: "At the end of each act, one must take care to bring all the characters together in a group, and to place each of them in the attitude that corresponds to the situation of his soul. For example: pain will place a hand on its forehead; despair will tear out its hair, and joy will kick a leg in the air. This general perspective is designated as *Tableau*. One can sense how agreeable it is for the spectator to take in at a glance the psychological and moral condition of each character."[6] The last sentence comes close to suggesting the motive of tableau: it gives the spectator the opportunity to see meanings represented, emotions and moral states rendered in clear visible signs.

The text of muteness is, then, pervasive in melodrama and central to the representation of its most important meanings. Gesture in all forms is a necessary complement and supplement to the word, tableau is a repeated device in the summary of meanings acted out, and the mute role is the virtuoso emblem of the possibilities of meaning engendered in the absence of the word. If it is relatively easy to grasp the effect created by tableau, it is much more difficult to talk about how gestuality in general, and the exclusively gestural language of the mutes in particular, creates meaning. The problems in the making and the reading of sense suggested by Eloi's trial remain to be confronted. Yet they may usefully be prefaced by some consideration of the origins of the text of muteness: the historical reasons for melodrama's constant recourse to silent gesture, and the aesthetics implied.

An Aesthetics of Muteness

The privileged position of muteness in melodrama in fact derives from the genre's own derivation, which is from pantomime by way of an intermediate form with the oxymoronic name of *pantomime dialoguée*. The emergence of pantomime as an important theatrical form in the late eighteenth century has to do in large part with the monopoly accorded to the official, patented theatres: the Italiens, the Opéra, and especially, the Théâtre-Français. They alone had the right to play both the classical repertory and full-scale new productions. The secondary theatres—most of which grew out of the acrobatic acts of fairs—were supposed to content themselves with ballets, puppet shows, pantomimes.[7] The pantomimes were accompanied by music from the beginning; they gradually began to become more elaborate and to incorporate pieces of dialogue, coming close to resembling *mélodrame* before the term had come into general usage. When the Revolution abolished the monopoly of the patent theatres and liberated the secondary theatres of the Boulevard to play whatever they wished, there was a rich flowering of spectacles of all types, but especially of *pantomimes dialoguées* and *pantomimes historiques* and *mimodrames*, and, more and more, *mélodrames*.

The monopoly of the patent theatres was hence a monopoly of the word. For some fifteen years, the Comédiens-Français indeed had the right to read all the scenarios proposed by the secondary theatres before their production, and to practice censorship where the word assumed a place beyond narrow confines. Restricted to the text of muteness, the secondary theatres and their authors exercised increasing ingenuity in the manufacture of its messages. We have some idea of the means employed from the *livrets*, summary scenarios of the action, that were hawked at the theatres. These sometimes give little more than the story line, indications of the following sort, from *La Forêt noire* by Arnold-Mussot (a prolific writer of pantomime): "After several tableaux, he captures Tony" (I,xi). But there is often, particularly in the later pantomimes, an attempt to describe the signification sought by each piece of action, as in Franconi's *Robert le diable*: "Elmgarde enters alone; her gait, her air, depict her melancholy. The memory of her liberator occupies her thoughts; she expresses the tender emotion that pushes her toward the unknown hero" (II,i). Or in the last scene of *Fayel et Gabrielle de Vergy* (by Félix and Franconi), "Couci arrives and holds Gabrielle in his arms; he lays her on a grassy bank. *Tableau.* Vergy, Raoul, Edmond lavish upon her the most tender care. Gradually she regains her senses, her eyes take in everything around her, her reason returns by degrees; recognizing both her suitor and her father, she throws herself into the arms of the latter; Vergy unites Raoul and Gabrielle; everyone surrounds them. *Tableau.* Finis" (III,xviii).

Subjects are evidently conceived for their plastic figurability, the dramatic interplay of posture and gesture. The spoken word is rarely used toward the formulation of significant messages; it is largely confined to emotional utterance, outburst, expressive cadenzas. When necessary, a further register of the message may be furnished by visible emblems and symbols. When Robert (of *Robert le diable*) falls to prayer, we know that his wishes are rejected by the divinity because the cross before which he has prostrated himself suddenly bursts into flame. Then, "a column rises out of the ground; on it are written the words: *Crime, Punishment*" (I,ii). Somewhat in the manner of titles in the silent cinema, emblems and inscriptions of this sort and messages imprinted on banners are frequently used to clarify the informational content of the action. In the first act of *La Main de fer*, by Cuvelier de Trie—a master of heroic pantomime—a flag is unfurled, reading "People of Dalmatia: Régilde, Duchess of Spalatro, gives her heart and her throne to young Prince Stephano" (I,x). The banner is quickly overturned by another character who, to "general astonishment," hangs in its place the message: "Having escaped from the daggers hired by his wife, the prince still lives." In Cuvelier's *Le Chef écossais*, a standard announces the engagement of combat: "War to the death against the Scottish Chief," to which is opposed the Shield of Trenmor, "at once standard and call to arms" (II,iii,xviii). By the end, it is the transfiguration of another emblem, the Lance of Trenmor, that will signify the victory of the right: "the Lance of Trenmor, like a shining meteor, rises near the ruins of the flaming tower." This in turns calls forth the final emblem of resolution and peace, the rainbow that stretches across the rear of the stage. Such spectacular, nearly cinematic effects are typical of heroic pantomime and melodrama alike. Ducange's *Elodie*, for instance, ends in an elaborate pantomime representing the death and transfiguration of Charles the Bold: lightning smashes the altar, which becomes the tomb of Elodie; the Furies seize Charles; the back of the theatre opens to reveal the specters of all Charles's victims; he disappears, and a tomb rises up, inscribed "He is no more"; but then his soul becomes a flame and rises heavenward to join Elodie's. It is a Fellini-esque conclusion.

Elodie is the melodrama of 1822; Cuvelier's work dates largely from the Empire and the Restoration, and he wrote melodramas as well as pantomimes. Pantomime, that is, survived alongside melodrama, and melodrama remained faithful to its silent origins in the recourse to gestuality. Born outside the legitimate theatre, from the populist tradition of pantomime, melodrama continued to be informed by the aesthetics of pantomime and to have recourse to muteness to express certain of its central meanings. When, in the late 1820s and 1830s, the *drame romantique* made its appearance and for a brief moment captured the citadel of the Théâtre-Français, aided by actors trained on the Boulevard, it too gave an important place to the text of muteness. And so would the nineteenth-century novel.

If we now address the question of the aesthetics of pantomime, the essential point of historical reference must (as in so many aesthetic questions) be Diderot. His attempted theatrical reform did not touch directly the popular theatre, but probably had a lateral influence on it, and is in any case relevant to it, since the popular theatre would be the true medium of a shift in dramatic aesthetics that would eventually affect the official stage.[8] In the principal texts of the "reform"—the *Entretiens sur le Fils naturel* and *De la poésie dramatique*—

Diderot mounts an attack on the performing style of the Comédiens-Français and the aesthetic that it embodies. The Comédiens are cold and rigid and formalized in gesture and movement; they tend to arrange themselves in semicircles and speak formally, with a minimum repertory of restrained and conventional gestures, to the audience. This is of course because the classical theatre—both tragedy and high comedy, *comédie de caractère*—is essentially verbal, its meanings generated almost exclusively from word, intonation, diction. Whereas for Diderot, not only must action and gesture be given an equal status with words, there are some scenes—particularly climactic ones—that should be played without words at all. He urges that playwrights follow the example of Richardson in the novel and write out their pantomime; he offers an example by recasting the end of *Le Fils naturel* as wordless drama, the effect of which he finds overwhelming.[9] He develops a full theory of the use of tableau, arguing for the grouping of persons in postures and gestures that show their reactions to a strong emotional peripety. He sketches the last scene of a hypothetical drama on the *Death of Socrates* where the phrases of the *Crito* are fleshed out with action. At the moment that Socrates drinks the hemlock, for instance, we have this tableau of reaction from his friends:

> Some of them had covered themselves in their cloaks. Crito had risen and was wandering about the prison, uttering cries. Others, rigid, immobile, were watching Socrates in dismal silence, tears running down their cheeks. Apollodorus sat at the foot of the bed; his mouth clasped in his hands, he was smothering his sobs.[10]

Plato has been made into the stuff of melodrama. Diderot compares the effect of his scene to that created by Poussin's painting of the *Testament of Eudamidas*, suggesting the relation of emotional charge to the plastic qualities of his tableau. If, as Roland Barthes has argued, literature today tends to demonstrate the supercession of the idea of *tableau* by that of *scène*, here, in the early pre-Romantic aesthetic, we have a movement from *discours*, from the model of the intelligible phrase, to tableau, the visual representation of meaning.[11]

The mute scene and gesture are clearly linked for Diderot to moments of acute passion. As the article on "Pantomime" written by Marmontel for the *Supplément* to the *Encyclopédie* puts it: "It is especially for the most impassioned movements of the soul that pantomime is necessary. There, it seconds the words, or takes their place entirely."[12]

What is it, asks Diderot, that moves us when we observe someone animated by strong passion? It is less the words that he speaks than "cries, unarticulated words, broken phrases, a few monosyllables that escape him intermittently, an undefinable murmur in the throat, between the teeth. . . ." And he goes on: "Word, tone, gesture, action, these are the actor's properties; and these it is that strike us, especially in spectacles that arouse deep passion." [13] Now cries, inarticulate words, and gestures, expressive of deep and primary passions, remind us of the terms given prominence by the eighteenth-century debate on the origins of language. The *Encyclopédie* sums up an important current of thought in the statement that gesture was "the primitive language of mankind in its cradle." [14] Rousseau himself, in the first chapter of the *Essai sur l'origine des langues*, identifies gesture as the first sign, the unmediated sign, dependent for its signifying on presence. Gesture appears in the *Essai* to be a kind of pre-language, giving a direct presentation of things prior to the alienation from presence set off by the passage into articulated language. In the mythical moment of "les premiers temps," man's primal language (Rousseau argues in chapter 9) consists of "gestures and a few inarticulate sounds." [15] Following, in this instance, Jacques Derrida's interpretation of this complex text, gesture, joined to the "cry of nature" in the moment of mythical purity, later becomes an adjunct to the word, an adjunct which represents an attempted recourse to immediacy of expression.[16] The dramaturgy of gesture and inarticulate cry urged by Diderot should, I believe, be seen in this context, as an effort to recover on the stage something like the mythical primal language, a language of presence, purity, immediacy.

Implicit in this proposition of a dramaturgy of inarticulate cry and gesture is no doubt a deep suspicion of the existing sociolinguistic code, as of its image in the classical theatrical code. As the meanings generated by the Comédiens-Français seem inadequate and impoverished, so, to Diderot as to Rousseau, the conventional language of social intercourse has become inadequate to express true emotional valences. For a summary illustration here, we could take a phrase from Crébillon's novel *Les Egarements du coeur et de l'esprit* (1736–38), where the narrator remarks about men and women engaged in the seduction game: "With a man of the world, a word, whose sense may be ambiguous, a look, a gesture, even less, will tip him off if he wishes to be loved. . . ." [17] This statement refers to a world in which the language of social intercourse has become so highly codified that all its signs—including a set repertory of looks, sighs, gestures—are fixed, and fully legible to the observer trained in the code. Human relationships in Crébillon's world can be fully articulated in terms of messages formed from this code; and this is true as well for the traditional dramaturgy of the Théâtre-Français; whereas the meanings which Diderot seeks in drama are simply not susceptible of manufacture, of *découpage*, from this code. For him—and at virtually the same moment Rousseau in the *Lettre à d'Alembert sur les spectacles* is carrying the same argument to a more radical conclusion—the expressive code of social relationships as represented in dramatic conventions constitutes an alienating mask rather than a medium for true expression. Diderot, like Rousseau, shows a suspicion of "understood" meanings, meanings implicit because conventional, and his cries and gestures look toward the melodramatic foregrounding and explicitation of meaning. Rather than deriving signification, like Crébillon's looks and gestures, from a conventional code, Diderot's cries and gestures posit the need for a new language, in which they are the radical utterances. If it is a postulate of any language system that it is sufficient for the generation of all meaning—that there is always an excess of the signifier in relation to the signifiable—language as socially defined, Diderot implies, may become inadequate to "cover" an area of the signifiable.

It is in this context that the recourse to inarticulate cry and gesture takes on its full importance. For they mark a kind of fault or gap in the code, the space that marks its inadequacies to convey a full freight of emotional meaning. In the silence of this gap, the language of presence and immediacy, the primal language, is born anew. It takes its place in the expressive ambition of those early Romantics—most notably Rousseau and Sade—who were obsessed by the idea that they must say all, *tout dire*, that nothing of the possible human response must be left unexpressed, that writing must be a continual overstatement.[18] Melodrama clearly offers a version of this ambition. But if gesture and primal cry do indeed stand in the gap of the traditional code, marking its inadequacy, we are forced to ask what the modalities of their signification are, what their status within the system of communication and expression may be. Here Diderot's implicit answer is clear enough: these cries and gestures signify because they are the language of nature, the language to which all creatures instinctively have recourse to express their primal reactions and emotions. This does not solve the semantic and analytic problem, however, which we need to address more closely.

THE LANGUAGE OF MUTENESS

The idea that gesture is the language of nature, and that pantomime is therefore the artistic use of a natural language, is pervasive. We noted the statement of the *Encyclopédie* on the naturalness of communication through gesture, and we find that a standard nineteenth-century *Manuel théâtral,* the Roret, maintains: "Pantomime is the universal language; it makes itself understood the world over, by the savage as by the civilized man: because physiognomy, gestures, and all the movements of the body have their eloquence, and this eloquence is the most natural." [19] Saussure indeed alludes to the possibility that gesture may be a language of non-arbitrary signs: non-arbitrary because "symbolic," in that gestures are supposed to be analogic to what they represent, "naturally" linked to it.[20] The major technical treatise written, at the end of the nineteenth century, by Charles Aubert, *L'Art mimique, suivi d'un traité de la pantomime et du ballet,* argues that gesture and pantomime constitute man's first language, and that it remains the fundamental language of the theatre because the spectator's own mimetic sense leads him "to share, to feel himself the emotions for which the signs are presented to him." [21] Aubert defines the language of pantomime as the language of nature supplemented by a few "artificial," conventional hand signs—kinds of diacritical marks. While starting from the premise of an analogic language, Aubert endeavors to analyze pantomime in quasi-linguistic terms and with a remarkable prescience of the distinction between *langue* and *parole,* or code and message. Postures of the body, hand movements, and facial expressions—themselves divisible into positions of eye, mouth, eyebrows, and angle of the head—are the essential elements of the code, and their various combinations and oppositions are used to form the message. Aubert is of course describing a highly codified "artistic" pantomime. Yet he also insists repeatedly on the limits of the code—the limits imposed by its being a "language of nature"—and on the kinds of messages that are outside its range. He claims that pantomime is almost exclusively a language of verbs, and so he provides, for instance, a table for the reinterpretation of adjectives as verbs. Nouns he considers unrepresentable unless they can be translated into the verb of the action in which they are employed (for example, a comb), or unless their referent is actually present on the stage. Pantomime is thus basically a language of action and presence. It is emphatically incapable of expressing abstractions, hypotheses, preferential or optative situations. Aubert gives some examples of sentences that cannot be articulated in pantomime, among them:

> "Formerly, I was virtuous."
> "When my father became a widower, he resigned."
> "My creditors are hard to deal with."
> "My mother gave me an example of devotion and self-sacrifice."
> "Art is difficult." [22]

While Aubert is talking about a pantomime which—though originally and still the language of nature—has developed its resources as code, presumably to their limits, we note that the mute gestures of the type staged by Pixerécourt in *Le Chien de Montargis* seem to endeavor to express the very sort of meanings that Aubert judges to be beyond the range of pantomime. The language of natural analogies seems, in Pixerécourt's play, to be employed to the representation of unanalogic abstractions, the language of presence used for the expression of absences. Eloi tries to show by pantomime that Aubri—not only not on the stage, but dead—gave him his effects to carry them to Paris, to give to his mother. This message is indeed obscure for its on-stage witnesses and requires the elucidation of cross-examination and the verbal interpretations of Dame Gertrude. What, then, is the status of the pantomime that closes the trial: "Eloi might accuse Providence, which lets him be condemned for a crime he hasn't committed, but he respects its decrees and awaits his fate with resignation. Without kneeling, he joins his hands and lifts his eyes to heaven with noble assurance. He seems to launch himself into the bosom of the divinity"? The message contains hypothetical clauses, abstract nouns such as "Providence" and "the divinity," and the intent to perform the (impossible) action of throwing himself into the embrace of heaven. To take another example, from *Coelina*, how do we perceive and read this moment, when "Francisque makes his daughter understand that they must never despair of the goodness of heaven" (III,vi)? Do we, as spectators, detect any analogic relationship by which the gestures on the stage necessarily refer to and represent these meanings? Do we rather apprehend them as forming a particular message from the elements of a known code? How do we read the text before our eyes?

These questions appear to place us before the problem of a gestural semiotics, which has engaged some recent theoretical analysis. The analysis of gestural communication according to a linguistic model encounters difficulties since, most analysts would seem to agree, we lack such normal characteristics of language as an identifiable code; a set of substitutable shifters; the possibility of commutation, which depends on the "double articulation"; the possibility of a retransmission of the message in its own terms.[23] According to Christian Metz, we must usually consider gesture as "an actualized linguistic statement": gestures do not refer directly to words, still less to phonemes and morphemes (which demonstrates the lack of the second level of linguistic articulation, that of phonemic combination), but rather to a whole phrase that cannot be further broken down.[24] This distinction is further elucidated by A. J. Greimas in his redefinition of the two relata of the linguistic sign, signifier and signified, in the analysis of gesture. The "semiosis" of gesture, he argues, will consist in "the relation between a sequence of gestural figures, taken as the signifier, and the gestural project, considered as the signified." [25] Greimas largely accepts the position of Julia Kristeva that gesture is "anaphoric," indicative. Gestures themselves are desemanticized, and the problem of signification is secondary. Hence analysis must be trans-linguistic.[26]

These considerations seem just and pertinent, and in particular Greimas' reformulation of the relata of the sign as "gestural sequence" and "gestural project" identifies accurately the elements with which we must work. But gestural semiotics in its current state does not solve the difficulties of approach to a gestural text for which specific meanings are proposed and are clearly of considerable importance for the global meaning of the play. Part of our problem in reading the text of muteness evidently derives from the procedures of the script, the stage directions, which, we noted, at times give us information pertaining to the "gestural sequence," the actual motions to be accomplished by the actor, and at other moments evoke rather the "gestural project," the effect to be rendered by the actor's gestures, their expressive result, their achieved message. There is indeed a shift in the script from description of the gestural signs required of the actor to a verbal translation of the signification of these signs. Hence the effort to analyze gesture into the relata of the sign, to see a pattern of signifiers covering a pattern of the signified, or a gestural sequence covering a gestural project, tends to break down: the gestural system is relayed by another sign-system, that of language proper, with its own relation of signifiers and signified. We can, of course, from our experience of the theatre, imagine generally the kind of gestures that an actor might use to render "respect for the decrees of Providence." Yet in the absence of any recognizable code in terms of which to identify this message (Aubert's estimate of the limitations of the code in the most highly developed pantomime indicates we cannot operate on the hypothesis of a code once operative and now lost), we cannot think of gestures themselves in terms of signifier and signified: too great a distance and too great an indeterminacy open up between the relata of the sign, however redefined, for any semiosis to be credible. This suggests why the script needs to relay one system by another, indicating verbal signs through gestural signs, yet specifying the gestural signs through their verbal translations. The gestural signs will themselves be exaggerated, hyperbolic (all that we know about Boulevard acting styles of course confirms this), because the signified in question is grandiose. But any specification of the conceptual meaning of the gestural sign must be relayed through the system of articulated language.

If, on the one hand, the symbolic or analogic relationship between gesture and meaning does not seem operative when gesture is postulated as conveying meanings of this type—that is, where any imaginable analogon must seem inadequate—and if, on the other hand, there seems to be no identifiable code of gestures, a semiotics of gesture on a linguistic basis should no doubt be set aside in favor of a more pertinent approach. We must recognize that gesture in the texts that concern us is being mediated by the context of articulated language, that the generalized indications of the gestural sequence exist to be translated into specific verbal articulations of the gestural project. This translation may in part be performed by other persons on the stage (as in the case of Dame Gertrude), by the context of action in which the gesture occurs (which must to some degree be true of gesture in pantomime proper), and, necessarily, by the spectator, whose interpretations are represented by those messages suggested in the stage directions. The operative code is that of articulated language, which alone provides the possibility of interpretation and hence of meaning; gesture is in fact desemanticized, it is anaphoric, in Julia Kristeva's term, in that it points *toward* meaning.

Mute gesture can then perhaps most pertinently be considered as a trope and analyzed on the plane of rhetoric. It is a sign *for* a sign, demanding a *translatio* between the two signs. It hence resembles metaphor, the transference or displacement of meaning. The gestures that we see on the stage, the visible movements, can perhaps best be considered, to use I. A. Richards' terminology, the vehicle of a metaphor whose tenor is a vaguely defined yet grandiose emotional or spiritual force that gesture seeks to make present without directly naming it, by pointing toward it. If we know from the script what a possible specification of the tenor could be (though this specification is of itself frequently metaphorical to a further degree), from the pit we apprehend it only through its hyperbolic vehicle, its indicator. In the gap of the language code, the grandiose, melodramatic gesture is a gesturing toward a tenor both grandiose and ineffable. Consequently, it is inaccurate to speak of *decoding* such gesture; we must rather *decipher* it, follow its directions, rename its indications in our translation.

The gestures which fill the gap reach toward other meanings which cannot be generated from the language code. They often take the form of the message of innocence and purity, expressed in an immediate inarticulate language of presence: a moment of victory of pure expression over articulation. In terms of Roman Jakobson's two poles of language, metonymy could represent the model of traditional *discours*, of the spaced, articulated phrase; while metaphor appears here as an effort to collapse spaced, articulated language back into a direct, presented meaning: a meaning made visible.[27] If the resemblance that we have detected between such gesture and metaphor is valid, we can now better understand the significance of the link to Diderot's dramaturgy of inarticulate cries and gestures, which, speaking in the gap of the language code, suggested an evocation of the mythic primal language. Recourse to gestural metaphor reënacts the original figure of language, the first hieroglyphs, or that "mouvement de baguette" which, in Rousseau's *Essai*, renders the presence of the beloved.[28] The use of mute gesture in melodrama reintroduces a figuration of the primal language onto the stage, where it carries immediate, primal spiritual meanings which the language code, in its demonetization, has obscured, alienated, lost. Mute gesture is an expressionistic means—precisely the means of melodrama—to render meanings which are ineffable, but nonetheless operative within the sphere of human ethical relationships. Gesture could perhaps then be typed as in the nature of a catachresis, the figure used when there is no "proper" name for something. In Roland Barthes's description, catachresis "restores the blank of the compared [the tenor], whose existence is completely given over to the word of the comparer [the vehicle]" [29] Yet of course it is the fullness, the pregnancy, of the blank that is significant: meaning-full though unspeakable.

We can perhaps clarify these formulations, and further suggest the importance of an attention to mute gesture, by moving momentarily from melodrama proper into an example from the *drame romantique*, to look at a play whose place in the literary canon is secure, and in which the metaphoricity of gesture in fact carries the most important and highly charged meanings. This is Alfred de Vigny's *Chatterton*, produced at the Comédie-Française in 1835. In a note written following the performance of the play, Vigny comments: "Never has any play been better acted than this one, and the merit is great. For, behind the written drama, there is a second drama which the text does not touch, and which the words do not express." [30] This "second drama" is first of all that of love that cannot speak its name: the love of Chatterton and Kitty Bell, which for most of the play is in a nascent state, unaware of its name, and blocked from articulation by the two characters' timidity and purity. Chatterton and Kitty Bell never in fact speak directly to one another until the next-to-last scene; and if Chatterton can then declare his love, it is because, as Kitty immediately understands, he has already chosen death—he has swallowed poison, and his articulation comes from the context of an impending silence. The whole of this second drama is played out in looks, in caresses displaced onto Kitty's children, in facial expression, bodily posture, and gesture. Vigny's very description of Kitty in the dramatis personae indicates the metaphorical charge that must be attached to her whole act: "Her pity for Chatterton is going to become love, she senses this and trembles from it; the reserve she imposes on herself is increased because of it; everything should indicate, from the moment we see her, that an unexpected grief and a sudden terror can kill her in an instant." The climax of this drama—when Kitty Bell has discovered the body of Chatterton in his upstairs room—is a silent scene, the celebrated *dégringolade* where she falls in a faint at the top of the staircase and slides to the bottom step.

The dégringolade of Kitty Bell is forever linked to the name of Marie Dorval, the actress (and Vigny's mistress) for whom the play was written. Marie Dorval was an actress from the Boulevard, trained in melodrama, the genre which she illustrated to perfection, and her translation to the stage of the Comédie-Française entailed violent conflict. The Comédiens made fun of her, found her mannerisms and her stage play vulgar. Attempts were made to drop her from the play—even the king, Louis-Philippe, hinted to the author that this might be the most diplomatic step—and it took all of Vigny's tenacity to keep her in the role. Given the hostility of her fellow players, Marie Dorval refused to rehearse her final *jeu de scène* with them; she studied it in private and unveiled it only on opening night, when it predictably brought down the house. She understood that it was a distinctly Boulevard effect, which would never be accepted by the Comédiens—until its reception by the audience had legitimized it. This point of stage history may serve to suggest how much the drame romantique owed to melodrama, not least in its sense of gesture, mute action, plastic representation, and hyperbolic expression that still in the 1830s were foreign to the style of the Comédie-Française.[31] And the foremost interpreters of the drame romantique—not only Marie Dorval, but also Bocage and Frédérick Lemaître, to name only the most famous—were formed, not at the Comédie, but on the Boulevard, in melodrama, in the aesthetics of expressionism. Marie Dorval was able to represent the "second drama" of Kitty Bell precisely because she was, and knew herself to be, in violation of the Comédie's codes.

Chatterton, the drama of the Romantic artist misunderstood and condemned by a materialist world, hence the drama of Romanticism itself, is in fact the drama of the ineffable. Not only the role of Kitty Bell, but even more that of Chatterton gestures toward the sublime and ineffable emotion at its moments of greatest intensity, which are in fact moments of muteness. Thus, at the end of the soliloquy during which he has finally swallowed the opium, we have this silent climax: "He lifts his eyes to heaven and slowly tears up his poems, in the grave and exalted attitude of a man who makes a solemn sacrifice" (III,vii). Or, in the preceding scene, when his maladroit and philistine patron, Lord Mayor Beckford, advises him to give up poetry and asks what good the poet is in the management of the ship of state, there is "a moment of arrest" before Chatterton speaks his one-line defense: "He reads in the stars the route marked out by the finger of the Lord." In this moment of silence, the defense of the art of the ineffable reveals itself as ineffable, and Chatterton—whose spoken justification will appear pure nonsense to his interlocutors—is caught, as much as Eloi, in a relationship of incommunicability with his listeners. The realm in which he is making sense is the realm *toward which* he gestures, the realm of "grave and exalted" emotion. When Vigny refers us to the "second drama" hidden behind the written drama, untouched by the words pronounced on stage, he means, finally, a drama that cannot be articulated in speech, the drama of the ineffable, which can be evoked only through mute gesture used as metaphor. The metaphor invokes a realm hidden to most of the characters on stage—those condemned to the social code and its language—but sensible to the *belles âmes*: the occult realm of true feeling and value, and unmediated, because inarticulate, expression.

Gesture   Writing   Meaning

The habitual recourse of Romantic drama and melodrama to the gestural trope of the inarticulate suggests, on the one hand, why these genres tend toward a full realization in opera, where music is charged with the burden of ineffable expression. On the other hand, it indicates still another reason for the emergence of the novel as the characteristic modern form. Diderot's dramatic aesthetics are subtended by his desire to introduce onto the stage some of the emotional immediacy achieved by Richardson in the novel, and the rise of *drame* and *mélodrame* would indeed bring the theatre far closer to the modes of fiction. The bourgeois and domestic novel gave a large place to transcribed pantomime. Most pertinently, the novel would allow an inscription of mute gesture used as metaphor. It would make of it a fundamental mark or trace in the creation of meaning.

The nineteenth-century novel is full of gesture, full of significant non-verbal signs that carry a great measure of expression—something that has no doubt long been recognized, but never much attended to. Many of the most highly charged meanings in the works of Dickens, Gogol, Flaubert, Dostoevsky, Proust, Lawrence, as well as Balzac and James, come to us through gesture, are postulated as being expressed through gesture. The most significant of these gestures do not derive their charge of meaning from a social code—as they do in Crébillon, or Choderlos de Laclos, or even still in Jane Austen—but are essentially metaphoric, punctuating the text with silent indicators invoking the presence of a moral occult. Sometimes these gestures are described, or at least characterized, as when (taking our examples for the moment from Balzac) Mme de Mortsauf, in *Le Lys dans la vallée*, bends "her face toward the earth in a movement of tragic slowness"

(8:913). Sometimes description is largely elided in favor of immediate translation: the gesture is seen through its decipherment, its interpretation, as when, in *Le Père Goriot*, an impatient Vicomtesse de Beauséant makes a "short gesture" which, underlining the inflection of her voice and her glance, allows Rastignac to perceive "the iron fist under the velvet glove" (2:946). Some gestures, moreover, are merely postulated and realized only in terms of their signification, as in this striking example from *Facino Cane*: "He made a frightening gesture of extinguished patriotism and disgust for things human" (6:71). Here, clearly, any *perceptual* approach to the vehicle of the metaphor has been abandoned. If the vehicle is characterized as "frightening," this is already metaphorical, because the "fright" derives not from the visible gesture but from its astonishing tenor: "extinguished patriotism and disgust for things human." The vehicle is virtually obliterated; it exists only as a concession to a system of motivation and to the constraints of rhetoric, so that it may permit the evocation of the tenor which could not otherwise be postulated within the text, precisely because of its sublime, undefined, ineffable nature. Finally, some gestures exist wholly in the medium of ineffability, as marks of an appalling significance beyond the power of interpretation, as when in *Le Colonel Chabert* the wife is faced with her husband's return from the dead: "The comtesse made an untranslatable gesture upon hearing the footstep of her husband" (2:1141–42). Why, we might ask, present the gesture at all if it is neither described nor translated? Precisely because it creates, makes present, an emotion and a moral dilemma all the more charged in that it is unrecordable and uninterpretable.

We could say that such gesture is not, to use a term of Roland Barthes', in the realm of the *operable*: one could not, however long one practiced before the mirror, learn to execute it in such a way that it necessarily carried the meanings attributed to it in the text.[32] Indeed, in the latter examples—in distinction to the stage directions of theatre—no indications for execution are provided. They need not and probably cannot be provided because such non-operable gesture is only pseudo-referential. It functions as a trope that permits the evocation or, more accurately, the postulation of meanings which are hyperbolic, in a state of excess, in relation to the narrative and descriptive language codes. Most gestures in nineteenth-century fiction are probably of this type. They are written in the form: "a gesture of . . ." (*un geste de*), "a gesture that . . ." (*un geste qui*). They are indicators, anaphoric signals, and rhetorical tokens whose presence in the text permits the construction of the audacious metaphors. Gesture in the novel, it appears, avoids naming its vehicle except in terms of its tenor. Yet this tenor itself is very often considered to be in the domain of the inarticulable: it is postulated through mute gesture precisely because it partakes of the ineffable. So that if in the theatre one charges the literal gesture hyperbolically, exaggerates it, in order to suggest the sublimity of its tenor, in the novel the hyperbole of the vehicle is merely implicit because shifted onto the tenor, which itself connotes more than it names a hyperbolic condition. The evident sleight of hand that takes place when gesture transcribed is so used as the token for the construction of unspecified yet grandiose meanings makes clear the special place of gesture in the novel. It is an important device toward the representation of conditions, concepts, forces held to be beyond the possibilities of rational apprehension and literal statement. Gesture appears as a way to make available certain occulted perceptions and relationships, to render, with the audacity of an as-if proposition, a world of significant shadows.

Gesture as transcribed in the novel appears to be a "betrayal" of theatrical gesture in that it refuses to actualize—through description, visual notation—the motions to which it gives such a significant status. If Balzac and Dickens and James often refer us to the theatre as the aesthetic model of their own representations, and clearly think of their written "scenes" and gestures in theatrical terms, they are nonetheless more concerned with the decipherment and translation of gesture than with its pure figure. Yet our attempts to analyze the status of mute gesture in a typical situation from melodrama should indicate that the novelistic use of gesture as trope in fact realizes—more completely than the theatre could—the deepest implications of the gestural sign. At least from the moment of its revaluation by the eighteenth-century debate on the origins of language, the gestural sign appears as a primary term in the indication or, more forcefully, the inscription of meaning. Gesture is that original trace of man's presence in nature, the mark of his quality as *homo significans*, the sense-maker in sign-systems.[33] Gesture is easily conceived as the initial sign in the construction of a sense-making system because of its anaphoric function (to use Julia Kristeva's perception again): it suggests an intention and a direction of meaning; it traces the first possibility of a meaning. An apt novelistic illustration of this is the scene in *Great Expectations* where Pip is first faced with an emissary from the yet unknown Magwitch who communicates only through gestures with a

file—the file which a still younger Pip had stolen and brought to
Magwitch so that he could free himself from the leg iron: "It was not a
verbal remark, but a proceeding in dumb show, and was pointedly
addressed to me. He stirred his rum-and-water pointedly at me, and
he tasted his rum-and-water pointedly at me. And he stirred and he
tasted it: not with a spoon that was brought to him, but *with a file*." [34]
The repetition of "pointedly" suggests the role of the "dumb show"
with the file in establishing a line or direction or intention of meaning
in Pip's life, tracing the first inscription of his "expectations" (the
emissary will in fact leave Pip two one-pound notes), plotting meaning
in the novel. Gesture may serve as the original pointing to meaning.

Gesture to such as Warburton and Condillac was inscribed in the
first written languages as hieroglyph.[35] It is in fact imaginatively
logical to think of the identity of gesture and writing, *écriture*, the
inscription of meaning. It is, then, within this fictive logic that the
novel should so often present its interpretations of human meanings as
the decipherment of gestures. Balzac, who typically had recourse to
pseudo-theory in order to justify his imaginative practice, was led to
concoct a *Théorie de la démarche*, which provides a "basis" for such
decipherments. Body postures and gestures, he tells us, "are imprinted
with our will and are of a frightening signification. This is more than
the word, it is thought in action." [36] What Balzac has perceived and
needs to explain is the close relationship between gesture and writing,
and how the creation of significance through the trace of the latter so
often follows the figure traced by the former. Man's gestures indicate
his intention to mean, and writing, retranscribing these intentions as
realized gestures of meaning, mimes and translates their indications.
Thus gesture in the novel becomes, through its translation, fully
resemanticized, and may stand as emblematic of the whole novelistic
enterprise of finding signification and significance in man's terrestrial,
even quotidian actions.

This emblem, and what we have said about the implications of
gesture to Diderot and in the larger eighteenth-century speculation
about the nature and origins of language, may suggest that we should
consider the frequent recourse to mute gesture within the broad
context of Romanticism as one effort to recover for meaning what
appeared to be in danger of being lost to meaning. With the suspicion
directed toward neoclassical linguistic codes and their understood
meanings, and toward a universe implicitly organized as discourse, the

potential for generating meaning had come to seem too limited. Gesture, a "return" to the language of presence, became a way to make present and available new, or revived, indications of meaning, emotional conditions, and spiritual experience. In the silence created by the "gapping" of the traditional language code, mute gesture appears as a new sign making visible the absent and ineffable. These grandiose, primordial significances are, we saw, democraticized; even more fundamentally, they are recovered for the system of meaning, for the sign-system. Recourse to mute gesture is a necessary strategy in any expressionistic aesthetics. Our very phrases "facial expression" and "bodily expression" suggest the belief that whereas language may have been given to man to dissimulate his thought, physical signs can only reveal. We may think of the importance given to bodily posture and facial grimace in the painting styles of Mannerism and Expressionism, or of what must be the modern aesthetic closest to melodramatic pantomime, the silent cinema, which deployed a full expressionist rhetoric. We should also note the importance of the revolution in the modern theatre urged by Antonin Artaud, breaking with the limited meanings of a conventionalized stage through a dramaturgy founded on "a new lyricism of gesture," using a language of gestural signs functioning as "animated hieroglyphs." [37] Artaud considered Romantic melodrama to be the last true theatre in Europe, and he recommended a drama in which articulated language would have "only the approximate importance it has in dreams." [38]

We should then recognize that the full logic of the text of muteness is in fact realized in Freud's discovery of the dream rhetoric, which treats words and concepts as plastic representations.[39] For with the dream text we reach what we must at present consider the deepest level of expressionism, the expression of our most basic and determinative meanings. Freud represents our most convincing modern breakthrough in the recovery for meaning of what might appear to be outside any systems of meaning. From *The Interpretation of Dreams* and *The Psychopathology of Everyday Life* onward, the Freudian enterprise is centrally concerned with finding the signs of meaning in all our silences, reinvesting meanings in the gestures we would like to think insignificant. The "conquistador," as he was pleased to call himself, Freud claims victory over voids of meaning, to ensure that the universe may once again become the seamless web of signification. The interpretive system of psychoanalysis is itself expressionistic in its premises, and it casts retrospective light on melodramatic expressionism, for it to some degree reformulates melodrama's concerns and realizes its possibilities. In the periodically renewed quest to reinterpret the modes of signification in the world, psychoanalysis relays melodrama, and it may provoke a further level of reflection on the rise of melodrama as a specific modern form of the imaginary, on its necessity, the gap it fills, its persistence through transformations.

Heroic pantomime, with its clashing emblems and blazing inscriptions, its hyperbolic and frozen gestures, its occasional verbal cadenzas, resembles not only a drama according to Artaud's specifications, but also a dream script. Melodrama in general, we saw, suggests the dream world in its enactments, in its thrust to break through repression and censorship, in its unleashing of the language of desire, its fulfillment of integral psychic needs. The text of muteness in particular suggests expression of needs, desires, states, occulted imperatives below the level of consciousness. Dickens reverts to muteness at the climactic moment of *Great Expectations*, when Magwitch reveals himself to Pip: Pip's recognition is the more profound and dramatic for not being played out on the level of consciousness; it is conveyed through a silent scene which reëvokes the novel's "primal scene":

> Even yet I could not recall a single feature, but I knew him! If the wind and the rain had driven away the intervening years, had scattered all the intervening objects, had swept us to the churchyard where we first stood face to face on such different levels, I could not have known my convict more distinctly than I knew him now, as he sat in the chair before the fire. No need to take a file from his pocket and show it to me; no need to take the handkerchief from his neck and twist it around his head; no need to hug himself with both his arms, and take a shivering turn across the room, looking back at me for recognition. I knew him before he gave me one of those aids, though, a moment before, I had not been conscious of remotely suspecting his identity.[40]

The preterition of the passage—the insistence that there is "no need" for all the signs in dumb show that are in fact detailed—merely serves to heighten the lack of sound and language in the scene, and to reinforce the impression that recognition of what is for Pip a cataclysmic moral condition forces its way up from the regions of the repressed. As in Balzac and James, the language of the moral occult often lies below consciousness, and surfaces in muteness.

4

Melodrama and Romantic Dramatization

On ne trouvait rien d'assez fort, d'assez hardi, d'assez passionné. Chacun allait au bout de sa propre nature.

—Théophile Gautier

"We cannot understand the romantic movement," writes George Steiner, "if we do not perceive at the heart of it the impulse toward drama. . . . The romantic mode is neither an ordering nor a criticism of life; it is a dramatization." [1] This is first of all true in the literal sense that the Romantics, especially in France but in Germany and England as well, constantly sought to realize their vision on the stage, in a theatre reborn. It is even more pertinent in that, as we have been attempting to illustrate in the domain of melodrama, a central impulse of the Romantic imagination strives toward making of life the scene of dramatic conflict and clash, of grandiose struggle represented in hyperbolic gestures. If in *The Death of Tragedy* Steiner illuminates the particular contribution of the Romantics to the decline of the tragic, his perspective is limited because he has not provided himself with the means to understand the new dramatization that comes to take its place. A fuller view of the expressive enterprise and mode of the modern imagination would, I think, have to balance the death of tragedy against the rise of melodrama as a pervasive aesthetic, and consider how the specific characteristics of the new mode fill the gap left by the demise of the old. [2]

Steiner is aware that in the Romantic theatre the melodramatic tends to replace the tragic: "Where the theatrical is allowed complete rule over the dramatic, we get melodrama. And that is what French romantic tragedies are: melodramas on the grand scale." [3] Yet since melodrama is for Steiner simply a term of pejorative judgment, since he gives little attention to the possible coherence and raison d'être of the melodramatic system of dramaturgy and expression, he is not in a position to say how and why melodrama succeeds tragedy, and to see its continuities with the highest achievements of the modern imagination. If Romantic endeavors in the theatre are strongly marked by a reliance on the elements of melodrama that we have considered, if their pretension to the tragic seems largely spurious, then it seems worth asking whether the label of failed or degenerate tragedy is not too limiting, and whether we should not rather look for the foundations of this art, and for its future implications, within the framework of melodrama as we have defined it. Such a discussion can perhaps best be pursued first historically—to articulate the relationship among the decline of tragedy, the rise of melodrama, and the flowering of Romantic drama—and then in confrontation with the problematics of a characteristic text.

THE RISE OF MELODRAMA

It should be recognized that the two illustrious forms of the traditional (neoclassical) French theatre, tragedy and high social comedy—*comédie de caractère*—were exhausted a century before the Romantic revolution came to pass. The tinkering with the tragic machinery performed by such as Voltaire in retrospect only makes the signs of decadence more apparent. The cosmic cause of the decline, I suggested earlier, may be located in the loss of an operable idea of the Sacred that set in toward the end of the seventeenth century and made it no longer possible for tragedy to act as a communal ritual of sacrifice. If high comedy survived somewhat better, its necessary basis in a unified audience committed to identical social and moral values was gradually undermined by liberal political thinking and was finally exploded by revolution.[4] The rise of the bourgeoisie entailed the privatization and "desocialization" of art and led to the novel as the characteristic modern genre. The evolution of a theatre freed from allegiance to the traditional genres and their prescribed styles itself had much to do with the simultaneous rise of the novel. As Diderot clearly perceived, the Richardsonian novel opened up the possibility of an aesthetics of the "interesting," a new exploitation of the drama latent in the quotidian and the domestic.

The life of the neoclassical genres was artificially preserved in France by the institutions: by the monopolies given to the patented theatres, and the training in dramatic art perpetuated for their members; by an audience that regarded the Théâtre-Français as a central institution in its intense sociability; and by the dominance of neoclassical critical theory, which rigidified the "Aristotelean" genres and unities, transmuting the idea of *vraisemblance* from a psychological and moral concept into a supposed natural law, and postulating that the genres as defined and illustrated were necessary and immutable. Efforts at reform all had to pass through the narrows of the generic argument and the debate about "the rules"—proposing and illustrating the possibilities of *comédie larmoyante, tragédie bourgeoise et domestique*, or *drame*; taking timid liberties with the unities of time and place, and with the *bienséances*.[5] One can, in retrospect, establish the importance of Nivelle de La Chaussée, Sedaine, Mercier, Beaumarchais, Diderot as proponents of a breakdown in genre distinction and exemplars in the formation of a more libertarian aesthetic, which would thereafter be taken up by Lessing and Schlegel in Germany, and be reintroduced into France by Mme de Staël.

Diderot in particular, as we have seen, was the prophetic theoretician of a drama revived through its renewed contact with those registers suppressed in a theatre giving exclusive valuation to the word. He wished to introduce into drama the emotional immediacy of the novel, its complex plotting and elaborately realized settings; and he saw drama as directly moral in its aim, concerned with the recognition of virtue, and based on a new relation of sentimental identification between spectator and character.[6] Posing explicitly as Diderot's disciple, Beaumarchais criticized tragic fatality as amoral, and proposed a drama of domestic disaster, which would touch our hearts more closely. "When I witness virtue persecuted," writes Beaumarchais, "the victim of wickedness, but ever beautiful, ever glorious, and preferable to all else, even amidst misfortune, the effect of the *drame* is unequivocal."[7] Clearly, Diderot's urging of a *genre sérieux* that would not be tragi-comedy but a new middle ground for serious treatment of private lives and their dilemmas—and that would depend for effect less on observing defined categories of the *vraisemblable* than on creating an illusion of lived experience—his arguments for an emotional rhetoric that would infuse sublimity into the ordinary, and for action and pantomime, in large measure announce melodrama. Yet Diderot's aesthetic gives no hint of the heroic dimensions of melodrama, its overt excitement (he did not like the coup de théâtre), its cosmic ambitions. His, and Beaumarchais' and Mercier's, theses belong to a more purely sentimental tradition. It is also not possible to call Diderot the father of melodrama in terms of the filiations of literary history. The movement to promote the *drame* was largely abortive. Diderot's own illustrations of his theories, *Le Fils naturel* and *Le Père de famille*, were not persuasive successes. The best plays of Beaumarchais and Sedaine do not really fall within the definition of the *drame*, with the possible exception of the latter's *Le Philosophe sans le savoir*, the one reasonably indisputable exemplar of the genre. That is to say, the reform postulated on the unfolding of the *drame* within the institutions of high theatre, though largely predictive of the future, seems to have had little immediate impact and influence. If one is to look for a movement of renewal that would prepare the Romantic theatrical outburst of the 1830s, it is to the popular theatre that one must turn. This is where (as in the Gothic novel) interesting things were happening.

Here the intricacies of literary and social history are such that radical foreshortening becomes necessary. It appears that, with the sclerosis of the traditional genres and theatres, more and more interest began to be shifted toward the secondary theatres. Obeying their own logic, which seems to have been largely independent of the evolution of the official theatres, the minor theatres were gradually being transformed from fair sideshows into something more permanent and theatrical. Nicolet's famous acrobatic and tight-rope act, the Grands Sauteurs du Roi, established itself in a comfortable permanent home on the boulevard du Temple in 1764. It was to become the Théâtre de la Gaîté. Then Audinot's puppet show settled permanently on the Boulevard in 1769, in the Théâtre de l'Ambigu-Comique. These two future temples of melodrama were, like the other minor theatres, still legally restricted to wordless drama and required for some time to display such reminders of their origins as a tightrope stretched across the stage. It was no doubt because of the restrictions on the word—as well as the uneducated nature of the bulk of their audiences—that these theatres paid special attention to the spectacular aspects of drama, to its visible signs: to decor, machinery, banners, inscriptions, gestures, action, music. While the authors of these theatres were probably innocent of acquaintanceship with Diderot's or Mercier's aesthetic theories (though some of this must have been moving into the public domain), they initiated their first, limited realization. The addition of dialogue apparently began in the early 1780s. *Pantomimes dialoguées* that came too close to full theatre were, however, subject to the somewhat quixotic enforcements of the monopoly by the Théâtre-Français, which—along with the royal censors—had the right to read all texts of the minor theatres before they were staged. What we find in these heroic and spectacular pantomimes of the 1780s is a theatre of action and visual image, frequently offering ingenious representations of meaning, and almost always presenting a dramatic conflict of clear emblems. The spoken word, when it is introduced, appears often more an emotional cadenza than a necessary element in the play's architecture.[8]

On the eve of the Revolution, there were some twenty-three theatres in Paris;[9] and by 1791 they had been liberated to show anything they wished. There followed a rich flowering of spectacles of all sorts, rewrites of the classics, borrowings from everywhere, *drames*, topical vaudevilles, fantasies, and all sorts of pantomimes—*dialoguées, heroiques, historiques, féeriques*—and sometimes *mimodrames*. The Revolution produced an immediate and ferocious realization of the moralism urged by Diderot: the theatre, like revolutionary oratory, was assigned a quasi-legislative function. It was considered a vehicle toward the instauration of the reign of virtue on earth; its language was held to be performative, imposing the ethical categories that it evoked. Through censorship and auto-censorship, it was forced to be doctrinally correct; and it regularly celebrated the advent of each new regime, and then the victories of the French armies. Yet, with the possible exception of the period of the Terror, the theatre was far from wholly politicized. It was also variously frivolous, heroic, sentimental, and especially Gothic, inhabited by dark Schillerian and proto-Byronic heroes, lascivious monks, and forced nuns. That drama in general prospered is suggested by the fact that in 1807, on the eve of the Napoleonic decrees, there were some thirty-two theatres operating in Paris. Napoleon, who considered high neoclassical tragedy a necessary representation of imperial glory—and found his stage counterpart in the tragedian Talma—reduced the total number of theatres permitted to eight and reinstituted strict control over the right to show various genres. Two houses, the Gaîté and the Ambigu-Comique, were assigned exclusively to melodrama (the third great home of melodrama, the Porte Saint-Martin, lost its privilege, which it only regained in 1814). Yet the theatre in general, and melodrama in particular, continued to flourish on the Boulevard. With the coming of the Restoration in 1814, freedom of the theatres was once again instituted and then generally maintained, possibly from a conscious policy of bread and circuses on the part of an insecure monarchy. By the 1830s, one could attend forty-four theatres in Paris.[10]

The period as a whole marks a time of prodigious theatrical efflorescence and creativity. There was a rich proliferation of dramatic genres. On the Boulevard du Crime—as the boulevard du Temple was

known from the high rate of murder and abduction in its spectacles—
theatre was in the street as well as on stage, as troupes lured spectators
inside through bits of the forthcoming play. People absorbed their
theatre-going in massive doses: an evening's entertainment would
consist of various curtain raisers and afterpieces, as well as one and
sometimes two full-length plays, and would last five hours or more.
Authors like Pixerécourt and Ducange were popular heroes; actors
and actresses such as Tautin, Marty, Mlle Levesque, Adèle Dupuis
("La fille aux larmes"), then Bocage, Marie Dorval, Frédérick
Lemaître were idols. The actors seemed to make a point of living their
lives with a full theatricality (well captured in Dumas' play on the
English actor: *Kean, ou désordre et génie,* acted by Frédérick Lemàître).
Stage theatricality was excessive, and life seemed to aspire to its status,
as if in a fictional representation of the historical epic of Revolution,
bloodshed, battle, and Empire that the nation had been playing out.
As Théophile Gautier would write in 1864 on the occasion of the
revival of *La Nonne sanglante,* a melodrama of 1835, this was a time
when "a splendid burst of poetry illuminated the darkest brains, a rich
sap penetrated to the smallest twigs, never has one seen such a
proliferation of the spirit. Nothing was strong enough, bold enough,
passionate enough. Everyone went to the limit of his own nature. . . .
The excessive seemed natural and wild lyricism the tone of conversation. . . . A furious life animates these strange works, and their
authors have a rare quality . . . complete seriousness, an implicit faith
in their work." [11]

The work, if we exclude the comic productions, falls principally into
the categories of pantomimes, melodramas, and *drames.* Their sources
are sometimes Germanic, though not those authors we most repute
today: the most translated and imitated German playwright was
August von Kotzbue, author of sentimental and thrilling dramas.[12]
Schiller was known through *Die Räuber* (adapted by Lamartellière in
1792 as *Robert, chef de brigands*). Goethe's *Faust* became an heroic
pantomime, remarkable chiefly for its machinery, and later a
melodrama. English sources were partly in the sentimental drama of
George Lillo, and principally in fiction, especially the Richardsonian
novel, Scott, and the Gothics, Ann Radcliffe and M. G. Lewis.
Melodrama itself then became a French export to England with
Thomas Holcroft's adaptation of *Coelina* as *The Child of Mystery: A
Melo-drame,* in 1801.[13] Melodrama pillaged happily in epic, legend,
and history for its subjects, but the principal source was probably

always the novel, the genre to which it is so closely related, the first medium to realize the importance of persecuted women, struggling to preserve and impose the moral vision.

The term *mélodrame* itself seems to have made sporadic appearances following Rousseau's original use of it to characterize his *"scène lyrique,"* *Pygmalion* (1770), where a dramatic monologue alternates with pantomime and orchestral accompaniment.[14] To specify the first "true" melodrama seems virtually impossible. A contemporary (and hostile) critic, Armand Charlemagne, names Cuvelier de Trie's *C'est le Diable ou la Bohémienne* (1798), officially still labeled a *pantomime dialoguée*. The *Traité du mélodrame* makes the claim for Lamartellière's *Robert, chef de brigands* (1792), called a *drame*. Pixerécourt himself reaches back to the *drame lyrique* of Sedaine (such as *Le Déserteur*, 1769) and calls his own play of 1798, *Victor, ou l'Enfant de la forêt*—originally written as an opera for the Théâtre Favart, then transferred to the Ambigu-Comique minus the singing but with the orchestral parts— the "first born of melodramas." Later critics have proposed: Mayeur de Saint-Paul, *L'Elève de la nature* (1781, possibly the first pantomime to employ dialogue); Boutet de Monvel, *Les Victimes cloîtrées* (*drame,* 1791); Loaisel-Tréogate, *Le Château du diable* (*comédie héroique,* 1792).[15] Although, clearly, proto-melodrama comes into being in the early 1790s, Charles Nodier probably offers the most convenient solution when he says that melodrama should be dated from *Coelina*, in 1800.[16]

Terminology in France undergoes another shift in the 1830s, as *mélodrame* tends to give way to *drame* (possibly under the influence of the Romantic dramatists' practice) to describe productions that retain a full use of music and are generically indistinguishable from melodrama. One begins to detect a certain contamination of melodrama by the popular themes of Romantic drama: a search for the paradox of the sympathetic villain—deriving from both the outlaw hero and the repentant sinner of earlier melodrama—incarnated by such as the hero/executioner of Anicet-Bourgeois' *La Vénitienne* and Victor Hugo's monster/mother, Lucrèce Borgia; the creation of endings that, while preserving the ideal of virtue, strive toward tragic deaths and dwell on the heavy price exacted in the struggle with evil. The role of social class becomes more conspicuous in plays like *La Grâce de Dieu* (by Adolphe Dennery and Gustave Lemoine, 1841) and *Marie-Jeanne* (by Dennery and Mallian, 1843): the heroines are daughters of the people who must struggle against a system of economic and social exploitation consciously manipulated by the villains. The theme owes much to Romantic socialism; and it would continue to inform much later melodrama, in England and America as well as France, in which villains were habitually landlords or factory owners. There came to be a true socialist and populist tendency in melodrama, best represented by Félix Pyat's *Le Chiffonier de Paris* (1847). The pastoral urge of earlier melodrama tends to be supplanted by a fascination with the city, either as the symbol of corruption lying in wait for peasant innocence (as in *La Grâce de Dieu*), or as an unexplored world offering layers of mystery (as in *Les Bohémiens de Paris*, by Dennery and Grangé, 1843). There is spectacular exploitation of the Parisian underworld, its geography and the annals of its crimes. The immediate cause of these Parisian plays— beyond the general Romantic attention to the urban landscape—was Eugène Sue's enormously influential novel *Les Mystères de Paris* (1842–43), probably of all novels the one most frequently adapted for the stage, and a direct novelistic counterpart to melodrama.[17] Melodrama became a natural vehicle for the staging of topical events—especially celebrated crimes, as in Anicet-Bourgeois' *La Dame de Saint-Tropez* (1860)—and even for political and social satire. The major point of reference here is the roguish figure of Robert Macaire, originally created by Frédérick Lemaître from the unpromising materials of *L'Auberge des Adrets* (1823, by Benjamin Antier, Saint-Amand, and Polyanthe), then sharpened in the *Robert Macaire* he wrote with Antier in 1834.

Signs of what might be called decadence begin to appear in the genre in the late 1830s. Compared to the classical examples of Pixerécourt, Caigniez, Cuvelier, Ducange, the melodramas of Joseph Bouchardy, Adolphe Dennery, Louis Desnoyers, Félix Pyat suggest a less cosmic ambition, an increasing orientation toward the social "problem play." Ducange himself appears a pivotal figure here: already his famous *Trente ans, ou la Vie d'un joueur* (1827) and *Sept Heures!* (1829) are more studies in the hyperbolic ravages caused by villainous passions than efforts to realize here below the struggle of transcendent ethical forces. There is a tendency for some melodrama to become more "domestic," a greater interest in situation and plot, and a certain repose on the well-worn tenets of bourgeois morality. We are moving closer to the world of Alexandre Dumas *fils*, Emile Augier, Victorien Sardou; and beyond that, to the "genteel" melodrama of Victorian England. Bouchardy, immensely popular in the 1840s, suggests another aspect of decadence in the baroque complication of his plots: the melodramatic recognition becomes so intricate as to require a prologue, generally set some twenty years before the main action, which establishes the situation, even presents the birth of the principal characters, and can itself run to over twenty scenes. "Bouchardy's poetics," wrote his admirer Théophile Gautier, "can be summed up by this example: 'You here! by what prodigy? But you've been dead for eighteen months!'—'Silence! that is a secret which I shall carry back to the tomb.' " [18] The source of our interest is more than ever in the breathtaking ingenuities of suspense and peripety. Melodrama, here and in all the later examples of the genre, remains a coherent expressive mode and dramaturgy, and a spectacularly impressive stagecraft. Yet the form is attempting to do less. Nodier's emphatic remarks about Pixerécourt's quasi-religious function could no longer apply, for even though there is still a constant appeal to moral evidence (when this touched the political realm, it led to censorship problems, as with *Robert Macaire*) and the rights of virtue, the systematic effort to dramatize the signs of a cosmic ethical struggle has been muted and diverted. The concern now is primarily plot, suspense, excitement, the search for new categories of thrills. But if it declines in ambition, melodrama never dies out. It rather transforms itself, for it is a remarkably adaptable form: its premises, of structure, rhetoric, vision, can be exploited for a range of subjects in many different media. It is still very much with us today.

Returning to the heroic period, approximately 1800–1830, to reflect upon the profligate production of melodramas, we become aware that the genre was forming a theatrical audience. This role fell to melodrama partly as a consequence of the Revolution and the emigration, which depopulated the theatres of those aristocratic connoisseurs who knew the classical repertory by heart. Pixerécourt is reputed to have said that he wrote for people who did not know how to read; and all that we have said about the importance of the visible and unambiguous sign in melodrama confirms this. Yet French melodrama—in distinction to English—did not remain a form for the populace alone: all sectors of the bourgeoisie began turning to the Boulevard for their entertainment, realizing that here was a theatre offering much more appeal than the bloodless official houses, and even the critics began to concur. Under the Restoration, the principal Boulevard theatres were respectable places where good manners were not offended; the Ambigu-Comique, the Gaîté, and especially the Porte Saint-Martin offered almost luxurious houses where one could be seen without embarrassment. The mixture of social strata that found pleasure in melodrama was being prepared to respond to, even to demand, new theatrical aesthetics long before the Théâtre-Français was ready for transformation.[19]

These points of theatrical history begin to suggest how much traditional literary history is in need of revision. The period under discussion is traditionally presented as a great void, a desert lying between the work of Chateaubriand and Mme de Staël published around 1800, and the arrival of the Romantic generation in the late 1820s, or, in terms of the theatre, virtually between Beaumarchais and Victor Hugo. Whereas in fact the period was one of intense creativity, and particularly of theatrical creation. But this creativity was unfolding, not in the official theatre nor in the recognized genres, but in popular forms, and most notably in melodrama—which is why a traditional literary history has been so blind to the profound intellectual evolution of this period.[20] Specifically, the burgeoning of Romantic drama was being prepared on the Boulevard, and the doctrines that would be presented in Hugo's *Préface de Cromwell* in 1827 were already partially in practice.[21] More generally, some of the fundamental premises of the modern expressive mode, in particular its representations of ethical conflict, were being given their first trial. It would only be a slight exaggeration to argue that in France melodrama quite literally lies at the source of Romantic aesthetics of dramatization, in the theatre and in the novel. It appears, in any event, as their first approximation and as their radical form.

Geoffroy, the leading theatre critic of the Napoleonic period and a man of essentially classical tastes, wrote of *La Femme à deux maris* in 1802: "If this play were translated into tragic style, if one ennobled the characters and gave them a philosophical and sentimental coloration, it would be far worthier of the Théâtre-Français than most of the novelties produced there." [22] What Geoffroy has perceived is that all the elements of a new serious dramatic mode are present in Pixerécourt's theatre, and that the only thing preventing its recognition as competitor and successor to neoclassical tragedy is a difference of what one might call class style: melodrama remains too petit-bourgeois, both in its characters and in its verbal style—principally, in its use of prose over verse—to take over the official stage. Geoffroy speaks from an aesthetic which still considers it impossible to approach high theatre without the *alexandrin* and without a cast of kings and queens. What is notable is that despite this bias he should be able to recognize in Pixerécourt's melodrama the stuff of a contemporary drama speaking to the audience, dealing with issues that matter, and altogether closer to what the theatre should be all about than the neoclassical imitations of the Théâtre-Français.

Geoffroy's remarks in some manner prefigure the battle engaged two decades later, that had its first manifesto in Stendhal's *Racine et Shakespeare*.[23] In arguing for an historical prose tragedy on national themes, Stendhal, himself one of the least melodramatic of authors, was preparing the possibility of an "ennobled" melodrama, and indeed his sketch of a play, "The Return from Elba," has many analogues among the numerous Napoleonic melodramas. The immediate occasion of the first part of *Racine et Shakespeare* was the visit of an English troupe playing Shakespeare, and particularly the revelation of the highly dramatic style used by the English actors in playing tragedy—a style that had never, in England, undergone the same purification by decorum that it had in France. In 1822, the English actors were hissed by much of the audience, partly for aesthetic and partly for political reasons (perfidious Albion being anathema to the liberals, who tended to be classical in taste, while the early Romantics were Gothic and monarchist). By 1828, another visit by English Shakespearians reached a wider and more enthusiastic audience and a group of young writers ready to carry the battle for the liberation of the theatre into the citadel of the Théâtre-Français. They would do so supported by actors trained on the Boulevard, enthusiastic about the new dramaturgy, and prepared to play it.

What matters to us here is not the details of the Romantic battle for the theatre, nor the attack on the neoclassical unities, or most of the other points of doctrine in the *Préface de Cromwell* and other manifestos. It is rather the continuities between this movement and the melodramatic enterprise as it had developed over the preceding thirty years. A few perceptive critics have worked out in some detail what the dramaturgy of Victor Hugo and Alexandre Dumas owes to melodrama, in the use of coups de théâtre, of the unexpected and the fortuitous, the hyperbolic and grandiloquent, tableau and plasticity of representation, the expressive effects of music.[24] There are masked and mistaken identities; lost and refound parents and children, the operation of the *voix du sang*; dramatic and spectacular apparitions; physical struggle and combat; conversion and redemption; bloody villains and innocent victims; rhetorical antitheses and a pervasive moral polarization of the universe. The problem with most critical commentary on the debt of Romantic theatre to melodrama is that it lacks any real sense of melodrama as a total and coherent aesthetic, a sense of what its repertory of devices exists for. The point is not simply that Romantic theatre is melodramatic, but that it must be so: that only the system of melodrama provides authors like Dumas and Hugo with the rudiments of what they need to realize their conceptions on the stage. Romantic theatre is, no doubt, to a degree limited by its reliance on the melodramatic, yet this is a condition of its very success. It is no accident that Hugo's most purely melodramatic play, *Lucrèce Borgia*, is also dramatically the most successful. When Romantic authors tried to invent something wholly other than melodramatic expressionism, they fell into bookishness and non-theatre.[25]

Passing over all that very definition of the *drame* as a form owes to melodrama, in the *Préface de Cromwell*, it is worth dwelling on the central Hugolian concept of the "grotesque." There are considerable ambiguities involved in Hugo's use of the term. In particular, are we to understand that the grotesque is the polar opposite of the sublime—as the *laid* is the opposite of the *beau*—or rather that it is a mixture of the sublime and the ugly or even the demonic? Sometimes the grotesque is presented as the result of a combination, the characteristic of "intermediate beings," and sometimes it seems rather the inverse mirror image of the sublime, and a necessary "temps d'arrêt" in its contemplation. The main point would seem to be that the grotesque is conceived as a principle of opposition in conjunction with the sublime: it is conceivable only in terms of bipolar relationships. It arises essentially from the message of Christianity which says to man: "You are double." The "discovery" of the grotesque—this aesthetic and moral concept that breaks so radically with the classical idea of beauty and verisimilitude—is the discovery of dynamic contrast. Hugo writes of the *drame*: "Is it in fact anything other than this continual contrast between two opposed principles that ever confront one another in life, and that fight over man from the cradle to the grave?" [26] And further: "The character of the *drame* is the real; the real results from the completely natural combination of two types, the sublime and the grotesque, which intersect in the *drame* as they intersect in life and in the creation." The definition of "reality" is striking: it is considered to be the place of continuous struggle and interaction between yin and yang, archetypally manichaeistic principles. The world is a magnetic field charged from opposite poles. The generation of drama, then, comes—as much as in melodrama—from polarized concepts and forces. Dramatic interest is the result of their clash, and the violent oscillation from one to another. As Didier will say of the heroine in *Marion Delorme*, in a characteristic and revealing line: "Oh God, the angel was a demon!" These are the terms, and the stakes, of the drama. What differs in emphasis, from Pixerécourt to Hugo, is the greater interest Hugo shows in the meeting point of blackness and whiteness, demonism and angelism. Whereas the confrontation of bipolar opposites in melodrama most often results in the reaffirmation of two integers, in Hugo there is a greater chiaroscuro as the opposites struggle for dominance. This effect of chiaroscuro, so characteristic of the coloring of all Hugo's writing, results in part, in his theatre, from the fact that the confrontation is not only between characters, but within one character, struggling with his own impulses to angelism and demonism. And yet, any illusion of interiority, depth, or psychological complexity that this struggle gives is dispelled upon close examination. The forces themselves remain integral, and the character who is the arena of their struggle never gains psychological coherence or consistency. He is himself a kind of theatre of the sign.

HERNANI AND HIS PROBLEMS

One might in illustration of this proposition turn to the most clearly melodramatic of Hugo's plays, especially *Le Roi s'amuse* (1832) and *Lucrèce Borgia* (1833). In the former, Triboulet (who was to become Verdi's Rigoletto) is a perfect realization of the grotesque: hideous physical deformity coupled to the sublimity of pure paternal love. Lucrèce Borgia, Hugo explains in his preface to the second play, stands as the other panel of a diptych: she is hideous moral deformity joined to physical beauty and inhabited by the redeeming sentiment of maternal love.[27] Lucrèce is the monster/mother, the theatre of utterly polarized forces in clash, which are spectacularly acted out. The first act of the play turns entirely on masks and unmaskings, on a voix du sang that cannot speak its name, on public nomination and identification of the villain, who is driven out, to prepare her return in vengeance. The second act stages the mother's struggle to save her child (who doesn't, of course, know that Lucrèce is his mother). The third act is brilliantly dramatic, as the orgiastic banquet is revealed to be the scene of a mass poisoning, and drinking songs give way to the funeral dirge of the chanting, hooded monks who will step aside to reveal the array of coffins prepared for the victims. Everything has prepared the final thunderous confrontation of mother and son, the mother who has unintentionally poisoned the son, the son who strikes in unwitting matricide. In the very last line, after Gennaro has stabbed Lucrèce, the monster reveals her motherhood in a spectacular nomination: "Ah! ... you have killed me!—Gennaro! I am your mother!"

But to dwell further on *Lucrèce Borgia* would be to rehearse too much what we have already said about melodramatic dramaturgy. It is perhaps more important to confront one of Hugo's dramas that is less obviously informed by melodrama, one that is written in verse and that has a great symbolic value in history since it first planted the standard of the *drame romantique* at the Comédie-Française.[28] In *Hernani*, we may detect the problematic of a melodramatism under tragic disguise. This problematic essentially concerns the hero and his mode of being. We might begin by noting, however, that *Hernani* is remarkable for the plasticity of its scenography, for the rich coloration and chiaroscuro of its spectacle. The setting of each of the five acts is chosen for its plastic possibilities, for the play of color, light, costume, symbolic architecture, and accessories that it allows. From the half-lighted bedchamber, with its crimson drapes, hidden doors, and closet, of act I, we move, in act II, to the patio outside; it is full night, with a play of lighted windows and torches. Act III, in the portrait gallery of the Castle of the Silva, is conceived for a sensation scene, since the hiding place in which Don Ruy Gomez will conceal Hernani to baffle the king's pursuit is directly behind his own portrait, representation of his place in the line of the Silva, hence of the ethical imperative that forces him to protect his rival-guest at any cost. Act IV is most spectacularly symbolic of all, the crypt of Aix-la-Chapelle sheltering the tomb of Charlemagne, a Piranesi network of arches, stairs, pillars, lost in the obscurity, lit temporarily by the arrival of the conspirators with their torches, plunged into blackness again with the appearance of the new emperor, then relit with the arrival of his troops to arrest the conspirators. In contrast, act V unfolds a panoply of light and color, music and movement, in the gardens of the Palace of the Aragon, decorated for the wedding feast, peopled by costumed guests, framed by fountains playing.

The plastic and expressive qualities of the settings support a dramaturgy of gesture and tableau, one is tempted to say of posture. From the start, with the introduction of the masked king, Don Carlos, through the hidden doorway, we are in a world of sweeping and expressive attitudes. When Don Ruy Gomez enters to find his protégée and fiancée between two unknown cavaliers, he rips off his collar of the Order of the Golden Fleece and hurls his hat on the ground—gestures that are met by the king's throwing off his cloak to reveal his identity, which produces a tableau of three different reactions, from Don Ruy, Doña Sol, and Hernani (whose "eyes light up"). In act II, as Don Carlos is about to use force in the abduction of Doña Sol, out of the darkness, apparently from nowhere, Hernani rises up: "The king turns around to see Hernani immobile behind him in the shadow, his arms crossed under the long cloak that covers him, the wide brim of his hat turned up. Doña Sol cries out, runs to Hernani, and folds him in her arms" (II,ii). Then in act III there is the grandiose piece of melodramatic dramaturgy as Don Ruy, put before the agonizing choice of giving up Doña Sol as hostage to the king or surrendering the bandit placed under the protection of the sacred law of hospitality, moves haltingly toward his own portrait, which conceals the secret hiding place, reaches his hand toward the button that will open it, then turns back to fall on his knees before Don Carlos: "No! Pity. Take my head!" (III,vi). Most impressive of all as tableau is no doubt the moment in act IV when the cannon sounds, three shots to announce the election of Don Carlos as Holy Roman Emperor. Don Carlos is within Charlemagne's tomb, the conspirators in the crypt:

> *A distant cannot shot is heard. All remain arrested, silent. The door of the tomb is half opened. Don Carlos appears on the threshold. Pale, he listens. A second shot. A third. He opens the door completely, but without taking a step, erect, immobile on the threshold.*
> *Don Carlos. Gentlemen, stand off. The emperor is listening to you. All the torches are extinguished at once. Profound silence. Don Carlos takes a step in the shadows, so thick that one can scarcely see the conspirators, mute and immobile.*
>
> [IV,iii–iv]

Light, shadow, mute posture, and plastic tableau are fully impressive and expressive.

It is directly following this moment that, with the separation of the conspirators into commoners and nobles—the latter to be executed by the aristocratic axe—Hernani steps forward to center stage and, for the first time in the play, names himself with his true name, reveals his hidden identity, in a fine roll of epithets, in a language that itself mimes his grandiose gesture:

Puisqu'il faut être grand pour mourir, je me lève.
Dieu, qui donne le sceptre et qui te le donna,
M'a fait duc de Segorbe et duc de Cardona,
Marquis de Monroy, comte Albatera, vicomte
De Gor, seigneur de lieux dont j'ignore le compte.
Je suis Jean d'Aragon, grand maître d'Avis, né
Dans l'exil, fils proscrit d'un père assassiné
Par sentence du tien, roi Carlos de Castille!

[IV,iv,1722–29]

[Since one has to be noble to die, I rise.
God, who grants the scepter and gave it to you,
Made me Duke of Segorbe and Duke of Cardona,
Marquis of Monroy, Count Albatera, Viscount
Of Gor, lord of domains that I cannot number.
I am Juan of Aragon, Grand Master of Avis, born
In exile, proscribed son of a father assassinated
By the order of your father, King Carlos of Castille!]

This is the kind of speech that makes George Steiner comment that
Hugo's dramas are "completely hollow to any touch of intelligence.
The shapes of drama are being invoked without the substance." [29]
These resounding gestures and rhetorical flourishes do in fact appear
empty when judged against the ostensible subject and the ostensibly
tragic universe of the play; the drama is indeed one of "shapes." But
the apparent emptiness belongs to the problematics of the hero, which
need closer attention. For Hernani himself provides a thematic
representation of tragedy become melodrama without a clear recognition of its changed status.

From the moment we first see him, Hernani announces that:

Chargé d'un mandat d'anathème,
Il faut que j'en arrive à m'effrayer moi-même!

[I,ii,103–04]

[Charged with a mandate of anathema,
I must manage to terrify myself.]

He conceives himself as a marked man whose life must be consecrated
to a horrendous undertaking, for which he must make himself
ferocious. He elaborates in act III:

Je suis une force qui va!

Agent aveugle et sourd de mystères funèbres!
Une âme de malheur faite avec des ténèbres!
Où vais-je? je ne sais. Mais je me sens poussé
D'un souffle impétueux, d'un destin insensé.
Je descends, je descends, et jamais ne m'arrête.

[III,iv,992–97]

[I am a force that drives on!
Blind and deaf agent of funereal mysteries!
A soul of misfortune made of shadows!
Where am I going? I don't know. But I feel myself driven
By a wild wind, by a mad destiny.
I descend, I descend, and never stop.]

The reason for feeling so driven, so subject to an uncontrollable and demonic destiny, is to be sought in the fact that Hernani's father was executed at the order of Don Carlos' father, and that Hernani as a child swore vengeance, to be carried out by the one son on the other. Never, however, has the entire motivation of a plot and a psychology been given in such cavalier fashion as it is here:

Les pères ont lutté sans pitié, sans remords,
Trente ans! Or, c'est en vain que les pères sont morts!
Leur haine vit. Pour eux la paix n'est point venue,
Car les fils sont debout, et le duel continue.

[I,ii,97–100]

[The fathers fought, without pity, without remorse,
For thirty years! But the fathers have died in vain!
Their hatred lives. Peace has not come for them,
For their sons are on their feet, and the duel continues.]

When we discover in act IV that Don Carlos has forgotten this ancient history, we are not surprised, for we have never found it very convincing as the motive force of the plot. Hernani's self-conceptions seem fabricated from the most tenuous of factual material. The ostensible justification of his "mandate of anathema," and the impossibility to be happy in life and love that it entails, seems a mere token to permit the construction of a character who conceives himself as the cursed agent of dark and satanic mysteries. As much as in melodrama, the realm of menace and evil appears pure and unjustified. It is true that in his self-flagellations and in his constantly deferred vengeance—which tends to become a merely verbal defiance, especially apparent in acts II and IV, where Hernani has every opportunity to strike Don Carlos—and also in his rhetoric of a time out of joint that he alone must set right, this hero makes implicit reference to Hamlet. Yet he receives no visit from an unshriven paternal ghost, no extraterrestrial imperative, and his metaphysical bombast appears unwarranted. The Shakespearean echo only makes it more evident that Hernani is, by any realistic metaphysical or psychological standard, an inadequate vehicle in relation to the weight of rhetorical assertion that he must bear.

We can perhaps best grasp the mode of existence of such a hero in soliloquy. When Hernani remains behind at the end of act I, as Don Ruy, Don Carlos, and Doña Sol exit, and speaks his impassioned monologue, what we have is in no wise a debate, or a meditation, a turning-inward to seek self-knowledge and resolution in action. The soliloquy is rather pure self-expression, outburst, the saying of self and the self's destiny. The soliloquy is a kind of emphatic verbal gesture in the designation of Hernani. It is constructed on a repetition of the verbs deriving from Don Carlos' last line, naming Hernani as "quelqu'un de ma suite," and plays on the definition of being ("je suis") as determined by pursuit of the designated target ("je te suis").[30] The soliloquy ends with the image of Hernani as specter lying in wait for the king:

Le jour tu ne pourras, ô roi, tourner la tête
Sans me voir immobile et sombre dans ta fête;
La nuit tu ne pourras tourner les yeux, ô roi,
Sans voir mes yeux ardents luire derrière toi!

[I,iv,411–14]

[During the day you will not be able to turn your head, king,
Without seeing me immobile and somber at your feast;
At night you will not be able to move your eyes, king,
Without seeing my flaming eyes shine behind you!]

That is, Hernani's attempted definition of being at this moment of self-communion produces no clear result, no adequate complement to the verb to be, but rather resolves itself into an image, indeed a tableau which makes of his person and his "character" a gesture and a posture, a sign of retribution and of "anathema."

At every decisive moment of confrontation and decision, Hernani seeks, not the definition of self through introspection nor the affirmation of self in action, but simply self-expression, victory over verbal repression. Both the liberation and the negation found in self-expression can be traced in his nominations of himself. The name Hernani, designating the proscribed bandit dressed as a shepherd, is both a disguise of original identity and signifier of the damned identity. The name conceals a mystery, which he is about to reveal to Doña Sol in act I:

> Il faut que vous sachiez quel nom, quel rang, quelle âme,
> Quel destin est caché dans le pâtre Hernani.
>
> [I,ii,168–69]

> [You must know what name, what rank, what soul,
> What destiny lies hidden in the shepherd Hernani.]

But Don Carlos arrives to prevent further explication. In act III, when further disguised as an itinerant beggar, he surprises the wedding preparations at the Castle of the Silva and concludes that Doña Sol is going to marry Don Ruy (not understanding that she has rather hidden a poignard in her bosom), he throws off his first layer of disguise and offers himself to Don Ruy and his servants, calling upon them to collect the bounty placed on the head of the bandit. It is in "a thunderous voice" that he proclaims:

> Qui veut gagner ici mille carolus d'or?
> Je suis Hernani.
>
> [III,iii,856–57]

> [Who here present wants to earn a thousand gold ducats?
> I am Hernani.]

He continues in lines that turn on naming:

> Vous vouliez savoir si je me nomme
> Pérez ou Diego? Non, je me nomme Hernani.
> C'est un bien plus beau nom, c'est un nom de banni.
> C'est un nom de proscrit!
>
> [III,iii,858–61]

> [You wished to know if I am named

Perez or Diego? No, my name is Hernani.
It is a handsomer name, the name of a man banished.
The name of a man proscribed.]

Revelation of name here fixes on his maledicted identity. He assumes
his false name in an act of nomination which is a call for extinction.
Yet what will finally provoke his nomination in his true name is also
the promise of extinction: he steps forth to make sure that the
hecatomb the new emperor is preparing won't pass him over:

Place à Jean d'Aragon! ducs et comtes, ma place!
Je suis Jean d'Aragon, roi, bourreaux et valets!
Et si vos échafauds sont petits, changez-les!

[IV,iv,1738–40]

[Make way for Juan of Aragon! dukes and counts, my place!
I am Juan of Aragon, king, executioners and valets!
And if your scaffolds are small, change them!]

Charles Quint's pardon, however, allows him to assume this "true"
identity and live also. "Changed," as he says, by the act of clemency,
he becomes "a covered volcano," and when Doña Sol in act V calls
him Hernani, he rejects the name as an image from a nightmare now
past. But with the apparition of Don Ruy, sounding the horn that
signifies his forgotten promise to death, he suddenly refuses her address
to him as Don Juan; he rises, "terrible," as the stage direction puts it,
to cry:

Nommez-moi Hernani! nommez-moi Hernani!
Avec ce nom fatal je n'en ai pas fini!

[V,iii,1989–90]

[Call me Hernani! call me Hernani!
I have not done with that fatal name!]

The successive nominations reveal, not the integral clarity of naming
in melodrama, but irresolvable conflict and contradiction. The hero is
ever saying "I am . . . ," but he can never complete the predicate in
any consistent or durable fashion. The contradictions, which are
neither justified nor analyzed, point to no psychological opacity (in
the manner of the implicit figure of reference, Hamlet), but rather to
incoherence. The hero's two names are in fact, like "sublime" and

"grotesque" in the *Préface de Cromwell*, or like "angel" and "demon" evoked in the final act here, or indeed like the black and the gold that adorn Hernani at the end, the designations of two forces that confront one another within the theatre of the "hero."

The problem could perhaps be stated in this manner: all of Hernani's rhetoric, and all his important acts in the play, appear postulated on the Rousseauian effort to say the self in its most intimate recesses, to render the self transparent. Yet expression opens no recesses and sheds little light. What is expressed seems literally superficial, unmotivated, unjustified. But only if we insist upon viewing the character as a psychological structure. If, recalling the Hugolian analysis of the grotesque, one conceives the character rather as that theatre for the interplay of manichaeistic forces, the meeting place of opposites, and his self-expressions as nominations of those forces at play within himself—himself their point of clash—the role of character as a purely dramaturgic center and vehicle becomes evident. Jean Gaudon speaks of the "transparency" of the Hugolian character. But Rousseau's transparency opens onto inner recesses, depths, whereas here we see onto a plane, a screen onto which is projected the clash of forces. Gaudon approaches this perception when he says of Hugo: "In substituting for the opacity of characters in French [neoclassical] tragedy a dramaturgy of transparency, he freed himself from the psychological mortgage. The return to a simple and coherent system of signs put an end to the exploits of emotional casuistry. . . ." [31] If "transparency" is a misleading word, the dramaturgy of signs, refusing depth analysis and conflict founded on psychology, accurately characterizes the Hugolian character and his dramatic life.

This dramaturgy of pure signs, however, has consequences that go beyond the problematics of "character," that implicate the very mode of existence of the play. *Hernani* is subtitled *L'Honneur castillan*, and the play is structured on a series of heroic gestures in illustration of the concept. Don Carlos and Hernani, though enemies, take turns saving one another's lives in the first two acts; while Don Ruy saves Hernani's life in act III, with the promise that Hernani will accept death when Don Ruy demands it. Then in act IV Don Carlos, become the Emperor Charles Quint, magnanimously grants pardon to all those—including both Hernani and Don Ruy—who had conspired against his life. We have a series of moments of intense confrontation in which heroic roles and identities are sharply defined. One such moment occurs in act III, when Hernani offers himself to Don Ruy's sword with the words:

> Taisez-vous, doña Sol. Car cette heure est suprême,
> Cette heure m'appartient. Je n'ai plus qu'elle.
>
> [III,v,1090–91]

> [Speak no more, Doña Sol. For this hour is supreme,
> This hour belongs to me. It is all that I have.]

The "supremacy" of this moment of heroic sacrifice depends upon its extremity, its height and grandeur. It echoes the heroic ethic of Corneille's tragedies, and particularly the moment when the Cornelian hero can seize his moral identity in a supreme act by which he immolates all lesser considerations. This characteristic moment is represented in Corneille's *Cinna* by the Emperor Augustus' decision for clemency as the supreme act of mastery: "Je suis maître de moi comme de l'univers; / Je le suis, je veux l'être." ["I am master of myself as of the universe; I am master, I wish to be."] [32] This moment will be imitated by Don Carlos–Charles Quint in his act of pardon, at the end of act IV, an act by which his own instantaneous conversion into a figure of truly imperial grandeur instantaneously changes the lives of all the quarrelsome and conspiratorial figures around him. The final act turns on what seems to be an analogous point of heroic ethical imperative. When Don Ruy arrives on Hernani's wedding night to exact fulfillment of Hernani's promise to give up his life, the hero—after protesting the bitterness of his fate and pleading for one night of love before emptying the poison vial—concedes:

> Laissez-moi, doña Sol. Il le faut.
> Le duc a ma parole, et mon père est là haut!
>
> [V,vi,2065–66]

> [Let me be, Doña Sol. I must.
> The duke has my word, and my father is above.]

He has indeed sworn his oath on the head of his father and to a man who saved his life at great peril to his own. Given the code of "Castillan honor," there is no escape for Hernani, and at the very threshold of paradise he is bound to turn away to death. But the very extremity and excruciation of the situation makes it all the more difficult for us to accept his forced suicide as the necessary consequence of Castillan ethics and ancestor worship. The suspension of critical intelligence cannot cover so much. For all of its being set in Spain in 1519, the play has not convinced us of the reality of Hernani's heroic bind. The scene indeed comes perilously close to foolishness. Don Ruy, whose deepest motive is pure sexual jealousy, is himself near to being a character from comedy; and when he arrives on stage in the last act, wearing a black masker's costume and sounding Hernani's horn, he is a simulacrum of extra-terrestrial vengeance rather than the real thing. Nothing convinces us that the tomb has op'd its ponderous and marble jaws, and that Hernani is constrained to obey a cosmic imperative. If the promise to Don Ruy has any meaning to us, it is not because of any putative heroic ethical system, but because of the impressive dramaturgy that framed the promise, at the end of act III, when Hernani detached the horn from his belt, gave it to Don Ruy with a solemn clasp of the hands, and Don Ruy called upon the portraits of his ancestors—those portraits which throughout the act have been the very determinants of his loyal conduct—to act as witnesses to the oath. It is the plastic and dramatic impression of the vow alone that gives it force and significance, not any moral, intellectual, or even historical reference that it may claim. By its impressive representation, it claims the status of the melodramatic vow: an absolute imperative (which also concerned fathers), an unalterable given, though here in a more precarious situation since the system of fidelities and ethical forces is much less clear in *Hernani* than in melodrama.[33] For the same reasons, we cannot "believe" in the necessity of the pseudo-tragic slaughter before us at the end of the play—as not only Hernani, but Doña Sol and Don Ruy lie dead—but we can respond to the poetic gesture whereby the ill-fated lovers define death as the true space of their union:

> Vers des clartés nouvelles
> Nous allons tout à l'heure ensemble ouvrir nos ailes.
> Partons d'un vol égal vers un monde meilleur.
> Un baiser seulement, un baiser!
>
> [V,vi,2151–54]

> [Toward a new shining light
> We will together soon open our wings.
> Let us set out in flight together toward a better world.
> A kiss only, a kiss!]

This lyric flight has nothing to do with Castillan honor, but with the dramatic equivalence of death and the maiden, the purely theatrical creation of the perfect final embrace.

The texture of references to Castillan honor, to a Cornelian heroic morality, to the supreme actions required to set right a time out of joint, to tragic necessity, must finally strike us, in Steiner's phrase, as "hollow to the touch of intelligence." The play simply has no coherent heroic and moral metaphysics to justify the appeal to such concepts. At worst, their evocation rings as false as the inevitable echo of Shakespearean heroic blank verse in English Romantic drama. But the very nonchalance and lack of justification in the reference should alert us to what else is going on in *Hernani*. When Steiner remarks of another of Hugo's plays, *Ruy Blas*, that it "erects an edifice of incident, passion, rhetoric, and grand gesture on the most precarious of foundations," he in fact touches on the core of Hugo's dramaturgy.[34] The "real" foundations of Hernani's actions and words are precarious indeed. All Hugo's interest goes to the structure reared above them, predicated upon them. Hernani's "supreme" confrontation with Don Ruy, the new emperor's act of clemency, Hernani's acceptance of the poison: these are gestures that fail to name ethical imperatives, that rather gesture toward meaning, toward a realm, or a medium, in which we could believe in their moral reality because we could believe them founded, grounded, justified. They are not grounded and justified in *Hernani*, and this makes the play a perfect example of T. S. Eliot's concept of sentimentality, of "excess" of claim in relation to what has been demonstrated.[35] What we are left with in *Hernani* is the interplay of the metaphorical vehicles themselves, the grand gestures in spectacular plastic confrontation. The drama exists principally on the plane of its representation and opens up no deeper or further signification. Hence it is truly a drama of "shapes" rather than "substance": a theatre using the simulacra of the heroic tragic universe in the manner of the melodramatic sign, but without even the clear system of references of the latter form. Hugo's theatre is effective finally because of its theatricality, its play of signs in spectacular representation, its clash of lyrically shaped "characters."

Hernani himself remains in our mind the hero of his lyric gestures:

> Monts d'Aragon! Galice! Estramadoure!
> —Oh! je porte malheur à tout ce qui m'entoure!—
> J'ai pris vos meilleurs fils pour mes droits; sans remords,

Je les ai fait combattre, et voilà qu'ils sont morts!
C'étaient les plus vaillants de la vaillante Espagne.
Ils sont morts! Ils sont tous tombés dans la montagne,
Tous sur le dos couchés, en braves, devant Dieu,
Et, si leurs yeux s'ouvraient, ils verraient le ciel bleu!

[III,iv,973–80]

[Mountains of Aragon! Galicia! Extremadura!
Oh I bring misfortune to everything around me!
I took your best sons for my rights; without remorse
I set them to fight, and now they are dead!
They were the most valiant of valiant Spain.
They're dead! They all fell in the mountains,
All laid on their backs, like heroes, before God,
And if their eyes were to open, they would see the blue sky!]

There is no true self-definition here, and the Byronic satanism that marks Hernani's self-conceptions is trivial. Its main interest is really functional: it serves as slender support for a rhetoric that unfolds a sweeping tableau, a gesture of attitude. If the rhetoric of the heroic ethic in Hugo is founded on the void, if even the expression of self refers to no coherent psychological being, rhetoric and expression nonetheless create a lyric and plastic theatre that is the medium for a clash of grandiose postures, sublime and grotesque, that define the space of their opposition.

The tendency toward a theatre of "shapes" is pushed to its outer limits in *Les Burgraves* (1843), the play that ended Hugo's active theatrical career. Here we have a theatre that has realized even further its spectacular and its architectonic qualities (*Les Burgraves* is first of all a certain architecture, that of the medieval Rhine) [36] and yet has simultaneously become more and more, in ambition, the drama of an otherness, whereby the action represented on the stage appears to be only a figuration of the true drama that is somehow behind or beyond. The literal drama is unremittingly overburdened by a weight of mysterious and grandiose reference beyond itself. The central conflict of the drama is played out by two men close to a hundred years old—one of them first revealed as a kind of mummy-like figure in the hollow of a pillar, the other a beggar who turns out to be the sometime emperor Frederick Barbarossa—as if to suggest that even the distanced and heightened actuality of the twelfth century is too narrow to accommodate the drama of the Idea. In some respects, this play is headed toward Symbolist drama, toward what Mallarmé would call "the theatre of our mind alone." [37] Yet there is this all-important difference, that Hugo is profoundly unclear what his Idea is—is simply attracted to the idea of Idea—and attention is once again shifted back to the plastic shapes of the represented drama, to the vehicles of a metaphor whose construction is failed. It is significant that the third and final part of the drama tends to become—as more than one critic has noted—unadulterated melodrama. Hugo can find no other way to dramatize the problematic he has endeavored to create earlier in the play; he is not yet Strindberg or Claudel, and the only means of dramatic resolution he has to hand are the means so successfully used in *Lucrèce Borgia* and *Le Roi s'amuse*: recourse to the heightened threat, confrontation, and struggle of melodrama.

We need not undertake the analysis of Hugo's other plays, nor need we enter into examination of the even more obviously melodramatic Alexandre Dumas, whose *La Tour de Nesle* might deserve special mention as creating a new subspecies, the monster play. Beyond the important surface resemblances—the Romantics' use of the properties and effects of melodrama—there is evidently a deep affinity in the very conception of drama as a plastic interplay of spectacular signs referring to a clash of cosmic imperatives. The difference lies in what one might call both a greater sophistication and a greater confusion on the part of the Romantic dramatists as to the ontology of the cosmic struggle and the possibility of expressing it. The robust confidence of a Pixerécourt that the signs of evil and virtue will become visible through the expressionistic gesture, and that these signs name imperatives that are thus themselves made manifest on earth, seems lacking in Hugo. The greater *démesure* of his drama, and particularly of its language, reflects a greater uncertainty about its true subject, a heightened sentiment of standing over the void, constructing fantastic structures on the most precarious of bases.[38] Uncertainty and démesure are also related to the claim to tragic dimension. Georges Lote has perceptively noted that if Hernani finished at the end of act IV, it would have a fully realized melodramatic structure, including conversion of the villain (Don Carlos, in the occasion), recognition and reward of hero and heroine. Whereas act V brings the tragic conclusion. From which Lote concludes that Hugo, unable to choose between the two subjacent models of his drama, simply proceeded by addition of one to the other.[39] More precisely, I think, there was no way to choose, because there was no possible reconciliation of the forces at play. Both "endings" are possible, neither is conclusive: the dynamism of the conflict alone matters. If the conclusion of act V may satisfy us, it is not because it resolves any of the forces in manichaeistic struggle in the theatre of the hero—on the contrary, it shows them as irreconcilable to the end—but because it finds a lyric, elegiac resolution in the equation of the lovers' embrace with death.[40]

The problem is not, as George Steiner would have it, that "the romantic vision of life is non-tragic," in that Romanticism promises a "compensating heaven" to "the guilt and sufferings of man." [41] Steiner goes astray, I believe, in his argument that Christian (or Rousseauist) redemption is incompatible with tragedy. Some form of a reconciliation to the Sacred is probably indispensable to the tragic, and this is no less true for *King Lear* or *Phèdre* than it is for the *Oresteia* or the *Bacchae*. It is thus not the rise of Christianity that makes tragedy impossible, but rather its decline, entailing the loss of the last operative system of embracing sacred myth—as Steiner appears in other pages of his book to recognize. Hence it seems inaccurate to say that Romantic "near-tragedy" represents "the desire of the romantics to enjoy the privileges of grandeur and intense feeling associated with tragic drama without paying the full price." [42] The problem is not so much an unwillingness to pay the price as an inability to say the price: an uncertainty as to what the price is, where it may be located, what makes its payment necessary. For men in the post-sacred universe, the mimesis of sacrifice no longer has clear referents. With the loss of sacred symbolism, only the uncertain constructions of dramatic metaphor remain.

Emblematic, then, of the Romantic dramatic enterprise are those plays constructed precisely around a central dumbness, an unspeakable darkness, which is not so much the void of meaning as the over-fullness of awful meaning, the fully sublime. *Lucrèce Borgia, Ruy Blas, Les Burgraves* approach this status—as does *Chatterton*—but the best example might be *The Cenci* (1819), by that most melodramatic of English Romantic poets, Shelley.[43] Beatrice Cenci, who answers incest with parricide, is imaged as

> She who alone, in this unnatural work,
> Stands like God's angel ministered upon
> By fiends; avenging such a nameless wrong
> As turns black parricide to piety. . . .

[V,i]

The point is less that the chosen crime and subject is unnameable, than that an unspeakable subject has been chosen and placed at the heart of the drama. The words can never designate it, yet they are charged by it, as the ethical imperatives and actions of the play are determined by it. And this will be true as well of the most ambitious novels in the melodramatic mode, in their effort to represent significances generated from a central meaning that is absent and occulted.

At its most exciting and successful, the Romantic theatre is superbly colorful plastic representation, the thunderous vehicle of a murky tenor whose very ineffability is portentous and further heightens the plane of representation. Exploiting, not pity and terror, but horror and admiration, it achieves a high and impressive theatricality. At its more modest and mundane, the Romantic theatre—like the later melodramas mentioned previously—points toward the bourgeois drama and the "well-made play" of the second half of the century. Dumas' *Antony*, with its domesticizing and socializing of melodrama and the tenebrous hero, is the symbolic pivot here, as several critics have noted, the play that most clearly prepares Sardou, Augier, and Dumas *fils*.[44] The revival of the theatre from such superficialities would be the work of those like Ibsen who could reinvest the social problem play with the moral and dramatic urgency of melodrama, a sense of its stakes and of the forces evoked by its gestures.

It seems important to understand that the death of tragedy is paralleled by the rise of what has here been called "melodrama," and that this will become an enduring mode of the modern imagination. The choice of the French Romantics to wage their major battle for literary recognition in what they considered the most prestigious and symbolic of genres, the theatre, enables us to perceive the articulation of the melodramatic to the Romantic enterprise, its role as the expressionistic dramatic ambition within the Romantic imagination. French Romantic theatre is of particular interest to us because it institutionalized the melodramatic without that name; it provides a particularly clear instance of an expressive mode that permeates much of Romanticism, and allows us to register the presence of melodrama in other Romantic and post-Romantic literature, whether or not it is literally in touch with stage melodrama. As consideration of *Hernani* suggests, the stage may not have been the best place to unfurl the melodramatic imagination; and this in fact was more or less clearly recognized, eventually, by the Romantics themselves. The possibilities of a drama of the moral occult, the clash of grandiose forces, must necessarily be limited in a form whose register of signs is so highly codified, where the restrictions of real space, real color and contour are so evident. The sweeping gestures and spectacular confrontations of *Hernani* tend to stretch the physical stage to its limits, and to look toward the novelistic. It is in the novel that writers of more complex melodramatic ambitions than a Pixerécourt will find the best medium for their dramatizations. In the novel, the struggle of ethical imperatives will open up convincing recesses in a world that no longer need be realized through visual simulacra, but in words alone.

5

Balzac: Representation and Signification

Tout est mesquin et petit dans le réel, tout s'agrandit dans les hautes sphères de l'idéal.

—Balzac, "Lettre à Hippolyte Castille"

I

The start of *La Peau de chagrin*, the first of Balzac's completely realized novels, presents, we saw, a narrator pressuring the details of reality, hammering at them to make them yield, release the terms and tokens of a truer, more intense drama, a super-drama both suggested in and hidden by the surface of reality.[1] We noted the narrator's effort to go through and beyond surfaces, to the locus of this fundamental conflict, to find the grandiose entities of a cosmic drama figured by Raphaël de Valentin's human drama. Similarly, the action of Balzac's novels tends to resolve itself, in moments of crisis, into tableaux of confrontation, where the actors stand at center stage and say their states of being, using a vocabulary that defines their positions and the sense of their lives, that sums up all they are in relation to one another in sweeping verbal gestures. The expressive formulations of the Comte and Comtesse de Restaud, in *Gobseck*, provide but one example of the victory over verbal repression that belongs to climactic confrontation. The power of nomination—of self and other—that they achieve permits a clarification of their drama through its resolution into pure verbal and dramatic signs. Their situation and their attitudes bathe in the stark lighting of moral manichaeism. The characters' gestures make clear the true stakes of the drama; and the narrator's gestures—particularly his construction of signification on gesture— suggest the charge of extraordinary and hyperbolic meaning postulated through the actions of the everyday universe. Gesture is essentially metaphoric, in that it is the token vehicle of a grandiose and sometimes ineffable tenor.[2] It claims to refer to a world behind and beyond the apparent world, to the realm of occult moral forces, forces hidden but also operative, that must be wrested into language. Balzac said of *La Peau de chagrin*—and could have said as much of any of his novels, including those considered the most meticulously "realistic"—"Tout y est mythe et figure." [3] The document is doubled by the vision; it is ready to release the vision under the scrutinizing pressure of the glance, with the insistent reading.

Balzac's melodramatic technique and vision in his fiction are not unrelated to literal, stage melodrama. His earliest literary ambition was to write a successful play, and throughout his life he returned with almost compulsive insistence to the idea that true literary glory was to be conquered only on the stage—a common Romantic ambition, as we noted. His numerous theatrical projects have been well documented, and on the whole they are essentially within the realm of melodrama.[4] His earliest completed play, *Le Nègre: Mélodrame en trois actes*—proposed to the Théâtre de la Gaîté—dates from 1822, when in the novel he was pursuing the related enterprise of Gothic fiction. There were many other projects of this type—*Le Mendiant, Le Lazaroni, Le Corsaire rouge, Le Corse*—and several abortive attempts at collaboration with such established melodramatists as Anicet-Bourgeois, Desnoyers, Dupetit-Méré, Frédérick Lemaître, and even Pixerécourt (who proposed a stage version of *Le Médecin de campagne*). Several of Balzac's novels attracted other dramatists who adapted them for the theatre. His own dramas that were staged—*Vautrin, Paméla Giraud, Les Ressources de Quinola, La Marâtre*—have generally been branded as failures.[5] The most successful is probably *La Marâtre* ("The Stepmother"), certainly the blackest of the lot, the most faithful to melodrama. The problem here—and it is even more exaggeratedly the case with *Vautrin*—is that the complication of the Balzacian vision, its concern with what is to be found beyond the gestures of the real, makes the literal stage too confining. For all the difference in tone and subject, these plays have an ambition similar to Vigny's *Chatterton*, a desire to suggest the "second drama" untouched by the words. Balzac's struggle to reach this realm leads to inextricable complication, multiple disguises, an exposition of relationships in which the spectator loses his way. The novel is a more successful medium for Balzac partly because he can offer a view of all that goes on, in the words of René Guise, "behind the drama offered to the spectators"; he can perform its "autopsy." [6]

Yet clearly the vision and the means for getting it across remain, in Balzac's fiction, profoundly theatrical. The tissue of references to the theatre suggests an awareness that he was writing for a public whose responses and taste had been formed by the theatre, and most of all by melodrama—the one genre that had filled the silence of the post-revolutionary period and offered a coherent aesthetic to an untrained audience. And the desire to see his texts realized on the stage by such as Marie Dorval and Frédérick Lemaître suggests a deep affinity between their acting styles and Balzac's novelistic style.[7] His is a dramatic and scenic art. "His novels are constructed of several *scenes*, strong moments between which he explains, analyzes, prepares," says Guise.[8] The novels work toward moments of confrontation conceived as *scènes à faire*, moments where grandiose signification achieves melodramatic representation. Style is conceived as a dramatization of reality, a heightening of effect in order to pass the footlights.

If the expressive means and premises of melodrama so predominate in Balzac's novels, it is because the melodramatic imagination is authentically central to his conception of life and its artistic representation. Like both Pixerécourt and Victor Hugo, he sees in the moral polarization of existence a fundamental law and an aesthetic principle. Man is "homo duplex," life "results from the play of polar principles," and art demands a confrontation of contraries.[9] The law of contrast could in fact be considered one of Balzac's most fundamental aesthetic canons, and the dramatizations that he creates are born from absolute and sweeping oppositions. The stakes played for in *La Peau de chagrin* are explicitly manichaeistic and hyperbolic: "*Vouloir* nous brûle et *Pouvoir* nous détruit; mais SAVOIR. . . ." (9:40).[10] The novel dramatizes absolute choices of ways of being: the Antiquary's exclusively mental orgies; Foedora's cold and inviolate egotism; Pauline's absolute self-abnegation and gift of self; the courtesans Aquilina and Euphrasie's choice of a brief, flaming existence; Rastignac's systematic dissolution. Raphaël chooses sequentially from among these, dedicating himself successively to austere meditation in the "aerial sepulchre" of his garret, then to the worldly courtship of Foedora, then to orgiastic debauch, then, after his reprieve from suicide, to an enclosed egotism for which he "castrates his imagination," finally to expire in a paroxysm of desire. The absoluteness of the choices to be made is symbolized by the series of three encounters with the gambling tables on which the novel turns.

The second of these (in terms of Raphaël's life; the third in presentation in the novel) is undertaken by Rastignac in Raphaël's stead, in an effort to save him from suicide by providing the means of "a profound dissolution," which Rastignac defines as creating a "new sort of death in fighting against life" (9:145–46). The meaning of this "profound dissolution" is first suggested by Rastignac's rooms, where

Raphaël waits for his friend to return from the life-or-death expedition. The organizing principle of the description is suggested by its first detail: "At the center of the mantelpiece rose a clock topped by a Venus, crouched on her tortoise, holding in her arms a half-smoked cigar" (9:147). The decor of the room reveals an underlying play of contrast between elegance and disorder, riches obtained through love or chance and a fundamental poverty and improvidence. "Opulence and misery coupled naively in the bed, on the walls, everywhere. You would have said a Neapolitan palace bordered by slums. It was the room of a gamester or suspicious character . . . who lives off sensations and doesn't worry about incoherences. The picture moreover was not lacking in poetry." This "poetry" is precisely derived from opposition, the "coupling" of breathless extremes, the images of a life turned on the wheel of fortune. The final sentence sums up: "How could a young man naturally hungry for emotions resist the attractions of a life so rich in oppositions, which gave him the pleasures of war in the time of peace?" The door is then thrown open, and Rastignac rushes in with his hat full of gold, twenty-seven thousand francs.

The descriptive passage, evoking the poetry and seduction of the life of violent and dramatic contrast, of frequent peripety and constant excitement, prepares Raphaël's experience of dissolution, and the theory of debauchery that he develops from it. "Debauchery is surely an art like poetry and requires hardy souls" (9:150). One must remake one's body, harden it, and forge a new soul. Debauchery is most profoundly an effort to transcend the quotidian by creating "a dramatic life within one's life," a melodramatic existence. War, power, art are forms of debauchery; and for private Mirabeaus or Napoleons, revolution and conquest assume the form of dissolution. As Balzac would later write to a critic, "Great works . . . endure by their passionate dimension. And passion is excess, and is evil." [11] "All excesses are related," says Raphaël. Their meaning is already that of the Baudelairian "gulf" or abyss, into which one plunges to find one knows not what, but at least something new, something to reinject drama into the gray ennui of existence. "Perhaps the idea of the infinite lies in these precipices? . . ." So that the plunge into debauch becomes a means of seizing—if it be seizable, if it exist—some arcane principle of life. "Debauchery comprehends everything. It is a perpetual close embrace of all life, or better, a duel with an unknown power, with a monster" (9:151). The debauchee, like Baudelaire's drunkard of "Enivrez-vous," defies the laws of ordinary nature (especially the laws of his physical organism) and, in his search for the rare and excessive sensation, recreates himself as anti-nature, as a creature who, like the Balzacian elegant or the Baudelairian dandy, makes life meet him on his own terms, who breaks through nature to a world where sensation, artifice, drama, the sense of the infinite, and death commingle. In systematic dissolution, man becomes his own maker: he creates himself "a second time, as if to mutiny against God." He is the dramatist of his own existence. Overcoming the repressions of the ordinary, he lives beyond the quotidian. In all senses, he lives beyond his means, in a constantly heightened drama.

The concept of "living beyond one's means" is played out in all relations of life in Balzac's novels. It is first of all the financial condition of many of the characters who interest him most, especially his young men on the way up, who are always in debt for the furnishings needed for their appearance in *le monde* to such a degree that they appear veritable speculators, whose windfall will be a rich marriage or liaison. The tailors, hatters, bootmakers, jewelers who deck them in the necessary accessories themselves understand that they are staking a kind of risk capital which will be repaid when and if success is forthcoming. (Rastignac's tailor in *Le Père Goriot* considers himself a "hyphen" between a young man's present and his future.) The construction of a social representation elaborated by such as Rastignac, Lucien de Rubempré, Maxime de Trailles, Godefroid de Beaudenord, and so many other young lions—the types Balzac qualifies as "pirates in yellow gloves"—[12] always rests on the most precarious of foundations, and failure to reach the payoff can start the chain of collection that compensates with a vengeance for the usurpation of what is not one's own: which gives the kind of total catastrophe and smash detailed in *Illusions perdues, Gobseck, La Cousine Bette*, and so many other novels. But living beyond one's means is not financial only: it is represented in a whole range of moral conditions, where people through passion, the will to power, or poetry try to live beyond what is normally allotted to man. The courtesan who, like Aquilina and Euphrasie or Coralie or Esther Gobseck, burns her life in a quick, spectacular flame of pleasure; those who like old Grandet or Lisbeth Fischer consecrate their life to gold or to vengeance; he who like Castanier of *Melmoth réconcilié* enters into a diabolical pact for pleasure and power; or those like Balthasar Claës of *La Recherche de l'Absolu* and Frenhofer of *Le Chef-d'oeuvre inconnu* who turn from ordinary life to the monomaniacal pursuit of creation or contemplation—all are examples of fundamentally similar excesses, of life lived with a superior intensity, not so much on borrowed as on usurped time, on the brink of the abyss which hides one of the integers of the occult moral world shadowed forth by the Antiquary's *Vouloir/Pouvoir/ Savoir*. Excess is necessary to approach the essential and the true, that which is hidden by what men ordinarily call "reality" as by a curtain. Living beyond one's means itself falls into two complementary polar categories, obeying the law of contrast: those who plunge into desire hyperbolically, exhausting life in the manner of the magic skin, in an orgy of *vouloir* coupled to *pouvoir;* and those who attempt to elevate themselves above experience, to achieve, like the Antiquary, the "sublime faculty of summoning the universe to appear within oneself . . . the pleasure of encompassing everything, of seeing all, of leaning over the edge of this world to interrogate other spheres, to listen to God" (9:41). The ultimate such figure in the *Comédie Humaine* is possibly the usurer Gobseck, who, through his control of the money flow, can make all the dramas of life pass through his bare chamber, and enjoy life as a perfect spectacle of which he is both the detached spectator and the prime mover, the perfect demiurge. The *Comédie Humaine* is in fact constructed on a basic metaphor of expense and conservation, which is both financial and sexual.[13] Both are reiterated in their extreme forms—on the one hand, the courtesan, the debauchee, the profligate, on the other, the miserly, inviolate, and sterile, like Foedora, who is "an atheist in love" (9:137) or Gobseck, who is of "the neuter gender" (2:627). Living beyond one's means signifies espousing one of the underlying metaphors of life, creating a "drama" in one's existence from the perception of a life behind and beyond the curtain.

Yet seeing behind the curtain, finding the significant vision, encounters the problem of expression. Can one say, can one incarnate, what one has glimpsed in the abyss? Can one achieve, in life and in art, that victory over repression which in Balzac most appears as a victory over the ordinary terms of "life" and "reality"? The whole of Balzac's work strives toward this question, the question of what is by its nature not directly representable, yet also the most significant. The paradigm is *Le Chef-d'oeuvre inconnu*, where the artist Frenhofer's search to render his exquisite vision results in the destruction of the language in which it must be rendered. "To be a great poet, it is not enough to know syntax thoroughly and to avoid grammatical errors," Frenhofer proclaims (9:392). This cavalier attitude toward the sign-system corresponds to an ambitiously expressionist aesthetic: "The mission of art is not to copy nature, but to express it!" (9:394). By "express," in this sense, Frenhofer means the articulation and representation of the occult principles of nature, the causes, he says, as well as the effects. He has been led beyond mimesis into the temptation to wield directly nature's own creative principles, the attempt to "force the arcana of nature" and to "steal the secret of God" (9:394,392). This explicitly Promethean effort is of course doomed, for Frenhofer's quest becomes a struggle with nature, the fight to redo the creation in a secular, and sacrilegious, *imitatio dei*, which inevitably entails the destruction of the very sign-system, line and form, in which he must embody his dream. To the spectators finally admitted to view the painting of "La Belle Noiseuse," nothing is visible but a great fog of overlaid colors, with one perfect foot emerging in the corner to suggest what the canvas was before Frenhofer launched himself beyond nature and language. It is not, finally, the possibility of mimesis, the imitation of nature, that the tale calls into question, but expression, the representation of causes and invisible principles.[14] Nor does the tale call into question Frenhofer's vision: we are persuaded that this exists, and Frenhofer himself can view his painting, momentarily, with inebriated exalta- tion, as the vehicle of his vision. It is on the plane of representation that disaster has occurred. The artist has been struck with aphasia and cannot tell what he has seen.

Frenhofer's is not the only story of the visionary and Promethean artist struck with aphasia. In *Gambara*, it is the musician, inventor of the *panharmonicon*—which produces only cacophonous sounds to other ears—who encounters the interdiction of expression. In *Massimilla Doni*, expressive blockage and sexual impotence are equated; and in *Sarrasine*, art opens onto castration. *La Recherche de l'Absolu* elaborates most fully the figure who neglects the vehicles of representation in the search for an ineffable tenor. Balthasar Claës is the very opposite of those young lions who invest everything in representation, hoping that it will of itself create and impose significance. Claës' clothes go to pieces, the rich materiality of his ancestral home is literally consumed in the crucibles of his laboratory as he quests in vain for his alchemical Absolute. Throughout Balzac's work, there is a haunting menace of expression blocked and prevented, the ever-threatening encounter with aphasia. Such is the dramatic center of *Louis Lambert*, the Ark of the Temple of the *Comédie Humaine*, its ostensible philosophical apex, the work which Balzac rewrote and polished more than any other.

Louis Lambert's more and more audacious analytic flights into the sphere of Will, Thought, and the Word Incarnate lead him, inevitably, beyond mankind into a perfect incommunicability that to men appears mere madness. On one plane, this inability to express is represented in his attempt, on the eve of his marriage, to castrate himself, thus blocking any physical incarnation of the spirit. When we last see him, lost in permanent meditation, his fiancée and guardian, Pauline de Villenoix, would persuade us that his mental life is by no means dead but rather transferred to another sphere. He is communicating with the extra-terrestrial and has paid the price of incommunicability in the human sphere.

In his earlier meditations upon human civilization and the decadence of societies, Louis Lambert finds a formulation that characterizes both his own later folly and Balzac's melodramatic enterprise: "When the effect produced is no longer in relation with its cause, there is disorganization" (10:413). This refers explicitly to the march toward chaos of a society no longer structured on organic relationships and hierarchical principles of authority—the world represented by the orgiastic banquet of La Peau de chagrin, with its proclamation that journalism, sensational and corrupt, has become "the religion of modern societies" (9:47). As Philarète Chasles wrote in preface to that novel, it is a world of convulsive egotism, consumed by the cult of the individual personality: "As [personality] increases, individuals become isolated; no more bonds, no more communal life." [15] Its rush toward the abyss is perhaps best figured in Splendeurs et misères des courtisanes, where we find the upper crust of society implicated in the darkest machinations of the underworld, and where Lucien de Rubempré's letter of farewell, written before his suicide in the Conciergerie prison, is dated 15 May 1830—two months before a revolution which to Balzac would seem both inevitable and a further confirmation of decadence. The Comédie Humaine is a paradoxical monument to a corpus in dissolution, and Balzac returns again and again to the difficulties of representation of a society where those very principles of a traditional drama—class distinctions, hierarchy, manners—have been flattened and have become idiosyncratic and intricate: a "time in which . . . there remain only nuances, where the great figures have faded, where distinctions are purely personal" (3:233).[16]

This situation demands the individual reorganizing gesture, both political and artistic. The artist, who must see and represent, is required to seek in disorganized and flattened reality for the terms of significant representation. On the one hand, this suggests his need for the device of returning characters: every novel will be peopled by beings who carry with them a weight of significance gained from other contexts. Each single novel, like an overcrowded menagerie, presents a concentration of significant presences. On the other hand, it suggests that the artist will (like his heroes) be attracted to the highest social sphere—to Paris and to Society—where "elegance dramatizes life." [17] He will interrogate gesture for meaning, to find the tokens that he needs—for instance, the gestures of the *femme comme il faut*: "There are artificial grandeurs obtained by superlative little things: she has let fall her hand nobly, hanging it from the arm of her chair like dew drops on the edge of a flower, and everything has been said, she has rendered a judgment without appeal that must move the most insensitive" (3:230). What this really indicates is that the artist, through the pressure of his insistence on meaning, has created significance in a world threatened by its loss.

Beyond the problem of social distinction and significant action, Louis Lambert's "law of disorganization" evokes the fundamental problem of the artist working in the domain of "effects" when the "causes" have become obscure, occulted, yet remain of primary importance—their represented relationship to effects indeed the very object of the artist's task. It is not sufficient to remain on the level of "social effects," Balzac argues in his *Avant-Propos* to the *Comédie Humaine*; one must study as well "the reasons or reason of these social effects, detect the hiden sense in this vast assemblage of figures, of passions, of events" (1:7). The causes, and then the principles underlying the causes, were to be the explicit domain of the *Etudes philosophiques* (where the tales of artists are in fact mainly grouped) and the *Etudes analytiques* (where we have the fragmentary formulations of Balzac's theory of meaning). Yet the need to refer to causes and principles is felt as much in the *Etudes de moeurs* and constitutes the very raison d'être of their melodramatism, their heightened representations. As Balzac wrote in defense against the accusation that his characters were touched with "gigantism," that his drama was not within nature: "How can one get across such a fresco [the *Comédie Humaine*] without the resources of the Arabian tale, without the aid of buried titans? In this tempest of a half century, controlling the waves there are giants hidden under the boards of the social third underground." [18] The image refers to the machinery of the theatre, hidden but productive of grandiose effects.

The effort at significant representation is thematically presented, again and again, as the preoccupation with hidden machinery, with the thing behind, the forms of its manifestation and the extent of its revelation. Any reader of Balzac is struck by the prevalence of secret societies and occult powers: organizations such as the Confrérie de la Consolation, Les Grands Fanandels, the Dévorants (otherwise Les Treize); and looser organizations of plotters, the bankers of *César Birotteau*, the Cointet brothers and their associates in the third part of *Illusions perdues*, the various secret police and counter-police in *Splendeurs et misères des courtisanes*, the formidable pair of Valérie Marneffe and Lisbeth Fischer in *La Cousine Bette*; and the single figure, benefactor or demon, who manipulates lives—Gobseck, Doctor Benassis in *Le Médecin de campagne*, Baron de Nucingen, John Melmoth, Vautrin. These organizations, groups, persons are all dedicated to the reorganization and manipulation of life. Their sphere of activity is behind the visible world—the stage of the novel—yet their actions decisively govern the play of the actors in the world. They exercise truly "occult power"—as Balzac names it in the preface to *Ferragus* (11:194)—in the sense both of hidden and of magical power. Already all the principles of occult power are present in *Ferragus* (the first of the three novellas comprising *Histoire des Treize*), with its secret lodgings, mysterious rendezvous, hidden parentage and relationship, slow-acting poisons and inexorable vengeance. Ferragus is in the line of the Gothic supermen of Balzac's early blood-curdlers, but his power is now exercised, significantly, behind the surface of modern Parisian reality. The occult power lurks more subtly behind in the other tales of *Histoire des Treize*. In *La Duchesse de Langeais*, Antoinette, hidden in the cloister like God in the "blinding rays of the sanctuary" (5:132), apparent only through the trace of her voice mingling in the nuns' chant, is pitted against the plot of ravishment conceived and executed by the "thirteen demons." While, in *La Fille aux yeux d'or*, unearthly pleasure and interdicted passion lie in the depths of a labyrinth ruled over, and violated by, contending occult powers: half-brother and half-sister linked finally in a kind of vicarious incest. "Here," writes Proust, "under the apparent and exterior action of the drama circulate the mysterious laws of flesh and passion." [19] A more mundane but no less effective exercise of occult power is recounted in

La Maison Nucingen, which tells the story of how Rastignac had his fortune made for him by serving as straw man in Nucingen's (his mistress's husband's) shady speculations. It is a tale of the *dessous des cartes*, the meaning hidden beneath what the public sees, an explication of the conspiracies that move history, the power of those who are powerful precisely because their actions remain invisible. In the most fantastic and, in some respects, the most revealing instance in the *Comédie Humaine*, *Melmoth réconcilié* shows Gothic and diabolical power exercised upon the world of contemporary Parisian reality, and eventually becoming a value of exchange for the financiers of the Bourse. In a less sinister vein, tales like *La Fausse Maîtresse* and *Un Prince de la bohème* give examples of lives ruled by secret relationships, of social effects whose apparent cause is not the true cause—which is visible only to the rare penetrating observer, the Sherlock Holmes-type character who, like the Countess of "Etudes de moeurs par les gants," can trace the filigree of hidden plots from the slenderest marks on the things of reality.[20]

Such are the models of life controlled, manipulated, given its true explanation and significance from behind, most often in a secret and conspiratorial realm. The model is indicative of Balzac's attraction toward a two-tiered drama, where life and acts on the surface of things are explainable only in terms of what is going on behind, in terms of those who know and control "the more dramatic existence." In heightened and spiritual form, this becomes the model of the hidden father and of life lived vicariously, or in the French expression, *par procuration*. The theme is central to Balzac, and we shall return later to the implications of paternity as the dominant metaphor of the *Comédie Humaine*. The most important representative figure is Jacques Collin, better known as Vautrin, whose vast and tenebrous underground power—conferred on him as the uncorruptible banker of Les Grands Fanandels, a society of thousands of convicts—does not alone satisfy him. For this underground power is indeed like the Promethean artist's vision: it is of no use without an expressive system, a means for its representation and exericse within the sphere of social reality, which for Vautrin, too, means recognized and respectable Society. That is why he needs Rastignac—whom he calls a "theatre" for the acting out of beautiful emotions—and Lucien de Rubempré as his creatures, those through whom he can act, whom he can make the expressive means of his will to power and to pleasure. Thus he says to Lucien de Rubempré, in the remarkable scene of their first encounter

—toward the end of *Illusions perdues* when Lucien is on the verge of suicide and Vautrin, under the alias of the Spanish priest Carlos Herrera, comes upon him on the road from Angoulême to Paris like "a hunter who comes upon a prey long sought in vain" (4:1014)—that he needs "an accomplice of his destiny." It is through this accomplice that he will taste the pleasures of the world of representation:

> I like to devote myself, I have that vice. . . . I want to love my creature, to fashion him, to mould him to my use, in order to love him as a father loves his child. I will ride in your tilbury, my son, I will take pleasure in your successes with women, I will say: "This beautiful young man is myself! This Marquis de Rubempré, I created him and put him in the aristocratic world; his eminence is my work, he is silent or speaks with my voice, he consults me in everything." [4:1032]

The story of Vautrin and Lucien, occult father and puppet son, is told in the sequel, *Splendeurs et misères des courtisanes.* No more decisive image of the double-tiered Balzacian world could be imagined than this, where Lucien holds forth on the principal floors of his apartment, while Vautrin directs his life from a hiding place in the garret. Lucien's life is built on an unstable structure of tiers: when, for instance, he leaves a social gathering in the Faubourg Saint-Germain —at the Grandlieus, whose daughter Clotilde has become his fiancée, while he sequesters his mistress Esther at home—he must change mysteriously from cab to cab to make his way back to the realm in which his protector reigns. Lucien's social representation reposes on vertiginous depths of significance, and when in those depths the shadowy struggle of Vautrin's and Nucingen's agents and counter-agents begins, the representation is doomed—and with it, ultimately, the ideal paternity of Vautrin, who will lose his creature. The final part of the novel will take us into what Balzac calls the "third-level underground" of society, the world of criminals and convicts, from his renewed contact with which Vautrin will emerge, in his "final incarnation," as one of the occult pillars of society, chief of the secret police. *Splendeurs et misères* thus elaborates to its fullest the model of the double-tiered drama, where what is represented on the public social stage is only a figuration of what lies behind, in the domain of true power and significance. But *Splendeurs et misères*, for all its highly colored pleasures, is not the example that most demands our attention, in part because the hidden tier, the world of the occult manipulators and agents, is too easily accessible and is also too facile, too much already predictive of the detective novel, cops-and-robbers model, with its recurrent and conventionalized version of supermen and dupes.[21] The more pertinent, and also the more difficult, question concerns figuration on the stage itself, the world of representation and what it is like when we know there are other tiers but are not in direct contact with them. This is much more the story of *Illusions perdues.*

The question of representation is at the very heart of *Illusions perdues.* Upon his arrival in Paris, with his first promenade in the Tuileries Garden, Lucien, living to its full the bitter experience of alienation, judges his own frowziness, his essential nudity, against the "world of necessary superfluities" that he discovers in the Parisian fashionables (4:608). To overcome alienation, to achieve a place in this world, it is first of all to the tailor, the bootmaker, the hatter that he must turn. Similarly, he must usurp an aristocratic name (from his mother's family) and make it stick. He must learn to parade in the procession of elegant carriages, to make of his life a show, a representation, not of what it is, but of what he wants it to become, of what he would wish it to signify. The opposite of representation is nudity, which in social terms is explicitly equated with vice. When Lucien first visits the journalist Etienne Lousteau's wretched digs, the description informs us that the room is "empty of any objects of value"; it is "furnished with negative things and of the strangest nudity" (4:684–85). At the end of Lucien's inspection, Lousteau breaks in with a witty remark "in order to mask the nudity of Vice." And his remark is: "Here's my kennel, my real representation is in the rue de Bondy, in the new apartment that our druggist has furnished for Florine." Florine is an actress and his mistress, the druggist Matifat her official lover and keeper, and the new apartment the furnished stage which will permit Lousteau's representation, his appearing—the situation that Lucien will find momentarily with the actress Coralie. Representation for the likes of Lousteau and Lucien—who refuse the "decent misery" of d'Arthez and his companions in the Cénacle—is constantly in excess of signification, in a disproportionate and unstable ratio to it. "Living beyond one's means," in this case, is the desperate hope that signification will be invested in the vehicles of representation.

The model of representation in life and personal style refers us inevitably to the theatre, a principal milieu, and perhaps the dominant metaphor, of the novel. The theatre, object of Balzac's repeated ambitions and possibly the key metaphor of the nineteenth-

century experience of illusion and disillusionment, is also the metaphor of Balzac's methods of melodramatic presentation. The theatre is
the fascination, light, erotic lure of the scene; and also the wings, the
world of backstage, which is both disenchanting and more profoundly
fascinating: here Lucien breathes "the wind of disorder and the air of
voluptuousness" (4:724). In its double aspect, the theatre seems to
offer the possibility of both representation and machination, of play on
the great stage and manipulation of the roles represented from the
wings. It is through his initiation into theatre journalism—by which
he is both in the orchestra and the wings, both before the spectacle of
the play and in relation with actors, directors, the claque, and all else
that goes into the "kitchen" of the theatre—that he seems with
hyperbolic rapidity to master the hidden mechanisms of the Parisian
world, to dominate not only among journalists and the half-world that
they inhabit, but to begin to impose himself among the fashionables
who earlier snubbed and denied him. Lucien's experience of fashiona-
bility and power is short-lived, largely because he is never able
adequately to distinguish representation from backstage manipulation. He comes to believe in appearances that he has himself put forth,
and which, to be operatively valid, would have to be treated with
sufficient distance and cynicism, with a sense of what is greasepaint
and what is not. Without tracing his whole career, one can give a few
instances. He condones Coralie's capricious decision to rid herself of
her protector, Camusot, in order to belong exclusively to him. To do so
is to misunderstand the nature of love for an actress, whose own
demands for representation precisely require a Camusot—as Lousteau
understands in his acceptance of Matifat. Then, when he is finally
admitted to Faubourg Saint-Germain society and again meets his
sometime protectress from Angoulême, Mme de Bargeton, he contents
himself with the seeming amiabilities of society and does not take the
decisive step that would give him real leverage in society: making
Mme de Bargeton his mistress. Finally, when he becomes a journalis-
tic turncoat, passing from the liberal to the ultra camp, he exposes
himself to mockery and vengeance from both sides, precisely because
he convinces himself of the sincerity of his switch: as Finot explains to
him, if only he had acted cynically and tipped off his former liberal
colleagues to the necessity of the reversal, all would have been well.
While thinking himself the Machiavel, Lucien is shown to be fatally
impercipient about the true ratios of representation and signification.
His fall is then as vertiginous, as hyperbolic, as his rise. He judges

himself, walking back on foot from a penultimate humiliation, as "the toy" of other men, and "the slave of circumstances" (4:867). It is at this moment that he perceives, in a book lender's window, the novel on which he had, in a more optimistic dawn, staked his hopes. But its title has been altered to something "bizarre," there has been no announcement of its publication, it is an alien and lost product. The moment is one of perfect self-alienation, loss of the products of one's own mind, and it prepares the final descent into destitution, nudity once again, as Lucien leaves Paris on foot, for the provinces, for suicide. Representation is finished.

The tale of Lucien's effort to penetrate into the machinery of Parisian dominance and his failure, his rejection back to the bare surfaces from which he began, appears as a thematization of the problematics posed to the melodramatic author. Lucien experiences melodrama—the manichaeistic extremes, the unbearable contrasts, the struggle of light and darkness, the accumulation of menace—[22] without ever mastering it, without himself becoming the dramatist of experience. Since he is trapped on the plane of surface representations, he is condemned to be the "toy" of significant powers and forces beyond his control. When all his debts, financial and moral, fall in on him in a final "fatal week," the melodramatic heightening of experience is something he undergoes rather than creates. He is exclusively the actor, never the director. In terms of Lucien's personal itinerary, it is clear why, at the end, the only solution, apart from suicide, is total surrender to another being, precisely one who presents himself as a master of backstage operations, of the secret machinery. As Lucien writes to his sister after his meeting with Vautrin, "I no longer belong to myself" (4:1048). When we find him again, in *Splendeurs et misères*, he is seated with his hooka in a narcotic reverie, voided even of ambition, a kind of stage property waiting to be used. "I am the author, you will be the drama," Vautrin says to him (5:727).

In terms of the authorial problematic, things are more complex. The world according to Balzac appears a *Welt als Wille und Vorstellung*. Meaning must be generated from the intersection of the two planes. It is in the realm of the Will—the subject of Raphaël de Valentin's first studies, and of Louis Lambert's fragmentary treatise—that the highest significations lie, and those protagonists who live on the plane of representation alone eventually fall into the void, the evacuation of signification from their lives. But to suppose this realm accessible—as it is to such as Louis Lambert and Séraphîta/Séraphîtüs—is not to conclude that its content can ever be revealed here below, incarnated in a word. Those who neglect the plane of representation and close themselves in the realm of pure significations are struck dumb. One cannot begin by placing oneself within the domain of full signification and hope also to speak. The generation of meaning must proceed in the contrary direction. The sign-maker, the author, must begin from a creative engagement of the plane of representation, the plane of the plastic, and of language.

Here we touch on the core of the Balzacian project and aesthetic: to make the plane of representation imply, suggest, open onto the world of spirit as much as can possibly be managed; to make the vehicles of representation evocative of significant tenors. Meaning is ever conceived as latent; description of surface will not necessarily and of itself give access to the inner world of significance. Hence the "pressure" applied to the surfaces of the real, the insistence of the recording glance, striving toward that moment where, as Albert Béguin has put it, "view becomes vision." [23] Balzacian description is regularly made to appear the very process of investing meaning in the world, demonstrating how surface can be made to intersect with signification. The first of the *Scènes de la vie parisienne, Ferragus*, rehearses the full process in its opening pages. The narrator begins with a simple assignment of moral qualifications to the streets of Paris. Then, the "physiognomy" of the streets opens into a full allegorization, as he calls the city "the most delicious of monsters" (5:18). The monster is anatomized vertically and horizontally: the garrets of Paris constitute a head, for they are full of thinkers; the second storeys are happy stomachs; the ground floor shops are active feet. Its activity is incessant: scarcely have the last carriages returned from the ball in the center of Paris than arms and legs start moving on the outskirts, as the workers begin their day; the city slowly shakes itself into life, moving like the articulations of a great lobster. Balzac's descriptions reiterate the mental operation upon landscape, the effort of optical vision to become moral vision and to create a stage for moral figurations. Everything in the real—facades, furniture, clothing, posture, gesture—must become sign. As the *Théorie de la démarche* claims, bodily posture and movement, for instance, can be "of a fearful meaning. It is more than the word, it is thought in action. A simple gesture, an involuntary tremor of the lips can become the terrible denouement of a drama long hidden between two souls." [24] As in melodrama, we are summoned to enter the world of hypersignificant signs. Our access to it is through a moral expressionism that could be defined as forcing the plane of representation to yield, to deliver the plane of signification.

The expressionist relationship of representation to signification also determines the characteristic narrative movement, the acceleration of peripety, the hyperbolic compression of time. Like description, narrative characteristically reaches a nodal point where it "takes off," speeds up, elaborates beyond the ordinary, irrealizes its material.[25] The language becomes charged and highly colored; time is foreshortened; experience becomes more intensely extreme. The gyrations of the wheel of fortune must be rapid for Balzac's heroes, for it is in the experience of extremes that most is revealed. Thus Rastignac will go from Mme de Beauséant's "delicate attentions" at her farewell ball to the tortured cries of Goriot's death agony; thus Lucien will arrive at one "fatal week" of catastrophic dimensions. Hyperbolic time in fact creates difficulties in fictional chronology: in several instances, we find Balzac introducing in his revisions a new set of time indications to make the action stretch over a longer, more "realistic" period (without always completely effacing the original set of references, thus creating inconsistencies). Most characteristic in this regard is *Illusions perdues*, where originally Lucien's Parisian career—his spectacular rise to eminence and power, his crisis, collapse, and ruin—took place in a few weeks. Balzac felt called upon in revision to introduce a more plausible time. That this creates incoherence as to seasons and temperatures is not of itself important. But the reader feels that the original time—the compressed, impossible, parabolic time—was in fact correct, the true dramatic medium of Lucien's experience.

Expressionism, as we have defined it, "justifies" the theatrical and heightened vehicles of representation: the summary gestures, excessive statements, extreme antitheses, hyperbole, and oxymoron. When Lucien is obliged to write Bacchic songs beside the corpse of his mistress, Coralie, dead at age eighteen, in order to pay for her funeral, we are in the realm of the excruciating, which seizes, reduces, and organizes Lucien's Parisian experience into its bare essentials. When the Duchesse de Langeais says that Goriot's daughters have squeezed their father like a lemon and thrown the peel in the street, she again summarily figures the essence of a relationship (2:911). When the Princesse de Cadignan has evoked her secret misfortunes for Daniel d'Arthez, we are told that d'Arthez "looked at the princesse stupefied, he felt a chill in his back" (6:48).[26] Such an image is almost like striking the boards in melodrama, an underlining, an appeal to attention, an alert to significance.

It is within the context of expressionism that we can best understand the insistent narrative presence in Balzac's novels, demanding that we see, measure, grasp the full dimensions of a universe inhabited by meaning. The reader is hammered at, harassed with solicitations to respond to the implications of everything. Thus, in *Le Père Goriot*, after the narrator's Dantesque approach to the Pension Vauquer, as if into the catacombs: "A true comparison! Who shall decide which is more horrible to see, desiccated hearts or empty skulls?" (2:848).[27] The rhetorical question insists that we espouse the narrator's understanding of his representations. The solicitation to the reader in many instances calls on a procedure of pseudo-explanation well described by Gérard Genette, the formulation of ad hoc pseudo-laws that appear to motivate details of behavior by placing them in an explicative tissue.[28] The tissue "really"—referentially—explains nothing; but it contributes to the internal portent of signification and significance in the textual details. Balzac's idiosyncratic "voici pourquoi"—the opening of the superadded explanation leading back into the machinery, and the machination—is usually less the sign of an explaining away than the start of a new raising of the ante of meaning, so that the plane of representation can bear even more weight of significance. Explanation and interpretation are as a consequence often in excess of the representation given, unstably related to it. Balzac himself characterizes the method in this definition of "*Parisianism* . . . which consists in touching everything lightly, in being profound without appearing so, in wounding mortally without appearing to have touched, in saying, as I have often heard, 'What is the matter, my dear?' when the poignard has been thrust in up to the hilt."[29] Proust's parody catches the essence of the formula: " 'Oh! darling,' answered the marquise with stunning ease, 'we can't hold back people of that sort. Lucien will meet the fate of young d'Esgrignon,' she added, striking confusion in the ranks of those present by the infamy of her words, each of which was a mortal shaft for the princesse."[30] Representation, we feel, has a long way to go to catch up with such a signification.

This excess of the signified in respect to the signifier places us once again before Balzac's essentially metaphoric enterprise, by which the represented gestures of the real (including here the significant detail of speech and language) both are that and claim to be something more. The visionary narrator of *Facino Cane* claims that his power of observation "penetrated the soul without neglecting the body; or rather, it seized so well the exterior details that it went at once beyond" (6:66). This is the power of extrapolation from the present to the invisible, from surface to depth. From the plane of representation, we begin to move into the tiers behind, which are themselves plural: some parts of the significant behind are more available—closer behind—than others.[31] Metaphor works in essentially two ways: by creating transactions from part to part, and from surface to behind. It hence both reorganizes, in a new provisional totality, and (sometimes the one is a consequence of the other) reveals, lays bare the causes and principles of the effects. Through the constructive play of metaphor, one can at least accede to the immediate behind—from stage to wings—to expose basic social structures and hidden controlling powers. By constructing metaphors upon metaphors, one may reach still further back, until one approaches the realm of a true spiritual occult. If this movement is doomed to a final falling-short of its goal, it is yet full of creative vitality in its approach toward the goal: it is the very principle of movement, the underlying force-field of desire of the *Comédie Humaine*. A more detailed demonstration could work through one novel's thematization of this movement, to emerge with closer definitions of melodramatic technique. Thematically, Lucien de Rubempré presents himself as the anti-image of the quest to move through effects to causes, the very type of failure in the *Comédie Humaine*.[32] The positive image whose career, fully as exemplary as Lucien's, offers the very type of success, is Eugène de Rastignac.

II

The narrative voice of *Le Père Goriot* overtly adopts the breathlessness of melodrama from the opening page, claiming for this tale the label of "drama" despite "the abusive and contorted manner in which it has been used in these times of painful literature" (2:847).[33] But the drama, the narrator adds, is no exaggeration: "this drama is neither fiction nor novel. *All is true.*" This is explicitly to be the drama of the real; and in the opening pages (as at the start of *La Peau de chagrin*) we can observe the narrator working upon the details of the reality he has framed in his "frame of bronze," to make them release latent significances. The famous furniture of the Pension Vauquer itself becomes the first token of the conflict: the furniture is "proscribed," placed in the Pension "as the debris of civilization are put in the

Hospital of Incurables"; chairs are "dismembered," or, in a suite of adjectives that moves from the objective to the fully animized, "old, cracked, rotted, wobbly, gnawed, one-armed, one-eyed, invalid, expiring" (2:851–52).[34] The very appearance of the boarders gives "the presentiment of dramas completed or continuing; not those dramas played before the footlights, between painted drops, but living and mute dramas, those icy dramas that touch the heart, perpetual dramas." Then individual figures—Mlle Michonneau, Poiret—lead to more audacious interrogations of the dramatic past lying behind the ravaged face: "What acid had stripped this creature of her female forms? . . ."; "What work could have so shriveled him up? what passion had blackened his bulbous face? . . ." (2:855–56).

The action of the plot, after the lengthy introduction of setting and characters, gets underway amidst darkness and mystery. Rastignac, who has returned from his first ball in Society and is pursuing ambitious reveries while attempting to study his law books, hears a groan coming from Goriot's room and looks through the keyhole to find the old man twisting silver bowls into an ingot. The questions raised by this operation are compounded by the phrase Goriot lets fall: "Poor child!" (2:876). Then, as Rastignac is meditating this mystery, he hears two men coming up the stairs; a light goes on in Vautrin's room, and he detects the clink of gold. Rastignac's first experience of what are to be the principal lines of plot in which he will be implicated comes, then, in the stage darkness, with all the mystery, of an encounter with the villains of stage melodrama. The plot then develops as a series of melodramatic encounters that tie the lines tighter, both explicating positions and relationships and creating a high degree of suspense about their resolution. Rastignac's temptation by Vautrin, and his interest in Victorine Taillefer, is brought to crisis at the same moment as his courtship of Delphine de Nucingen and also Vautrin's detection and arrest; Mme de Beauséant's ball, her farewell to society, coincides with Goriot's death agony, Anastasie de Restaud's breakdown before her husband, and the final scene in Rastignac's "education." Everything moves toward, prepares, a few thunderous and decisive scenes.

Melodramatic representation indeed touches on the central experience of the novel; it constitutes much of what the book is about. We can best grasp this through the first major "scene" presented; it occurs when Rastignac, leaving behind him the sordid mysteries of the Pension, goes to wage combat for entry into "le monde." His first social call, at the hôtel de Restaud, is structured on two verbal gestures, the first of which opens doors, produces a sense of belonging and a flood of light on society; the second, obscurity, rejection, and a permanent barring of passages. If his arrival is obviously a nuisance to the Comtesse Anastasie de Restaud—who is receiving her lover, Maxime de Trailles—when the Comte de Restaud enters she nonetheless introduces Rastignac with the "magic" phrase that he is "related to Mme la Vicomtesse de Beauséant through the Marcillac": a formulation which is a "stroke of the wand," opening "thirty compartments" in Rastignac's brain, restoring to him "all his prepared wit," and providing a "sudden light" to make him "see clear in the air of high society" (2:895–96). The comte is then all polite attention and discusses ancestors until Rastignac announces his acquaintanceship with someone he has just perceived leaving the hôtel de Restaud, Père Goriot: "At the mention of this name, prettified with the title of *père*, the comte, who had been attending to the hearth, threw his tongs into the fire as if they had burned his hands and stood up. 'Sir, you could have said Monsieur Goriot,' he cried" (2:898). In a moment, Rastignac notes that there has again been a stroke of the wand, but this time with the "inverse effect" of "related to Mme la Vicomtesse de Beauséant." The subject is changed, Rastignac's departure hastened; and upon his leaving the hôtel, we hear the comte give his valet the order that they will never again be at home to Monsieur de Rastignac.

An understanding of what has really gone on in this scene can lead us to a clearer grasp of the kind of dramatization that interests Balzac. At first glance, Rastignac seems to have made (without his or our quite knowing why) an impolite social gesture, what he qualifies as a "gaucherie." Such an outcome to a first venture into society by a young provincial would appear normal to the point of banality. We might think we were in the medium of comedy of manners, witnessing a scene that could be found, doubtless with much greater subtlety, in Marivaux or Laclos or Stendhal, Jane Austen or E. M. Forster—any of those novelists whose attention and efforts at representation are directed to the texture of social life, the significant gestures of actors on the public stage of society. Balzac does refer us to this stage and this texture when he notes the "magical effect" of social formulae, the supposed importance of an omitted "monsieur," or when, a few pages later, he comments that Rastignac has made progress in the "Parisian code which is not talked about, although it constitutes a high social jurisprudence which, well learned and well practiced, leads to everything" (2:905–06). Yet the crudity of Balzac's rendering—the excess of the comte's successive reactions, the rapidity of Rastignac's complete acceptance and complete rejection—make the labels of comedy of manners and social realism inadequate and misleading. If we see the scene as such, we will be forced to conclude that it is bad social realism: the gestures dramatized by Balzac are the motions of the bull in the china closet; more is broken than need be to make the "point" about Rastignac's social inexpertise (an image which the narrator himself suggests when he comments that Rastignac is like someone in a curiosity shop who has bumped into a cabinet of figurines and "knocked off three or four badly glued-on heads"). As James indicated in his comment on the very similar scene of social rejection in *Illusions perdues*, Balzac's social gestures do not have the volume and opacity of those we find in the novel of manners. There, gestures are counters which have value in terms of a system, a social code which forms their context and assigns their meaning. If the first "magic phrase," evoking Rastignac's relation to Mme de Beauséant, seems a reasonable equivalent to any social identification found in Austen or Stendhal or Forster, his disastrous mention of Père Goriot cannot be assimilated to Emma's insult to Miss Bates, or Julien Sorel's failure to change into silk stockings for dinner. These refer us to the code, in terms of which they are inappropriate, embarrassing, in violation. Rastignac's gaffe is other, it is charged in a different manner. It is more than social: it is revolutionary and revelatory. To understand how this is so is to see why Balzac is not writing a crude and uneven comedy of manners, but something very different, a melodrama of manners.

The very "Parisian code" that Rastignac must master is only on the surface a code of manners. This is indeed suggested by the preliminary circumstances of his visit to the Restauds, which we passed over. Seeking to show that he is a familiar of the house, Rastignac opens the wrong door out of the entrance hall and stumbles into a dark corridor ending on a hidden staircase, from which he hears the voices of Mme de Restaud and of Père Goriot, and the sound of a kiss. Then, from a window looking down on the courtyard, he sees Père Goriot barely escape being run down by the comte's tilbury, entering the court, and a greeting proffered by the comte, a gesture in which is painted "the forced consideration that one accords to usurers of whom one is in need, or the necessary respect toward a man of bad repute, of which one is later ashamed" (2:893). These circumstances already situate us in a realm beyond the idiom of social comedy; they call into play mystery and melodrama. The possible meanings read in the gesture of salutation already suggest dark and unavowable relationships, a thing behind; and Rastignac's mention of Goriot is explicitly an effort to discover what is behind. "He wanted to penetrate this mystery"—that of Anastasie's relation to Goriot—"hoping to be able in this way to reign as sovereign over this eminently Parisian woman" (2:897). So that the "gaucherie" is in fact motivated by the intimation of a dark and sinister drama, first suggested by Vautrin's "frightful reflections" on society. It cannot be considered to fall within the framework of manners; it raises other, threatening questions.

Rastignac will begin to discover why in the course of his next social call, on Mme de Beauséant: Goriot is of course the publicly repudiated and secretly exploited father of Anastasie de Restaud (as of Delphine de Nucingen), a man who has been banished from his daughters' drawing rooms, where he appeared, in the Duchesse de Langeais' phrase, "a spot of grease" (2:911), but who is frequently called to the backstairs for cash. Rastignac's mention of Goriot in the Restaud drawing room is then like the creation of the grease spot. It marks a public social style with what lies behind it, with its unavowable backstage. It puts into question the very closure and self-sufficiency of the Restauds' world by juxtaposing it to its financial and genetic substructure. Hence it rends the fabric of manners to reveal truer stakes, more significant gestures. Rastignac's gaffe in fact has the effect of a metaphor juxtaposing surface and depth, before and behind, through a "transaction between contexts." He has violated the single context of codified social manners, has conjugated together two contexts that the Restauds, and all of the upper class, wish to keep hermetically separate.

Rastignac's draft "metaphor" is, on the social plane, potentially revolutionary, for it brings a new totalistic vision whereby superstructure reposes on substructure, the sordid realities of labor and economic exploitation become visible through the veneer of manners. Society becomes a tiered or layered structure, and the level of manners no longer is an autonomous system. So that Rastignac's verbal gesture, so heavy with consequence, first suggests inclusiveness, approach toward totality of perception in the analysis of society. Uncovering the structure of society is simultaneously discovery of the true ethical terms of the drama: Goriot's exploitation and betrayal by his children.

There is no separation for Balzac between socio-political truth and ethical truth: the sinister structuration revealed in the former domain points directly to a moral degradation. Rastignac's draft metaphor points, on the ethical plane, to the locus of the real drama. The scene of his gaffe in the hôtel de Restaud hence thematizes Balzac's metaphoric method and its relationship to melodramatic representation. Like the novelist of manners, and like his own protagonists, Balzac is attracted to the social sphere that yields the most exciting and significant representations: the highest circle. This sphere, however, can no longer—in post-revolutionary society—be understood alone: its representations depend on, take their sense from, what is going on behind and beneath. Therefore the theatre of Balzac's drama cannot have the closure and self-containment of the novel of manners. It must be metaphoric, based on a drama of interacting contexts. This being so, it is evident that the manners dramatized, the gestures, cannot themselves have the opacity, codification, or subtlety of those in a novel of manners. They exist rather to reach beyond, to violate the autonomy of their primary context, and to raise other, deeper issues: to raise from "beneath the boards" those "buried titans," explicitly figured in this text by Goriot and Vautrin, whose shadowy presence materializes within Society through Rastignac's gesture. Hence, necessarily, a melodrama of manners.

Rastignac's own experience in the novel moves toward the clarification of his unwitting draft metaphor, toward proof of its validity and the importance of its revelations. The measure of Rastignac's perceptual achievement in the novel is his clear final articulation of the metaphor, expressing the clear vision of life and society that he has gained and on which he is to found his future behavior. The most decisive formulation of the perception comes during Mme de Beauséant's farewell ball, where Anastasie and Delphine are decked in diamonds bought or redeemed with their father's last money, while he lies dying in the meanest room of the Pension: Rastignac "saw then beneath the diamonds of the two sisters the pallet where Goriot lay stretched in pain" (2:1061). The essential words here are *beneath*, which expresses the relation of superstructure to substructure, the way in which the representation of the upper social sector is dependent on exploitation of the lower, the surface dependent on the sinister and sordid thing behind, the drama of paternity betrayed; and *saw*, which suggests that the substructure is implicit in the superstructure, Society hence threatened by the structure of society, and that the thing behind, the most telling conflict, can become visible. Rastignac's perception here is *vision*, almost in the sense of the X-ray glance possessed by Castanier, in *Melmoth réconcilié*, and some of Balzac's early Gothic supermen: he has seen behind the curtain, and he can articulate what he has seen.[35]

Rastignac's experience, in antithesis to Lucien de Rubempré's, will be one of learning to understand and master the social melodrama rather than simply acting in it. This means first of all understanding polarities and extremes. When his first lesson in the ethics of Parisian success, furnished by the exemplars of Faubourg Saint-Germain society—Mme de Beauséant and the Duchesse de Langeais—receives immediate confirmation in the lesson offered by Vautrin from the social depths, the form of the necessary learning is clear. "He told me crudely what Mme de Beauséant told me in observing the forms" (2:942): Vautrin's cruder analysis is really a further melodramatization—a grandiose, revelatory articulation—of the other, and as such the more admirable, and the more useful, of the two. The structure of the lessons points to their message, which is about structure. "Society is a mudhole," the Duchesse de Langeais summarizes, "let us try to stay on the heights" (2:911). The image of heights and muddy gulfs dominates the novel. The streets of Paris are a literal mudhole, and if, like Rastignac, you have to cross them on foot, your boots get dirty. This has moral implications: "Those who get muddy in a carriage are honorable men, those who get dirty on foot are crooks," says Vautrin (2:886). To which we could juxtapose Mme de Beauséant's comment that Delphine de Nucingen "would lap up all the mud" of the streets between her house and the Faubourg Saint-Germain to be admitted to a truly aristocratic drawing room (2:913). To go into the streets represents a descent, the descent of a woman like Anastasie, who after the ball goes to seek out the usurer Gobseck, a condition generalized by Vautrin as a continual vertical movement between extremes: "Yesterday at the top of the wheel at a duchess's . . . this morning at the bottom of the ladder at the moneylender's: that is your Parisienne" (2:884). When the Goriot daughters come to the Pension in search of money, melodramatic extremes touch. The Pension itself is the very bottom, the subterranean: near the start of the novel, the narrator evokes the start of Dante's journey when he compares approach to the rue Neuve-Sainte-Geneviève to descent into the catacombs: "as, with each step, light fades and the song of the guide goes hollow . . ." (2:848).

Structurally, the novel reposes on its two most widely separated, polarized terms, both horizontally and vertically: the Pension Vauquer and the Faubourg Saint-Germain. The urban landscape is already manichaeistic, expressive of exclusive integers which repel each other yet nonetheless, in the manner of the Hugolian grotesque, must be embraced in a total imaginative possession. It is Rastignac who almost daily experiences the distance between the two, who journeys like a shuttle from one to the other. The ethical experience of the novel is constructed on his returns from the upper world to the lower, the journeys (mostly night journeys) that bring to consciousness his moral choices and the possible formulae for leaving permanently the one world for the other. With his return from his first call on Mme de Beauséant, hesitating between the career in law for which he has been sent to Paris and the splendors of Society to which he has just been exposed, he makes a decision to "open two parallel trenches leading to fortune, to brace himself both on learning and on love, to be a doctor of laws and a young fashionable" (2:915). To which the narrator replies that parallel lines never meet.

The structural polarity is indeed doubled by a moral polarity. Rastignac is faced with a choice of means which, according to Vautrin's exposition of the situation, is an absolute and total commitment of the self. "Virtue, my dear student, is not divisible: it either is or it isn't" (2:941). Hence he offers Rastignac the choice between two summary, integral stances toward life: Obedience or Revolt. "Here is the crossroads of life, young man, choose" (2:935). At the core of the novel, Vautrin—certainly the villain, but at the same time almost the wise and understanding généreux of melodrama—is a moral absolutist who offers a thoroughly manichaean image of moral reality. Pitiless critic of "a gangrened society," disciple of Rousseau who protests against "the perversions of the social contract" (2:1014,1016), he articulates a "puritan" ethic which makes Rastignac's choice ineluctably take on the coloring of a moral melodrama or even allegory. When Rastignac restates Vautrin's proposition to his friend Bianchon, it is in a melodramatic parable and conundrum: if one could become rich simply by willing the death of one unknown and aged mandarin in China, should one accept? The parable accurately identifies the terms in question: Rastignac need only consent to Vautrin's assumption of the role of "Providence"; he will have the worthless young Taillefer killed in a duel; Victorine Taillefer will become her immensely rich father's sole heir; and she is already in love with Rastignac.

Vautrin's exposition of the world engenders within the novel—more effectively than could Rastignac's draft metaphor—a secondary system of moral absolutes. He raises the metaphysical stakes of the drama and provides another, starker version of Rastignac's social experience. At the moment of his arrest, he becomes an "infernal poem" and "the fallen archangel dedicated to incessant warfare" (2:1015). He more and more assumes a Mephistophelean guise, and the moral dilemma takes on classic and grandiose form, temptation. "What kind of a man are you?" Rastignac cries out; "you were created to torment me" (2:981). The moral crisis and climax of the novel is played out as a *Walpurgisnacht*, an infernal celebration where Rastignac, numbed by drugged wine, listens to his tempter's projects without being able to summon the force to protest, a nightmare experience where gesture cannot be made to accord with conscious intention, and unconsciousness supervenes to create a fatal gap in time—Rastignac awakens only at eleven o'clock the next morning to find that all has been consummated. During the gap, Vautrin, with a nice sense of the fitting irony, has taken Mme Vauquer to see Pixerécourt's melodrama *Le Mont sauvage* at the Théâtre de la Gaîté.[36] Rastignac will not have to face the criminal act directly, for the following morning Vautrin is arrested and, before that, is himself drugged by Mlle Michonneau, so that he falls to the floor at the very moment he is announcing the successful completion of his plot. "So there is a divine justice," says Rastignac at this point. The echo of the melodramatic heroine is fully ironic: this justice is no more than the stool-pigeon Michonneau's wiles, and Vautrin will soon revive; but it is significant that Rastignac wishes to believe in it.

We may want to see in Rastignac's drugged lethargy at the moment of crisis an image of his desire to achieve moral unconsciousness, to believe in the workings of an ethical mechanism, and to avoid personal choice. For he has from the start sought ways to attenuate the moral polarities presented by Vautrin, to reduce the distance between structural extremes, to evade the secondary system of moral absolutes. He has, curiously, himself chosen the role of the metaphorist intent to find viable transactions between contexts. His path is first indicated by the tailor he convokes after remarking what a negative quantity his suits are compared to Maxime de Trailles', the tailor who considers himself "a hyphen between a young man's present and his future"

(2:927). A hyphen, that is, constitutes the beginning of a relationship, a link, eventually a passage from depths to heights, a crossing from one context to another. It could be considered the first step in the construction of a ladder out of the mudhole. Rastignac's perceptual progress in the novel must be doubled by such a construction, a kind of metaphor in action that will allow him to escape the confines of the primary context. Yet the construction of such a metaphor requires as its grounds the medium of money, which Rastignac discovers to be the *"ultima ratio mundi"* (2:914): what we might call (pushing the metaphoric model to its limits) the "esemplastic power" of society, the medium of transaction, encompassment, passage.

The acquisition of money threatens to return Rastignac to Vautrin's moral polarities. Yet he manages to mediate between them through the identification of two parallel columns, between which he must choose, on an implicit moral table that could be written out in this manner:

"Vice"		*"Virtue"*
Revolt	(moral stance)	Obedience
Vautrin	(father)	Goriot
Victorine	(woman)	Delphine

What is curious about the table is that by all usual moral standards Victorine and Delphine would have to change columns: the one is innocent and virginal, the other worldly and corrupt. But Victorine has been chosen by Vautrin as the vehicle of his scheme, which allows Rastignac by bipolar opposition to place Delphine in the virtue column. This is useful, for Delphine will, precisely, allow him to escape the absolutism of Vautrin's ethics and to preserve his efforts at mediation between polarities, his avoidance of true choice. For Delphine is the very principle of non-choice: the luxury/love that she incarnates, the "voluptuous elegance of the rich courtesan" (2:970), provides both the solution to Rastignac's moral dilemma and the necessary term of his passage from the Pension to what we know, from subsequent novels, will be the highest positions imaginable. Through her, Rastignac's ambition can be translated into love, solving the moral problem by remaining faithful to his early decision that "the heart" is his best "guide" (2:943), while his love can simultaneously be translated into cash and fashion, solving his problem of transition— and in a completely literal sense, it is Delphine's husband who will make Rastignac's fortune. Each of the two terms "means" the other; Rastignac saying love also says money and begins to construct his metaphoric ladder.

All of Rastignac's exertions in the novel are in fact deployed toward softening the melodramatic terms of choice, toward mastering them through mediation, masking them by his web of metaphoric transactions. By the end of the novel, when he has overtly recognized Vautrin's grandeur and the inescapable accuracy of his message, Rastignac nonetheless surreptitiously adds a third term to the symbolic polarity: now it is Obedience, Revolt, and *Struggle* (2:1057). Struggle is precisely the effort to answer the two polarized stances with a third term which, like metaphor, is postulated on a constructive and mediative effort that rejects exclusive commitment to one or the other, masks choice in perpetual movement.

Rastignac as metaphorist cannot, however, permanently blunt the polarities. For the final metaphoricity of reality lies, not in a possible mediation of social polarities, but in the possibility of access from surface to depth, from representation to signification, where irreducible and contrary forces inhabit. Rastignac's perceptual progress, cannot but uncover this access. The inescapable reality of Vautrin's version of experience requires that Rastignac learn to see and to encompass ethical integers, rather than mediate and mask them, so that he may eventually act with the heightened perception of the melodramatist. Such, particularly, is the evolution of his consciousness in the final section of the novel, "La Mort du Père." When, at the end of the quarrel among the two sisters and their father, Anastasie returns to throw herself on her knees and ask for Goriot's pardon, Rastignac reads the true meaning of her gesture: " 'She came back for the endorsement [of the check Goriot has given her],' he whispered to Delphine" (2:1048). Then, when he has gone to tell Delphine that her father is dying, and she has sent him home to dress, refusing to hear his report, he understands that he is faced with what he calls an "elegant parricide" (2:1056)—a phrase that once again juxtaposes manners to their stark signification. As he returns to the Pension to dress, his meditation yields a full consciousness of his relation to Delphine, expressed in an image of remarkable brutality: "Infamous or sublime, he adored this woman for the pleasures that he had brought her in dowry, and for all those that he had received in exchange; just as Delphine loved Rastignac as much as Tantalus would have loved an angel who came to satisfy his hunger, or quench the thirst of his burning throat" (2:1057–58). Their relationship is barter and brute alimentary need. But as such, it is all the more necessary. Infamous or sublime—infamous and sublime—she is the way out from Vautrin's alternatives, the term of struggle, now to be carried on with the superior lucidity suggested by Rastignac's capacity to produce such summary images.

These images of his relation to Delphine stand as prelude to Mme de Beauséant's ball, her farewell to society, which recapitulates structurally the ball near the start of the novel that stirred Rastignac's desire for the heights. It is with this final ball that we have his ultimate coming to consciousness about the structure of society and the melodramatic terms of the world in which he must live. Not only is there his vision of Goriot's agony "beneath the diamonds," but also his perception that Anastasie has "discounted even the bill of her father's death" (2:1061), his image of Mme de Beauséant as "the gladiator who knows how to smile in dying," his statement to Bianchon that Society is "horror covered over in gold and jewels" (2:1063).[37] If he has managed to avoid commitment to Vautrin's ethics, he has achieved and allied himself with Vautrin's perception. As the narrator states, "His education was nearing completion" (2:1062). To which is juxtaposed his conclusive statement to Bianchon: "I am in hell, and I must stay there." The struggle continues with its stakes laid bare. It only remains for Goriot's cries of rage in his death agony to explicate the cosmic betrayal of life, and for Rastignac to play out through Goriot's funeral—pawning his watch while Restaud and Nucingen give nothing, following the corpse while they send two empty emblazoned carriages—the final extremities of the drama.

At the very end, Rastignac returns, in disillusioned consciousness and heightened lucidity, to his mediative and constructive effort, on a stage setting which, like the sets of the last acts of melodramas, provides a symbolic locus for a final acting-out. He stands on the heights of Père-Lachaise cemetery following Goriot's burial, and looks down on Paris. The final passage is preceded by an image of baroque complication and excess announcing the end of Rastignac's youth: "He looked at the grave and buried there his last tear of youth, a tear brought forth by the sacred emotions of a pure heart, one of those tears which, from the earth where they fall, rebound into the heavens." After this last gesture of mediation with the realm of moral essences, Rastignac is spiritually complete for his encounter with the real antagonist:

Alone now, Rastignac took a few steps toward the heights of the cemetery and saw Paris lying serpentine along the two banks of the Seine, where lights were beginning to shine. His eyes fixed almost avidly between the column of the Place Vendôme and the dome of the Invalides, the dwelling place of that fashionable society into which he had tried to penetrate. He threw at this murmuring hive a glance that seemed in advance to suck out its honey, and spoke these grandiose words: "Now between the two of us!"

And as first act in the challenge hurled at society, Rastignac went to dine at Mme de Nucingen's. [1:1085]

This exemplary conclusion demonstrates both Rastignac's achieved understanding of the melodramatic terms of his situation and struggle, and the capacity to control and use the terms in such a way as to master his future destiny. Rastignac's situation is excessively grandiose, of itself hyperbolic: standing on the literal heights of the cemetery whose name reminds us of the novel's title, a mountain of the Parisian dead (the theme is developed by Balzac at the end of *Ferragus*), facing and looking down on the Paris of the *beau monde* stretched out with a contained reptilian energy along the Seine, between the two commanding beacons of the Vendôme column and the Invalides, both recalling the colossal Napoleonic drama. Its heightening and excess permit Rastignac to raise Paris itself to the status of meaning, to see society and the city as a landscape endowed with clear, represented significations, and hence to pass to a visionary taking of possession: the city becomes a beehive which his glance seizes in its vital richness, sucking its honey. His challenge to Paris aims, not at revolt, but at encompassment, as its institution in going to dine at Delphine's shows. It is the melodramatic command of Paris from his height and the grandiose terms in which he obtains his *vision* of reality that allow his gesture of seeming revolt to become the gesture of possession, that subsumes revolt within possession, because society and the city have been seized in their totality and essence, in a gathering together of essential structures, relations, meanings made legible. Rastignac's gesture is fully expressionistic: it forces the plane of representation to yield its full charge of ethical signification. Rastignac has indeed at the last achieved a position analogous to that of the author: master of his material, capable of recognizing, through the visionary glance, the terms of the true drama hidden behind façades. From his state of limited vision in the "valley of plaster," he has risen to dominating heights, seized the knowledge of his way into and through the world, and become master of his destiny.

Rastignac's final gesture is a necessary demonstration of his ability to play in the Parisian drama with a sufficient awareness of the thing behind, the superdrama which is figured in the drama of the real. In moving from his original desire to "penetrate" the mysteries surrounding Anastasie de Restaud's relationships, and his unwitting draft metaphor of the relation of heights to depths, through to fully articulated statements of relationship which are also articulations of the large moral entities figuring in the drama, Rastignac moves from the exposure of the naked provincial struggling for survival in what Vautrin has described as the "jungle" of Paris to the strength and encompassment of the man of fashion and political power. His ability to see—to uncover structures, relations, meanings—is the precondition of entry onto the higher stage: not only that of high society, but also that of the higher stakes. He has achieved melodramatic consciousness. Like Vautrin now—or at least approaching that superman's prescience—he knows what he is dealing with.

The world, said Paul Claudel in a phrase relevant to Rastignac's final vision, is before us like a text to be deciphered. For Claudel the legibility of the world is never in doubt, because each discrete element of physical reality can in the end directly be related to—since it originally derives from—a unified spiritual reality. For Balzac and his characters, this legibility must be conquered, the world must first be invested with meaning; and the way through to spiritual reality is more problematic. With the interrogation of surfaces, we open first onto the melodrama of social experience and the mystery of passion. Particulars of reality both speak of the mystery and conceal it, soliciting the quest to understand it, then to go beyond, to the realm of a drama that itself implicates the underlying spiritual principles. Rhetorically, we pass from description to increasingly audacious efforts to construct metaphors for the total organization of society, the total human ethical experience, then for the forces that shape and determine all that is real. It is the *Oeuvres philosophiques* that provide the final metaphors of the arcane spiritual forces: the magnetic power of the Will in animating the world, the fecundation of matter by spirit, as Albert Béguin summarizes it,[38] Balzac's "angelism," straining toward the ultimate metaphor predicted by Louis Lambert: "Perhaps one day the reverse of the *Et Verbum caro factum est* will be the summary of a new

Scripture proclaiming: *And flesh will be made Spirit, it will become the Word of God*" (10:452). That this should be the final ambition of Balzac's most illuminated thinker is significant, for it suggests that the whole of Balzac's own enterprise tends toward such a reverse incarnation, or disincarnation: that finally reality exists to become spirit and vision, to reveal and discharge its significant essence.

Such is of course the ideal place of arrival only, and we have already noted that those who achieve its luminous perfection are struck dumb. We are most often left with the various stages of approach on the plane of representation, the play of metaphor, from the most local verbal instance to the grandiose and summary metaphor of basic relations and truths. *Le Père Goriot* is itself inhabited by one such pervasive metaphor that encompasses and interiorizes the novel's social melodrama. The form that this takes is implicit in the title; it is the drama of paternity and of creation. "When I became a father," says Goriot, "I understood God. He is complete everywhere, since all creation came from him. Sir, so am I with my daughters" (2:957). This transcends what we ordinarily think of as vicarious existence, to move onto a higher plane, that of the creator who lives in his creation: not simply through the other, but in an otherness which is a new realization of the self, a new incarnation of the spirit. It is Vautrin who takes this assertion of individual deification to its next analogical stage, that of literary creation: "I am a great poet. I don't write my poems, they consist in actions and sentiments" (2:938). Rastignac is the necessary signifier of this poem, the vehicle for the realization of Vautrin's dreams of creation, the metaphor by which his word may be made flesh. "A man is everything or nothing. He's less than nothing when he is named Poiret: you can squash him like a bedbug, he's flat and he stinks. But a man is a god when he looks like you; he is no longer a machine covered with skin, but a theatre where the most beautiful emotions are acted out . . ." (2:982). The sterility implied by Vautrin's homosexuality is hence transcended in a larger creativity, the power to make life, the temptation to godhead. His dream of a patriarchical life in the southern United States is to be realized through Rastignac's ascension to the highest social sphere: two poems, in fact, to be enacted through the same metaphor— Rastignac as beauty and ambition translated into Rastignac as money and power (Victorine's dowry). Yet his relation to his creature-metaphor will be thwarted: man will fall off from his creator, be unequal to his conceptions (or free from his intentions), and institute distance between them; or else, in the case of Lucien de Rubempré, betray God. (The more successful self-deification achieved by Gobseck results from his never having attempted a creation, from his resisting the allure of an "accomplice of his destiny"; miserly, self-contained, sterile, he represents a pure *logos* never risked in incarnation.) Goriot, too, is betrayed by his creation, and in his deathbed monologue this "genius of fatherhood" reinvents Hamlet's interdiction of marriage: "Fathers, tell the Assembly to make a law on marriage! . . . No more marriages!" (2:1073). Marriage is accursed because it destroys the vertical, genetic relationship of father and child, creator and creature, to substitute for it a horizontal social relationship which, the novel has amply demonstrated, is a denatured contract, a barter, commerce, institutionalized prostitution. In his final rantings, Goriot reverts to another, precedent, primary social organization: "I protest. The nation will perish if fathers are trodden underfoot. That is clear. Society, the world turn on paternity . . ." (2:1070).

Society does not perish, it merely moves deeper and deeper into chaos. Obeying Louis Lambert's law of disorganization, it succumbs to secularization, class stratification, commercialism, legalism, the contradictions of substructure and superstructure: the whole network of relations which the novel has sought metaphors to express. Vautrin, who takes as his motto "There are no principles, only events; there are no laws, only circumstances" (2:940), understands that the disproportion of cause and effect opens up possibilities for the grandiose personal gesture by which the superior being proposes his personal reorganization. "I will take upon myself the role of Providence," he says to Rastignac; "I will force the will of God" (2:940). The gesture may rather be in the nature of Rabourdin's plan to restructure the bureaucracy (in *Les Employés*),[39] Doctor Benassis' utopian community (in *Le Médecin de campagne*), Felicité des Touches' novelistic manipulation of her friends (in *Béatrix*), Rastignac's cosmic challenge to Paris, or Balzac's own insane effort to "compete with the civil registry," to know and to conquer the world through his fictions, to represent it all in language.[40] The struggle to organize the mass of metaphors of the *Comédie Humaine* calls into play new metaphorical efforts—new transactions between ever-larger contexts, and the ever-renewed attempt to work through such transactions to essential structurations, to the basic drama and the very principles of creation—which finally have the effect of making the whole opus an exacerbated nerve center, where a touch on one strand provokes reactions through many different chains, where one particular object or person or destiny can constantly be seen in a chain of metaphoric mutations.

III

We have perhaps gained a position from which we can usefully reformulate Balzac's need for the melodramatic mode. Melodrama is first of all a mode of heightening which makes his novelistic texture approach the overt excitement and clash of theatrical drama. When those two paragons of Faubourg Saint-Germain society, the Duchesse de Langeais and the Vicomtesse de Beauséant, exchange gossip, the duchesse, "transmitting floods of malignity in her glances," reveals the impending marriage of the vicomtesse's lover, and the narrator comments: "This blow was too violent, the vicomtesse went pale . . ." (2:907). The narrator's explicit translation of words into blows is characteristic and revealing. We must be made to see the real nature of the exchange, its quality of naked pugilism; we must conceive of the interlocutors not only as elegant and costumed aristocrats in their salon, but also as antagonists stripped for battle. Balzac's heightening allows us to read, in and through manners, the more basic postures, allegiances, conflicts. Heightening is the art of the summary and the essential; it extrapolates from the surface of life into a dramaturgy of purer signs. The measure of crudity involved in such representations is the necessary price of delivering the essential. The capacity to be crude—to think, like Rastignac when he takes Delphine's money to go to the gambling table, "She's compromising herself with me, she'll not be able to refuse me anything" (2:967)—is the capacity to distinguish representation from signification.

The latter is implicit rather than explicit in the former, which accounts for the dominating presence of the narrator, his need to weave his tissue of explanatory references. The complexity and charge of the plane of representation itself—in its texture and its movement—compensates for the summary nature of the signs it indicates. Balzac is crude, and never more so than when he is endeavoring to be refined (where he gives the impression of an elephant dancing on tiptoe), but he is not simplistic or uncomplicated. The simplistically melodramatic stance and attitude is in fact repeatedly viewed ironically, as when Rastignac's judgment that Vautrin's seizure is the action of a divine justice is juxtaposed to the real cause in Mlle Michonneau's adminis-tration of drugs. When Rastignac poses his melodramatic moral conundrum to Bianchon, the question of the death of the mandarin, Bianchon's immediate reply is refreshingly cynical and deflationary: "Bah, I'm up to my thirty-third mandarin" (2:960). Balzac does not let us be duped by the sublime gesture and attitude: their reference may be self-interested, sinister, or mundane. When Valérie Marneffe plays a scene of the self-sacrificing "virtuous woman," in *La Cousine Bette*, and reduces Crevel to tears, it is only to turn on him with a shriek of laughter and mock both the role and his gullibility.[41] Such irony toward the fraudulently melodramatic is related to a larger complication and transvaluation of melodramatic values, which we can detect in the figure of Vautrin, the traditional villain who is also the *généreux*, whose response of revolt to a mean and corrupt society seems the most admirable moral position in the *Comédie Humaine*. For Balzac melodramatic consciousness and modes of representation do not mean a reduction of the ethical complexity of reality, but a clarification of it.

The device of the *"retour des personnages"* is in similar manner both complicating and clarifying, creating a rich interweaving of persons and destinies in a legible pattern. The device is melodramatic in its insistence that coincidence is fate, that the same benefactors and the same villains return as in a nightmare, that in looking for the Other we find the Same. Balzac's plots are like Pixerécourt's or, even more, Bouchardy's, in that reality is always a machination, a true plot linking everything in a running noose. One might reflect here on the fate of Gobseck's fortune, perhaps the most considerable of the *Comédie Humaine*, which unites different stories, persons, and social situations (he appears in a dozen novels or tales) finally in high dramatic irony: the fortune destined to his nearest living relative, Esther (whom he does not know), arrives too late to save the reformed courtesan from a forced return to prostitution, and suicide. Willed by her to Lucien, it again arrives too late to save him from infamy and suicide. It finally passes, in varying amounts, to Lucien's virtuous but defeated provincial relatives, and to Vautrin. From its complex itinerary emerges a clear symbolic pattern in reality.

The Balzacian narrative tends to move toward moments that clarify the signs it uses, moments of confrontation and explication where signification coincides, momentarily, with representation. These can be moments at which, as in the scene from *Gobseck* quoted in chapter 1, characters say all there is to say about themselves and each other, breaking through repression to an irremediable expressionism. They can be simply instants of spectacular nomination, as when Vautrin, at the end of *Splendeurs et misères*, presents himself before the Comte de Grandville, the incarnation of the judiciary, to announce: "Sir, I am Jacques Collin, and I surrender!" (5:1109). They may also be moments of significant posture, where characters assume a pose as if in permanent expression of their lives' meanings, as when (in a passage that in fact complements the scene from *Gobseck*) Rastignac enters the Restaud drawing room, seeking to bring Anastasie to her father's bedside, and finds her fallen in an armchair: "Before looking at Rastignac, she gave fearful glances toward her husband, glances that announced a complete prostration of her forces, crushed by a moral and physical tyranny" (2:1075). Scenes may have the quality of revelation. An instance is Vautrin at the moment of his arrest, when his wig is knocked off and his true physiognomy becomes visible: "Everyone saw the meaning of Vautrin, entire: his past, his present, his future, his implacable doctrines, his religion of egotistical pleasure, the royalty conferred by the cynicism of his ideas, of his acts, and by the force of a constitution ready for anything" (2:1013). Latent and disguised meanings break through the mask of representation in an instant of extravagant expressionism.

If we have repeatedly referred to the role of gesture in the making-present of signification, it is because Balzac's efforts at representation culminate here. The whole of that curious text belonging to the *Etudes analytiques*, the "Théorie de la démarche," offers a "theoretical" basis for the reading of significance in gesture. "For me, from then on, MOVEMENT included Thought, the purest action of human beings; the Word, translation of their thoughts; then Gait and Gesture, a more or less passionate accomplishment of the Word." [42] The somewhat tortuous language suggests a vocabulary not wholly adequate to describe Balzac's discovery of what we might now call "the presentation of self in everyday life" or even "kinesics." [43] Everything, subjected to the interrogating glance of the visionary narrator, speaks, reveals. Here in answer to Louis Lambert's "new Scripture" of disincarnation is a reincarnation of meaning. Gesture may be, where all else falls silent, the final vehicle of expressivity, the irreducible indicator of signification. At the climax of *La Duchesse de Langeais*, for instance, Montriveau shows the duchesse the brand with which he intends to mark her—punishment for her coquetry and refusal of his total passion—and her reaction, where she "claps her hands in joy," is sign of an instantaneous and total conversion of self, of her passage into a state of erotic and spiritual dependency on Montriveau (5:216). A whole scene may be played out in gesture, as in *Autre Etude de femme*: "The young woman involuntarily made an indescribable gesture which painted at the same time the contrariety that she must have felt to see her liaison exposed without any human respect, and the offense given to her dignity as a woman, or to her husband; but there was also in the puckering of her traits, in the violent drawing together of her eyebrows, a kind of presentiment: perhaps she had a premonition of her destiny" (3:241). This moment of mute expression implies the entire trajectory of the story's plot.

There are moments at which gestures are of themselves so fully inhabited by meaning that they achieve the fixity and transparency of symbol: Valérie Marneffe, for instance, gives Crevel a glance "which passed, like a glint off a cannon barrel in the smoke, through her long lashes" (6:408). Such—stretching somewhat the term gesture—is the moment when the empty emblazoned carriages of the Comte de Restaud and the Baron de Nucingen suddenly appear to follow Goriot's funeral convoy. At the other extreme are the tenuous cases where, as we noted, the gesture recorded stands merely as a token of the expression predicated on it. "Here the princesse shook her head, moving her beautiful blond ringlets full of heather, in a sublime gesture. What she expressed in harrowing doubts, in hidden miseries, is ineffable. Daniel understood everything and looked at the princesse with lively emotion" (6:32). If the Princesse de Cadignan's interlocutor sees and understands, we must remain content with only the most uncertain grasp of both vehicle and tenor, a vague, but effective, impression of mystery and sublimity. Another kind of example occurs with Anastasie's arrival at her father's deathbed, too late to ask his pardon: "At this moment, Goriot opened his eyes, but only as the result of a convulsion. The gesture that revealed the comtesse's hope was not less horrible to behold than the eye of the dying man" (2:1080–81). The gesture is completely unspecified, it exists only through its heavy charge of signification. Yet the signification could not be managed were it not ostensibly extrapolated from gesture, and really predicated on gesture, for it could not be articulated directly.

As a form of representation that stands in the relation of a trope to the word- and sign-system, gesture can be the most direct expression of communication, or the attempt at communication, with the world behind. Such is Facino Cane's gesture "of extinguished patriotism and disgust for things human" (6:71). An elaborate instance is found in *Le*

Lys dans la vallée, at the moment when the Comte de Mortsauf has fallen seriously ill, and Mme de Mortsauf and Félix de Vandenesse are watching over his sickbed. The comte makes the first gesture: "His trembling hands were seeking to pull the blanket up over him." Mme de Mortsauf turns to Félix: " 'They say that this is the gesture of a dying man,' she said. 'Ah, if he were to die from this illness that we have caused, I would never remarry. I swear it,' she added, extending her hand over the head of the comte in a solemn gesture" (8:930). The "solemn gesture" marks a pact with the sacred, a consecration of self within a spiritual order beyond. Much might be said, however, about the context and ontology of this vow sealed by the gesture: the structure of the entire novel offers a deconstructive reading of Mme de Mortsauf's sublime virtue, and the attentive reader is bound to see in her vow a psychological payoff, a large measure of unconscious fraud.[44] It stands as another example of Balzac's capacity to complicate the melodramatic through ironic context. That Balzac is capable of so deconstructing his melodramatic gestures is further evidence of his complex awareness of the means of his art.[45]

That he should choose the melodramatic mode even so, that he should rework and exploit its expressive means, suggests that he knew he could not do without melodrama. The problematic of meaning as Balzac conceived it postulates a world of representation and a world of signification that do not coincide and do not necessarily offer access from one to another. The effort to make the one yield the other belongs to an ambitiously expressionist aesthetic that relies on the heightening and hyperbole of melodrama. We can in fact interpret Balzac's statements about the difficulty of creating meaning from disorganized and flattened reality as perceptions concerning the very difficulty of writing a novel: the problem of putting human action and motive into significant form, so that they may be intelligible. The model of significant human action was to be found, not in "life itself," but in the theatre, essentially in melodrama. Here was a complete repertory of situations, gestures, tropes that did confer heightened meaning on life, made its mimesis a signifying and significant enterprise.

Melodrama is hence part of the semiotic precondition of the novel for Balzac—part of what allows the "Balzacian novel" to come into being. We can best understand this novel when we perceive that its fictional representations repose on a necessary theatrical substratum— necessary, because a certain type of meaning could not be generated without it. It is a novel from which we most retain a series of summary attitudes and gestures in high relief, a breathless insistence on the dramatic semantic potential of all our actions. Its words and deeds are conceived on the scale of actors like Marie Dorval and Frédérick Lemaître and confound reference to a naturalistic context.[46] It is a fiction that is totalizing and Promethean, reorganizing the world in new unifying contexts, and extrapolating from the phenomenal world and its clouded signs toward what Balzac in the "Lettre à Hippolyte Castille" calls the "high spheres of the ideal": what we have identified as the world of purified signs.[47] The document is the vision; from the obscure fragments of the one is wrested the lucid totality of the other.

An ultimate demonstration of Balzac's engagement with the substance of melodrama might be found in a repeated structure of his short stories and novellas. It has never been much remarked how consistently Balzac's short fiction makes use of the traditional device of the framed tale. The first narrator may himself become the listener to a tale (the principal narrative) related by another, to reappear at the conclusion with the teller of the tale. Or the authorial voice may introduce a narrator and his circle of listeners, who at the end will comment on the tale told. Or there may be a succession of narrators and tales offered to one audience, which comments on their significance in the interstices. *Gobseck, Honorine, L'Auberge rouge, Z. Marcas, Facino Cane, Sarrasine, Adieu, Un Prince de la bohème, Autre Etude de femme,* are all examples of short fiction in which one of these methods of framing is of major importance. The list is no doubt incomplete, and among the full-length novels *Le Lys dans la vallée* and *Louis Lambert* employ a similar form. What is most significant in the use of the device is the final reflection on the tale or tales told by listeners and tellers, the registering of effect. In *Facino Cane*, for example, the story told by the blind musician who is convinced that he is the rightful doge of Venice leads to his extortion of a promise from his interlocutor to set out with him for Venice to recover the lost treasure from the depths of the Doges' Palace—a promise that results less from the interlocutor's conviction that Facino is telling the truth than from his magnetizing narrative presence. Facino dies soon after, leaving in suspense the question of the reality of his vision and the reality of his listener's promise. What we are left with is the force of Facino's tale itself, the haunting vision of treasures piled high in dark vaults, the strength of a belief. More complex and more remarkable still is *Adieu*. General Philippe de Sucy rediscovers, in a retired country estate, Stéphanie,

Comtesse de Vandières, whom he lost at the crossing of the Berezina, on the retreat from Moscow, and who lapsed into madness at that horrific moment, into amnesia and an aphasia from which she can pronounce only one word, her parting cry to Philippe, "Adieu!" Her uncle, the doctor who has been taking care of her, recounts the story of the crossing of the Berezina. This is then followed by another fiction, not recounted, but staged by Philippe, who has the idea that a perfect reconstruction of the moment of crippling trauma might lead to its reversal, to cure. He constructs in his park a reproduction of the banks of the Berezina, complete with its devastation, cannon, and carnage; hires peasants and costumes them as soldiers and cossacks; then, on a December day when snow has fallen, brings Stéphanie to the site. The fiction succeeds: Stéphanie recognizes Philippe, memory and consciousness return, she throws herself into his arms—but only to speak once again her word "Adieu!" and to die. The fiction has proved both curative and mortal, potent and dangerous. It devastates, bringing not only Stéphanie's death but Philippe's suicide as well.

There is in *Adieu* a striking dramatization of the potent effect of fiction making, of the stories we tell and enact. Fictions count; they act on life, they change it. As much as in the stage enterprise of a Pixerécourt, there is in Balzac's tale-telling a consciousness of action on a listener, of a life affected. With Balzac, this is not simplistic moralism, but rather a recognition that fictions are, or should be, engaged with the ethical substance of life and should take a moral toll on the reader. Another instance of this is represented in *Sarrasine*, which plays off fictions against their effect with considerable complexity. The narrator is asked by the Marquise de Rochefide, whom he is courting, to account both for the aged spectral person found at Mme de Lanty's soirée, and for the *Portrait of Adonis* by Joseph-Marie Vien they have found in Mme de Lanty's boudoir. His satisfaction of her desire implies her reciprocal satisfaction of his (erotic) desire when the tale has been told. His story recounts the sculptor Sarrasine's love for the Roman singer Zambinella, whom he takes for a woman but then discovers to be in fact a *castrato*, whereupon Sarrasine feels himself stricken by sterility, dead to both art and the erotic forever. He attempts to destroy the statue he has made of Zambinella and lifts his sword to punish the singer, but is instead himself struck down by the emissaries of Cardinal Cicognara, Zambinella's protector. The plaster statue is then executed in marble; the *Adonis* of Vien is subsequently copied from the statue (and this canvas in turn is imitated by Girodet for his *Endymion*), while Zambinella lives on, a neuter being who achieves great longevity, a kind of animated specter. Now that all is elucidated, the Marquise de Rochefide imposes silence on the narrator and tells him that he has created in her a disgust for life and love. Passion has been marked by castration in the narrator's tale; art has been discovered to originate, not in the plenitude of "ideal beauty," but in lack, in emptiness. This generalized mark of castration now transgresses the boundaries of the narrator's story to enter his life. As Roland Barthes well demonstrates, castration passes into the very relationship of narrator and interlocutor and renders their liaison impossible.[48] "You know how to punish," the narrator says to the marquise, recognizing that he has been struck (6:110).

The last sentence of the novella—"And the Marquise remained pensive"—stands as an emblem of the expansion of the fiction into the lives that it touches. Fiction, in Balzac's conception, exists to make us "pensive," exists to make us reflect on the substance of life and its principles. Implicit here is a theory of reading and the nature of fictional referentiality. If the literary sign is interreferential, without transcendent referent—as the complex interlockings of *Sarrasine*, leading us back to an original emptiness, perfectly dramatize—it nonetheless ought, in the view of a writer concerned with the moral substance of life, to provoke this "pensiveness," this reactive reflection in the reader. Fiction is transmissible, and its transmission takes a toll. Through their structure, the tales reveal most clearly the function that Balzac assigns to storytelling. In the simplest and possibly the most pertinent terms, this has been designated by Walter Benjamin, in his essay "The Storyteller," as "Wisdom." [49] Wisdom derives precisely from the carry-over of experience told—told as "counsel" in the living voice of the storyteller—into the experience of the listener; it depends on his remembrance of and reflection on the tale. Balzac is intuitively close to the traditional role and function of the storyteller described by Benjamin.[50]

The analogue of the short fiction's tellers, listeners, commentators in the novels is of course nearly always the insistent narrative presence, with its constant intervention, explanation, emphasis. The narrator articulates both the meaning of his dramatized life and its intended effect. "Consider this: this drama is neither a fiction nor a novel. *All is true*, it is so true that anyone can recognize its elements close to home, in his own heart perhaps" (2:848). This clarion call from the start of *Le Père Goriot* has many echoes throughout the texture of the narrator's speech. We should not be embarrassed by its excess but consider it as a necessary sign pointing to the melodramatic enterprise, engaging us in a melodramatic reading of the text to follow. Sainte-Beuve accused Balzac of conquering his public through its secret infirmities, as though he brought (as Freud would announce arriving in America) a kind of irresistible plague.[51] It is certain that this is a literature that wants to act on us, not in the predicative manner of Pixerécourt ("Pixerécourt, you write a drama and we believe in God!"),[52] but through an active solicitation of the reader to enter into the highly colored drama played out behind the banalities of quotidian existence. We know that Balzac was haunted by a feeling that his excessive creation was almost a sacrilegious imitatio dei, a Promethean enterprise for which there would surely be a punishment.[53] This could not have been the case had he not believed in the importance of fictions, and in their danger. Fiction making became itself a dangerous enterprise for him precisely because it meant working in the domain of discovery, revelation, laying bare. The motto of the utopian and pastoral *Médecin de campagne*, culled by Doctor Benassis from an inscription in a cell of the Grande Chartreuse—*"Fuge, late, tace"*— stands as a temptation to repose, silence, and the unmelodramatic existence. Yet the very hyperbole of the motto's form suggests the impossibility of its message for Balzac himself. The work had to go on: uncovering, unmasking, pressuring reality to reveal the terms of its drama, capturing the drama through large summary gestures, reorganizing the effects in terms of their causes, wresting meaning from chaos, proclaiming a world inhabited by significance.

6

Henry James and
the Melodrama of Consciousness

"For if he *were* innocent what then on earth was I?"

—*The Turn of the Screw*

The plunge of civilization into this abyss of blood and darkness by the wanton feat of those two infamous autocrats is a thing that so gives away the whole long age during which we have supposed the world to be, with whatever abatement, gradually bettering, that to have to take it all now for what the treacherous years were all the while really making for and *meaning* is too tragic for any words.

—Letter to Howard Sturgis, 4 August 1914

I

James's earliest fictional exercises have been described by Thomas Sergeant Perry as lurid stuff: "The heroes were for the most part villains, but they were white lambs by the side of the sophisticated heroines, who seemed to have read all Balzac in the cradle and to be positively dripping with lurid crimes. He began with these extravagant pictures of course in adoration of the great master whom he always so warmly admired." [1] That such overtly Gothic and melodramatic elements should have characterized James's juvenilia will not surprise anyone attentive to the plot, situation, and issues of such early novels as *Watch and Ward*, *Roderick Hudson*, and *The American*; or indeed, anyone who has reflected on the continuing dark strain in the Jamesian imagination, its unremitting concern with the menacing, the abysmal, the violent, and the unknown. "I have the imagination of disaster," he wrote in 1896, "and see life as ferocious and sinister." [2] If there is in his fiction an evolution away from some of the more obvious and external devices of melodramatic representation and rhetoric, the underlying melodramatic ambition remains, and indeed reasserts itself with the "major phase."

The evolution of James's judgments of Balzac is significant in this respect. What we find is not a progressive turning away from Balzac's

153

grandiose representations, his "lurid documents" and his "visions," but rather a greater acceptance of them. If the principal essay on Balzac in *French Poets and Novelists* (an essay first published in 1875) reveals a certain discomfort with the novelist's lapses from "realism," with his visionary and "romantic" side, in the essays of 1902 and 1905—"Honoré de Balzac" in *Notes on Novelists* and "The Lesson of Balzac"—he has come to terms with his unremitting admiration of his master. Balzac is imaged with a certain nostalgia as "the last of the novelists to do the thing handsomely," a prelapsarian giant whose lesson must be studied if the novel is to recover its "wasted heritage." [3] James unhesitatingly concedes that "Balzac's imagination alone did the business," that the observer and the visionary are inseparable, that Balzac's heightened mode of representation is the necessary vehicle of his subject.[4] The passage where James in the 1902 essay makes implicit reparation for his strictures of 1875 (the passage quoted in chapter 1) follows a discussion of "the romantic" in Balzac that shows a relaxation and a broadening in James's attitude, a conscious acceptance of a mode beyond conventional realism. "He has," writes James, " 'gone in' for his subject, in the vulgar phrase, with an avidity that makes the attack of his most eminent rivals affect us as the intercourse between introduced indifferences at a dull evening party." [5] The phrase, in its implicit reference to the milieu exploited in much of James's own fiction, suggests awareness and acceptance of the necessary heightenings and extrapolations of the melodramatic mode.

Close to the time he was composing the late essays on Balzac, James undertook his celebrated discussion of "romance" in the preface to *The American*. Shortly before the much-quoted passage on "the balloon of experience," he worries about the definition of "the romantic" and its use, virtually from an epistemological perspective. "The romantic stands, on the other hand, for the things that, with all the facilities in the world, all the wealth and all the courage and all the wit and all the adventure, we never *can* directly know; the things that can reach us only through the beautiful circuit and subterfuge of our thought and our desire." [6] This striking characterization of "the romantic" as the realm of knowledge reached through desire recalls central themes in our description of melodrama, a form that facilitates the "circuit" of desire, permits its break through repression, brings its satisfaction in full expression. As he proceeds in his attempt to isolate and delineate the romantic element, James rejects any definition dependent on traditional accessories or characters ("as a matter indispensably of boats, or of caravans, or of tigers, or of 'historical characters,' or of ghosts, or of forgers, or of detectives, or of beautiful wicked women, or of pistols and knives") and on the number and magnitude of dangers. What he calls "the dream of an intenser experience" may be found in common occurrences "that 'look like nothing' and that can but inwardly and occultly be dealt with, which involve the sharpest hazards to life and honour." The phrase images clearly James's commitment to a mode that would render a sense of the inner melodrama played out in reaction to life and conferring intensity and value on life. The "intenser experience" is a matter of vision and of treatment: if Flaubert's Emma Bovary is herself of a romantic temper, "nothing less resembles a romance than the record of her adventures": a phrase that strikes close to the heart of James's lifelong critical reserve about Flaubert, his repeated preference for Balzac. The discussion terminates on a parenthetical note which suggests that, whatever the difficulties of finding the demarcation of the real and the romantic may be, "I am not sure an infallible sign of the latter is not this rank vegetation of the 'power' of bad people that good get into, or *vice versa*. It is so rarely, alas, into *our* power that any one gets!" (p. xx). Such is the force of personalized evil and, potentially, of its opposite.

The Jamesian definition of romance, then, encompasses many of the elements, and indeed the very terms, that we found basic to melodrama: the confronted power of evil and goodness, the sense of hazard and clash, the intensification and heightening of experience corresponding to dream and desire. If the discussion of romance is advanced partly in criticism of his early novel, there is clearly at the same time both a "discovery" of the romantic element in his work and an acceptance of its necessity. It is not simply that James in 1907 has recognized the romantic nature of his novel of 1877, but that he has recognized, and stated more clearly than previously, the romantic element inherent to all his work, and his need for it. The point needs making, because the inclusion of James in a discussion of the melodramatic imagination will to many readers initially appear perverse. James is of course reputed for his subtlety, his refinement, his art of nuance and shading; and his world is preëminently the highly civilized and mannered. What sense then does it make to conceive him as a melodramatist and to claim particular illumination of his work from this source?

The term *melodrama* when it is employed by critics of James usually points to more or less deplorable characteristics encountered in such early works as *Roderick Hudson* or *The American*, though not entirely eliminated from *The Portrait of a Lady*, *The Bostonians*, *The Princess Casamassima*. Jacques Barzun and Leo B. Levy are the main exceptions. Barzun proposes to use melodrama as an inclusive term for "those fictions that record man's horror in the face of evil" and notes James's representation of "panic, fear, the mystery of the horror." [7] Levy, whose study is focused on the relation of James's melodrama to his experience as a playwright, instances the "failure of communication between different moral states" in James's fiction; he refers us to literal melodrama with the statement that " 'outraged virtue' and depravity in open conflict is the essential Jamesian melodrama"; and he suggests the underlying reason for recourse to melodrama as the means to infuse "his most deeply felt moral concerns with a sense of peril and crisis." [8] These are useful perceptions; we can hope to extend them from a more thorough grounding in the nature of melodrama and the uses of the melodramatic mode. Though neither Barzun nor Levy discusses James's late fiction in any detail, they are both aware that the melodramatic persists in it. We must work toward this late and complex melodrama, a melodrama at the service of what James calls "the author's instinct everywhere for the *indirect* presentation of his main image," to say how in his transmutations of melodramatic materials and techniques James remains faithful to its premises.[9]

The American can stand for the use of melodrama in the early fiction. As we noted in the first chapter, Newman's experience in that novel brings into play a number of melodrama's specific devices, even its claptrap. James is not content to have American innocence baffled and betrayed by the manipulations of decadent French aristocrats in their fortress-like hôtel in the Faubourg Saint-Germain. He must further intensify the clash by creating a hidden crime in the Bellegarde heritage, the murder of the old marquis by his wife, who has denied him his medicine and transfixed him with her fully Balzacian glance: "You know my lady's eyes, I think, sir; it was with them that she killed him; it was with the terrible strong will that she put into them." [10] The deed is recounted by old Mrs. Bread, the English governess, as the dusk gathers on a bleak hillside by the ruined castle of Fleurières; and Newman is provided with documentary evidence in the form of the deathbed accusation scribbled by the old marquis. Underlying the social drama played out in Newman's courtship of Claire de Cintré is this bloodcurdling deed, rendered with all possible shades of horror, supported by sure signs to the determination of guilt. After his encounter with Mrs. Bread, Newman appears to be in a position to act as the providential hero of melodrama: he possesses the signs necessary to expose the villain and perhaps to free the innocent heroine from her claustration in the convent of the rue d'Enfer, to purge the poisoned air of the social order.

That Newman does not so rout the villains is a first sign of the typical Jamesian transmutation of melodrama, his primary interest in the melodrama of consciousness. The clash of good innocence and sophisticated villainy in this novel at the last works to an intensification of the terms of Newman's choice between revenge and renunciation, a choice that is the final test of his inner being, that must call upon his deepest moral inwardness for a difficult victory of generosity and natural nobility. Newman's renunciation of revenge should not be construed as James's renunciation of melodrama. It marks on the contrary a deep understanding of the fundamental concerns of melodrama and its possible uses. If melodrama as a form exists to permit the isolation and dramatization of integral ethical forces, to impose their evidence and a recognition of the force of the right, the mode and terms of Newman's choice stand squarely within the tradition. What differs is that the melodrama of external action—the suspenseful menace, pursuit, and combat—all are past by the time he resolves the ethical conflict.[11] External melodrama has been used to lead into the melodrama of ethical choice.

In later novels, the melodrama of external action will tend to be more and more superseded in favor of a stance, from the outset, within the melodrama of consciousness. Such for instance is the case with *The Portrait of a Lady*, where all of Isabel Archer's career is framed in terms of choices, and the terms of choice are themselves progressively polarized and intensified, so that Isabel's final decision to return to Gilbert Osmond in Rome is freighted with lurid connotations of sacrifice, torture, penance, claustration. Leo B. Levy argues that "the real subject of the novel has become the intensification of oppositions for its own sake." [12] It might be more accurate to say that oppositions are intensified for the sake of the choice between them, so that the adventure of consciousness can be fully melodramatic. James in his preface to the novel draws our attention to the crucial episode of the melodrama of consciousness, Isabel's "extraordinary meditative vigil," as an example of "what an 'exciting' inward life may do for the person leading it" (1:xx). Here the stuff of consciousness becomes explicitly dramatic and exciting: "Her mind, assailed by visions, was in a state of extraordinary activity . . ." (2:204). It is probable that the discomfort felt by many readers and critics faced with the ending of the novel derives from the absolute terms that James has staked on Isabel's choice, a feeling of moral assault or psychic scandal of the type that we found literal melodrama to produce.

The melodrama of consciousness that reaches its first maturity in *The Portrait of a Lady* will be pursued by James in his subsequent fiction, with the indirection provided by an increasing rigor of "point of view," and yet also with deepening intensity. The greater inwardness of the drama will be matched on the plane of external action by an effort to make those gestures or acts that are executed and recorded fully paying, fully charged with meaning. Critical reserve has been voiced about such overtly melodramatic endings as that to *The Bostonians*, where Basil Ransom hurries Verena Tarrant out into the night while Olive Chancellor rushes onstage to offer herself to the well-bred furies of the disappointed Music Hall crowd, or that of *The Princess Casamassima*, where the German revolutionary Schinkel and the princess batter down the door to Hyacinth Robinson's room, to find him lying in gore, shot by his own hand with the bullet designated for the Duke. If James uses such strong and violent action in these endings—as later he will use the violent, exorbitant evocations of the last encounter between Strether and Mme de Vionnet in *The Ambassadors* and the storm-burst of evil at the Venetian climax of *The Wings of the Dove*—it is because such action best correlates to and delivers, over the footlights as it were, the intensity of his melodrama of consciousness. If in *The American* we feel to a degree the outer, manifest melodrama working to shape the dimensions of Newman's final inner choice, later in James's career we sense the inner melodrama reflecting upon and charging the outer action. External action tends more and more toward the revelatory, toward rendering of the critical moment and gesture that summarize and release the significant vision: Isabel's discovery of Gilbert Osmond and Madame Merle "unconsciously and familiarly associated" (2:205), Strether's discovery—"a sharp fantastic crisis that had popped up as if in a dream"—of Chad and Mme de Vionnet in the rowboat (2:257–58), Hyacinth Robinson's view of the princess and Paul Muniment standing at the door of her house—while Hyacinth feels "his heart beat insanely, ignobly"—then entering together (2:324). The exiguity and restraint of the external action is overborn by the weight of revelatory meaning that the novelist, through his preparations, juxtapositions, and use of a post of observation, has read into it.

The reasons for outward and inward melodrama in James are the same: his desire to make ethical conflict, imperative, and choice the substance of the novel, to make it the nexus of "character" and the motivation of plot. Yvor Winters approaches this question in terms similar to ours when, in his consideration of Jamesian "obscurity," he notes that James's virtues are closely related to his defects: "His defects arise from the effort on the part of the novelist and of his characters to understand ethical problems in a pure state, and to understand them absolutely. . . ." [13] The heightening of experience and the intensification of choice are motivated by the desire of the novelist, and those characters who act as his "centers of consciousness," to find, to see, to articulate and eventually to dramatize in their actions moral problems seized in their essence, as pure imperatives and commitments. This must not be construed to mean that characters are themselves integral, representative of pure moral conditions, black or white. Especially in James's mature work, there is always a subtle mixture of motive and fine shadings of ethical coloration in his major characters, and most of all in his "villains." It is rather that characters, whatever their nuances, make reference to such absolutes, recognize, more or less clearly, their existence and force, and in their worldly actions gesture toward them. The movement of the typical Jamesian plot from complex and often obscure interrelationship to crisis imaged as revelation signals his need to disengage from the complications of reality a final confrontation, however nuanced, of moral integers. Good and evil do exist, and an inability to see and understand them, even when they are exquisitely alloyed, is to fail in the reading of reality, to oversimplify in the manner of a Flaubert, to misestimate what life is really about and art is really for.[14]

The conflict of good and evil—terms that we must further explore and refine—must hence be led to confrontation, articulation, acting out. As Balzac's novels regularly worked toward the scenic "showdown," the *scène à faire*, so James developed more and more consciously his conception of the novelistic "picture," which, as in the examples cited from *The Princess Casamassima* and *The Ambassadors*, can be a tableau of represented meaning, and the "scene," the dramatized significant moment. The scenic method is part of James's technique from the very beginning, yet evidently sharpened and made more conscious by his experience in the theatre, his struggle to write stage drama. When he wrote to himself in his Notebook, in 1896, "I realize—none too soon—that the *scenic* method is my absolute, my imperative, my *only* salvation," he was recording a final coming to consciousness of what he had as an artist known for a long time.[15] Theatrical conventions, enactment, theatricality itself were the semiotic preconditions for the novel as James understood it.

James was attracted to the theatre for other reasons similar to Balzac's: because it promised a sociable, institutional glory, and because it offered the possibility of popular and financial success. The latter motive has bothered some critics who wish to see James as confined to the rarified medium and emotion; yet there is abundant evidence that James throughout his career longed to succeed in popular forms, to meet a Balzac on his own terrain. And it is clear that he envisioned success in the theatre as a way to reëstablish contact with a glorious public tradition extending back to Romanticism. But he was forced to work in the wrong theatre, to write for the London, rather than the Paris, stage. His admiration for French acting and drama is fully evident in the articles he contributed as a young man to the New York *Tribune*, in the ideals he advances in his critiques of the London theatre, in numerous passages of the Notebooks. Of the Comédiens-Français he wrote, in a phrase that suggests his own continuing ideal in both theatre and novel, "they solve triumphantly the problem of being at once realistic to the eye and romantic to the imagination." [16] When he began work on his stage adaptation of *The American*—which was in fact to reduce the novel's complex melodrama to the most schematic and stagy melodrama—he invoked uniquely French masters: "*A moi*, Scribe; *à moi*, Sardou, *à moi*, Dennery!" [17]

The three playwrights mentioned delineate with fair accuracy James's conception of his theatrical tutors. Scribe and Sardou, to whom one should add Alexandre Dumas *fils*, so often discussed by James, represent the tradition of melodrama domesticated, melodrama become the "well-made play." We have mentioned earlier (in chapter 4) the elements of this domestication, its preservation of the hyperbolic dramaturgy of melodrama together with its search for greater "realism" of detail and situation, and its falling off from the cosmic ambitions of earlier melodrama. Scribe, Sardou, and Dumas offered to James models of impeccable construction, plotting, suspense, and confrontation. Dennery, on the other hand, was a true melodramatist throughout his long career, and James's admiration for him is significant. We in fact find James responding with pleasure to the New York production of Dennery's *Les Deux Orphelines*, a melodrama of 1874 that is one of the latest representatives of the genre to preserve quite intact its conventions: it offers a compendium of melodramatic themes and devices, foundlings, poverty, blindness, disguised identities, culpable parents, incipient revolution, conversion, renunciation, and heroics.[18] We should recognize James's nostalgia for the grandiose possibilities of Romantic melodrama. As he wrote in tribute on the death of Frédérick Lemaître, in 1876, "The theatre of our own day, with its relish for small, realistic effects, produces no more actors of those heroic proportions." He closes that article with an evocatory flight: "But Frédéric Lemaître, as we see him in his *légende*, is like a huge, fantastic shadow, a moving silhouette, projected duskily against the wall from a glowing fire. The fire is the 'romantic' movement of 1830." [19] As Balzac represented the prelapsarian novelist to whom all was possible, the French Romantic stage suggested a prelapsarian theatre.

That James was actually obliged to work within conventions at once narrower and more vulgar, for an audience more socially segregated (such was the case in London) yet less conditioned to the possibilities of the dramatic art, was the assurance of failure, whether for *The American* or for the curiously late-Romantic *Guy Domville*. Only Ibsen, who can be said to have reinvested in the structure of the "well-made play" some of the intense ethical concern of melodrama—transmuted in his late plays into the melodrama of consciousness—offered a valid contemporary example, though one socially too foreign to James to be of immediate use. As Leon Edel has pointed out, it was to Ibsen that James looked in creating Rose Armiger in that curious melodrama, at once mannered and sensational, *The Other House*.[20] Rose Armiger drowns the small child Effie Bream in the hope of marrying Tony Bream, who has made his late wife a promise not to marry again during the life of the child—a promise extorted on her deathbed, at the close of act I, which dominates the play as a fully melodramatic absolute vow. *The Other House* was originally written as a play, then revised into a short novel for serialization in the *London Illustrated News*, the most "popular" medium for which James ever wrote, then once more reworked as a play for Elizabeth Robins, but never staged. It is lurid fare, and an interesting demonstration that James still in the

162   THE MELODRAMATIC IMAGINATION

1890s was attracted to the possibility of doing something popular, and
something that would give overt expression to the most melodramatic
elements in his imagination.

Years later, in 1910, as he worked with the pieces of an outline for a
new fiction, James wrote in his Notebook: "Oh, blest *Other House*,
which gives me thus at every step a precedent, a support, a divine little
light to walk by." [21] The "divine light" shed by his melodrama was
that of a fully developed scenic and dramatic technique translated
into novelistic form. The original transcription of *The Other House* from
play to novel was the most telling demonstration for the author of how
the lessons of his grim theatrical years could be put to use in fiction.
Leon Edel and Leo B. Levy have well described the direct effect of the
theatrical experience on James's novelistic technique from *The Spoils of
Poynton* onward. Levy refers us to "the scenic intensities that are the
primary literary experience of the reader of James," and while this is
characteristic as well of the fiction before the theatrical years, the
practice of the theatre confirmed and sharpened James's sense that to
"dramatize" a subject—as he so often exhorted himself, and others, to
do—meant to have almost literal recourse to the dramatist's tools, and
especially to the direct verbal and physical encounters that the stage
allows and needs.[22]

What James called "the little drama of my 'Spoils' " (p. vii) stands
at the inception of the line of James's most theatrical fiction, and its
climactic scenes convey a sense of drawing room melodrama at its
best. Place is conceived as stage set, and within its confines a limited
number of selected stage properties and gestures are made to bear the
weight of an impassioned drama. At the end of chapter 14, for
instance, Owen Gereth, who has come to tea with Fleda Vetch, breaks
through his long muddlement and reserve to declare his love for her,
and his desire to break his engagement with Mona Brigstock. At the
moment of declaration, "as the door opened the smutty maid, edging
in, announced 'Mrs. Brigstock!' " (p. 168). With this inopportune
arrival of Mona's mother, a new scene begins—chapter 15—and with
it our attention, like Mrs. Brigstock's, is drawn to a trivial object that
is given disproportionate dimensions, made into a stage property that
stands for a "real" object that in turn acts as a sign of human action.
Mrs. Brigstock's eyes attach themselves to the barely nibbled biscuit
that "in some precipitate movement" has been brushed to the floor. It
was, we are told, "doubtless a sign of the agitation that possessed
[Fleda]. For Mrs. Brigstock there was apparently more in it than met

the eye. Owen at any rate picked it up, and Fleda felt as if he were removing the traces of some scene that the newspapers would have characterized as lively. Mrs. Brigstock clearly took in also the sprawling tea-things and the marks as of a high tide in the full faces of her young friends" (p. 169). The biscuit and then the tea-things (which can only metaphorically be "sprawling") are, in the manner of stage properties, signs *for* signs: they are hyperbolic conventional signs, magnified in order to release to scrutiny "more than meets the eye." [23] The scene is an exemplary instance of James's capacity to invest his confrontations with revelatory excitement without apparently violating decorum and the surface of manners, through imprinting on the objects and gestures rendered the stamp of hyperbolic and theatrical meaning.

The scene develops from this encounter over the sign of the biscuit into a vivid interchange which at the end explicitly reminds us of its "staginess," when Mrs. Brigstock announces that she came to see Fleda in order to "plead" with her, and Fleda replies: "As if I were one of those bad women in a play?" (p. 177). Here is a typically Jamesian procedure of ironizing dramatic conventions all the while suggesting their imaginative appropriateness: a way of having one's melodrama while denying it. If Fleda may be cast in this stock role (a role, no doubt, from Dumas *fils*) by Mrs. Brigstock, she in no wise fills it in the reader's mind. Yet James's evocation of the possibility allows us to respond to her situation *as if* she were so theatrical a character. As in his metaphors, another context is brought to bear on the literal context. Fleda's own self-consciousness about her role frees her to act with a higher awareness of the significances that may be read in her enactment: she is aware of the signs that her actions generate, of her embodiment of meanings. Hence in her subsequent climactic encounter with Owen, in chapter 16, she plays in full consciousness of her words and gestures as heightened and interpretable signs. The scene unfolds in her sister's shabby living room, and we are repeatedly made aware of the characters' movements within a space conceived as a stage. Its most important property is the staircase, ever ready for Fleda's flight from Owen—her renunciation of him unless he first obtains his grant of freedom from Mona—up which she at the last will scramble. By making his readers live so consistently in a theatrical medium, and respond to the performances of his characters as if on the stage, James prepares and legitimates his "strong" ending, the burning of Poynton. This final scene reproduces the physical cataclysms typical of melodramatic third acts, strikes the set in a fully realized symbolic enactment.

Even more totally theatrical and scenic in their presentation are *What Maisie Knew* and *The Awkward Age*. The latter James recognized as his most finished play-as-novel, patterned on the practice of the French writer Gyp, and bringing to culmination all his studies in the dramatic form. The climactic scene of *The Awkward Age* is one of the most accomplished pieces of confrontation and cataclysm that James ever wrought. It is, again, realized without rending the fabric of "manners"—though it sends tremors through the social order—while yet opening up depths of violence, hostility, and conflict. The scene turns on an unidentified "French novel," the nexus of moral "horrors," [24] which, it will be revealed, Nanda has borrowed from Vanderbank, has read, and then has recommended to Tishy Grendon. The book is another stage property, passed from hand to hand and commented upon by the characters. Aggie wants it, but Lord Petherton (who, we gather, from being the Duchess's lover has become Aggie's, now that she has "come out") keeps it from her, only to have it snatched by Harold Brookenham, who reads Vanderbank's name inscribed on the cover, whereupon it is grabbed by Mrs. Brookenham, who announces that the handwriting isn't Van's and passes it on to Mr. Longdon for confirmation; then Nanda confesses that she wrote Van's name, intending that the novel be returned to him. Mrs. Brook, recovering the volume, presses Nanda for a public declaration of whether or not she has read it. Mr. Cashmore takes possession of the book as Mrs. Brook continues to insist to Nanda:

> "Have you read this work, Nanda?"
> "Yes mamma."
> "Oh I say!" cried Mr. Cashmore, hilarious and turning the leaves.
> Mr. Longdon had by this time ceremoniously approached Tishy. "Good night." [p. 434]

End of scene, and end of act. The unspeakable horrors of the unspecified French novel have moved through the group like a tracer dye, revealing relations, making clear positions and motives that have thus far been uncertain. The terrifying role is Mrs. Brook's, for her insistence upon a public avowal from Nanda is a conscious effort to show her daughter up before the assembled set—and particularly before Van, the man who should be Nanda's suitor, whom Mrs. Brook desires for herself, and Mr. Longdon, the man who in compensation will offer her a retreat from the world—as corrupted and hence as unsaleable goods on the London marriage market. To the alert reader, the scene has all the shock of villainy unleashed. Mrs. Brook has created what Van will later call a "smash." His image for the scene is accurate: "It was a wonderful performance. You pulled us down—just closing with each of the great columns in its turn—as Samson pulled down the temple" (p. 439). The *scène à faire* of the novel has been Mrs. Brook's to do, and the narrowness of the stage, the conventionality of the characters and props involved, cannot blind us to its thunderous effect.

The technique of such revelatory dramatic confrontations, bathed in the "divine little light" shed by the composition of *The Other House*, is particularly appropriated to the kinds of situations repeatedly dramatized in James's fiction, especially at this period. Nanda Brookenham's dilemma, her showing up, and her defeat at the hands of the society orchestrated by her mother constitute one of the many versions of the Jamesian obsession with sophisticated versions of innocence and corruption. Nanda's story is one of the most subtle and pessimistic of these because it becomes evident that innocence as "purity" and as ignorance cannot survive in so treacherous a world (and Aggie, brought up in ignorance of good and evil by the Duchess, becomes the most inconsequential of strumpets upon her marriage); at the same time, the world insists on maintaining the hypocrisy of innocence. What supplants innocence as purity is necessarily consciousness, at root the knowledge of good and evil. This Nanda gains, but at the price of losing worldly rewards, losing in particular Van. It is on Van that the novel suggests the sharpest moral judgment: worldly, himself one of the corrupt and the conscious, he is unwilling to accept consciousness in Nanda. He draws back from her knowledge of good and evil, he fears consciousness as inseparable from corruption. The ironic result is to drive him once more, at the end, back to the solace of the fully conscious and corrupt Mrs. Brook. It remains for the gallant and betrayed Mitchy, and Mr. Longdon—the *vieillard généreux* of melodrama, the representative of an earlier and nobler generation —to recognize (but not to reward) the quality of Nanda's virtue within corruption.

The clash of untenable innocence with sophisticated corruption and evil also provides the theme and structure of *What Maisie Knew*. As in *The Awkward Age*, in this novel innocence cannot long maintain the state of purity if it is to survive. The point so often missed in discussion of *What Maisie Knew*, it seems to me, is that if the novel is about the limitations of the child's vision, it is also about its precocious sophistication, Maisie's premature but necessary education in "handling" people whose motives and intentions she may not understand, but whose relations to herself, whose greater or lesser utility to herself, she most uncannily masters and by the end manipulates. The final scene of the novel, where she turns the tables of the agonizing choice presented to her against her would-be protectors—demanding that Sir Claude give up Mrs. Beale if he wishes to keep her, Maisie, then choosing Mrs. Wix when it becomes apparent that Sir Claude can't and won't give up Mrs. Beale—registers her arrival at a sophisticated and usable practical knowledge of what is in her best interests. What is never seen—and is queried in the last line of the novel as in its title—is the extent to which Maisie knows what lies *behind* the behavior of the different adults, and combinations of adults, in her regard. If she has become an expert in human relationships as they affect her destiny, she is, we estimate, still largely ignorant of their overriding motivation—which here, as in *The Awkward Age*, is essentially sexual. So that her position in regard to the various sets of "parents" in the book is much like our position in regard to the "French novel" of *The Awkward Age*: like Maisie, we know the effects but not the content; we know the "horrors" only through their effect. Such knowledge through effect rather than cause and substance is indeed one of the voluntary constraints of the purely scenic form, "the imposed absence of . . . 'going behind,' " as James states it in the preface to *The Awkward Age* (p. xvii). This constraint means that the melodrama of consciousness can here be known only insofar as it suffuses outward action, speech, and gesture.

More generally, such an evacuation of the content is typical of the "horrors" at issue in the clash of innocence and evil in James's fiction at this period and in most of the later novels as well. If *The American* enters upon a full specification of the Bellegardes' black deed (though not in fact on specification of the reasons for Claire de Cintré's renunciation of the struggle), the fiction of the 1890s tends to exploit an evil all the more oppressive in that it is unnamed, undesignated, detectable only in its effects. Evil is a kind of blankness into which we read the content that we need, as with the misdeeds that cause little Miles, in *The Turn of the Screw*, to be sent home from school: misdeeds persistently guessed at by the Governess, posited, shaped, figured, invented. That such "ambiguity" was James's intent is sufficiently clear from the preface to The Turn of the Screw: "Only make the reader's general vision of evil intense enough, I said to myself . . . and his own experience, his own imagination, his own sympathy (with the children) and horror (of their false friends) will supply him quite sufficiently with all the particulars. Make him think the evil, make him think it for himself, and you are released from weak specifications" (pp. xxi–xxii).

The Turn of the Screw is exemplary of the tendency in all James's later fiction to intensify the manichaeistic struggle of good and evil, light and darkness, through a reflection of effect that does not designate cause, yet in not doing so creates a large and portentous menace that evokes a tremendous cause. It is as if James had discovered that to maintain the melodramatic terms of his vision and his presentation, in particular to maintain the conflict of polarized moral conditions, while at the same time escaping the limitations of overt, explicit melodrama (of the type of The American), he must make his confronted terms rich in perceived and felt possibilities, emanations, effects, while elaborately refusing designation of their ontology. The Turn of the Screw shows the consequences of this decision to a high degree. The ontology of the evil whose undoubted effects are chronicled in the story is so uncertain that some readers, led by Edmund Wilson, have been led to see it as a study in pure, and pathological, subjectivity.[25] The logic of the Wilsonian position is clear: if there is no objective evidence of the presence of evil at Bly and of the corruption of the children, then we should look in the very consciousness that is perceiving such evil, to see if it may not be a projection of that consciousness; and here he finds hints enough to establish a plausible, if extrapolated, case. The Wilsonian emphasis is a necessary corrective to the excessively theological view of Dorothea Krook, for whom the story is a Faustian struggle of corruption and attempted salvation, for she tends to ignore the epistemological complication.[26] Both views are in fact too limited in their exclusive form. It is important to recognize that both the perceiving eye and the field of perception are shifting and unreliable; or rather, that there is a perfect relativity of movement, since one can never say at any given moment which has shifted. The result is never a clear decision about the nature of the horror, but rather a kind of moral ratio that is stated by the Governess in a rare flash of self-doubt just before the end of the tale, as she presses Miles for a designation of the horrors for which he

has been expelled from school: "It was for the instant confounding and
bottomless, for if he *were* innocent what then on earth was I?" (p. 307).
The statement is hypothetical, and to try to give it a clear answer
assigning guilt and innocence is the wrong approach. What is most
important is the formula of the ratio itself, the either/or in the struggle
of darkness and light. The either/or assumes its melodramatic form as
the all-or-nothing; there can be no compromise in moral terms: if
Miles is innocent, the Governess is the agent of damnation. The logic
here is that of the excluded middle, which we encountered repeatedly
in melodrama. It once again images a world of cosmic forces in clash
where choices of courses of action and ways of being are absolute.
What has changed from the world of primary melodrama is that we
no longer know how to choose because of our epistemological doubt:
we no longer can or need to identify persons as innocence or evil; we
must respond instead to the ratios of choice themselves.

It is necessary to address a closer scrutiny to the terms corresponding to "good" and "evil" in the Jamesian melodrama. The Jamesian
"theology" evidently gives a large part to the forces of blackness. "If
ever a man's imagination was clouded by the Pit," writes Graham
Greene, "it was James's." Greene goes on to suggest that experience
taught James "to believe in supernatural evil, but not in supernatural
good." [27] James's sense of evil and what he called his "imagination of
disaster" is remarkably intense. It has led critics to a comparison with
Hawthorne and the American puritan tradition, the haunted sense of
original sin and the intellectual preoccupation with "the unpardona-
ble sin." Yet the manifestations of blackness in James often remind
one less of Hawthorne than of Poe; or, since Poe was an author for
whom James had little use, Balzac. They have a flamboyant and
Gothic sense of the *tremendum* rather than the quiet anxiety of
puritanism. As the "ghostly tales" most evidently demonstrate, James
can be very close to the conventions and spirit of Gothic romance, its
settings, characters, and oppressive atmosphere; the Governess's logic
of the excluded middle looks directly back to Matilda's in *The Monk*:
choices of allegiance to blackness or whiteness are absolute and
irremissible. When, at the end of *The Turn of the Screw*, Miles's heart is
"dispossessed," it can only stop. Nor is the Gothic feeling of
tremendum confined to the ghostly tales; the "horrors" are present
within the most polished and mannered social frameworks, and when
they manifest themselves, it can be with thunderous force. James's
prose makes recurrent use of terms that image the menace of evil:

"sinister," "appalling," "portentous," "lurid," "chilling," "abysmal" return to invest superficially quiet crises with a sense of metaphysical darkness. We can often detect in James's prose the effort to give adequate representation to what he feels to be the latent sinister implications of an event, to shadow forth the inner horror. An example among many would be the series of letters that he wrote in August 1914 in reaction to the outbreak of the World War. We find a concern to make his prose adequate to the occasion, to make his statement live up to what he conceives as a monstrous betrayal of all the "civilization" that he, his friends, his class, his characters had believed in. The war is an "abyss of blood and darkness" that "gives away" civilization and progress, transforming the years of his maturity—and of Victorian and Edwardian glory—into "the treacherous years," whose meaning must now be read as totally other, on the far side of the excluded middle. Or, as he puts it to another correspondent, the war "seems to me to *undo* everything, everything that was ours, in the most horrible retroactive way."[28] The possession of an imagination of disaster includes the capacity to respond fully to disaster, to reflect its lurid colorings in one's life and art.

The theme of betrayal is central to James's fictions, he is fascinated by what Graham Greene calls "the judas-complex"; or, as J. A. Ward states it, the problem of "improper intervention in the life of another."[29] The villain of classic French melodrama was commonly called *le traître*, no doubt because his villainy included a full measure of dissimulation and dupery. James's usage, for all its subtlety, shows a certain fidelity to this tradition. Evil is treacherous in that its darkest intent is dissimulated under layers of good manners or even beneath the threshold of consciousness in the evildoer himself; and evil is treachery in that it means denying to someone the means to free realization of his (or so much more often in James, her) full potential as a moral being. What opposes such treachery is not simply innocence, but more forcefully loyalty, what might best be characterized in James's own terms as "kindness": the refusal to do hurt, the refusal to betray, a full awareness of the independence of other beings.

If the "tremendousness" of evil in James may make us concur with Greene's judgment that he believed in supernatural evil—at least supernatural psychic evil—it is not quite accurate to suggest that the good opposed to it hasn't the same absolute value. In the face of evil, good appears in James's fiction increasingly tenuous, privatized, interior, and complex. Good is not innocence and certainly not purity, for a failure to incorporate the consciousness of evil is simply to be a victim and a fool. Nanda Brookenham's story is again exemplary here, for it is both her superiority and her worldly tragedy that she encompasses knowledge of evil within her virtue. This is necessary if goodness is to assert its autonomy, its resistance to the manipulative demands of evil, its interpretation of life. Nanda is potentially both Milly Theale and Kate Croy. She looks back to Isabel Archer, for whom the mature consciousness of good and evil is both a chastening lesson in how to be, in how to carry on the struggle of existence, and its own reward. And she looks forward to Maggie Verver in *The Golden Bowl*, who almost alone among Jamesian heroines can use the knowledge of good and evil to restore the reign of good, a postlapsarian good tempered by terrible wisdom.

It is remarkably difficult to talk about "goodness" in James because it is so tenuous, so private and interior, based so exclusively on an individual commitment to a subjective perception of ethical imperatives that may have no shared or community value. The moral sense for James and his characters, as Yvor Winters states it, "was a fine, but a very delicate perception, unsupported by any clear set of ideas." [30] At its least persuasive, such an ungrounded subjective moral sense can produce Strether's decision, at the end of *The Ambassadors*, to return to Woollett, a decision based on his desire "to be right," on his "only logic," which he states as "Not, out of the whole affair, to have got anything for myself" (2:326). This renunciation smacks too much of a narrowing puritanism—exactly what one thought Strether's adventure of consciousness had led him beyond—to be entirely satisfactory. It is dangerously close to renunciation for its own sake: like Olive Chancellor's favorite line from *Faust, "Entsagen sollst du, sollst entsagen!"* (which she repeats in Bayard Taylor's translation: "Thou shalt renounce, refrain, abstain!"), an attitude which James clearly recognizes in its unsupported state to be perverse and unbalanced.[31] On other occasions we are persuaded by the individual sacrifice to an ideal which the individual alone may barely perceive, and which he may not be able entirely to model his actions on, but which nonetheless achieves the status of a moral imperative. Such, I think, is Isabel Archer's return to Osmond—if one is willing to accept the idea of marriage as a sacrament, at least a human sacrament, and the principle of responsibility for one's acts—or Merton Densher's refusal to take Milly's legacy.

There is nonetheless throughout James's fiction an apparent

discrepancy between motive and action, cause and effect, in the moral decisions that determine plot and character. As Yvor Winters again states the case, "There is a marked tendency . . . on the part of James and of his characters alike to read into situations more than can be justified by the facts as given, to build up intense states of feeling, on the basis of such reading, and to judge or act as a result of that feeling." [32] This judgment corresponds to our characterization of melodrama, particularly as put to the ambitious use of a Romantic dramatist such as Hugo or such a novelist as Balzac. In both cases, we noted, the emotion and signification found in the gestures of reality, extrapolated from them and postulated on them, is in excess of the representation itself, in excess of the "objective correlative," or more simply the vehicle, presented as embodying it. The need for melodrama, on this basis, is the need for a form of statement and dramatization that will make the plane of representation yield the content of the plane of signification. This means in practice a pressure on the surface—the surface of social forms, manners; and the surface of literary forms, style—in order to make surface release the vision of the behind: as Strether's pressure of imagination applied to Mme de Vionnet's hôtel conjures forth "the smell of revolution, the smell of the public temper—or perhaps simply the smell of blood" (2:274). The technique is expressionistic in that surface forms are treated, not for themselves, in their interrelation and as ultimate integers, but as signs of what lies behind them and charges them. Laurence Bedwell Holland has employed the term *expressionism* in a related sense to characterize James's use of form; citing Herbert Read, he talks of an expressionism whose "distinguishing feature is *pressure* and which is founded on the 'desire to exceed the inherent qualities of the medium.' " [33]

One of the media whose "inherent qualities" are exceeded in James's expressionism is social manners, the order of human interchange within an established social code, complete with its register of coherent, because conventional, signs. As F. R. Leavis has written, "It is doubtful whether at any time in any place he could have found what would have satisfied his implicit demand: the actual fine art of civilized social intercourse that would have justified the flattering intensity of expectation he brought to it in the form of his curiously transposed and subtilized ethical sensibility." [34] The fictional answer to this demand was the invention of a medium of social intercourse and manners that would allow the observer to read into it, to extrapolate out of it, the significances he needed, and to do so largely through the pressure of an insistence that distorts the literal forms. Thus indicators or tokens such as Eugenio's "slight, too slight smile," in the passage from *The Wings of the Dove* discussed in chapter 1, or the nibbled teabiscuit confronting Mrs. Brigstock on the floor, in *The Spoils of Poynton*, achieve a charge of hallucinated meaning. At its most elaborated, this technique of pressure and metaphorical extrapolation can give passages that on any literalistic level must be considered grotesque, and which work at all only because the context of consistent expressionism legitimates them. To confine ourselves to a relatively brief example, there is this passage between Maggie and the Prince, in *The Golden Bowl*, following the breaking of the bowl:

> She had done for him, that is, what her instinct enjoined: had laid a basis not merely momentary on which he could meet her. When by the turn of his head he did finally meet her this was the last thing that glimmered out of his look; but it none the less came into sight as a betrayal of his distress and almost as a question of his eyes; so that, for still another minute before he committed himself there occurred between them a kind of unprecedented moral exchange over which her superior lucidity presided. It was not however that when he did commit himself the show was promptly portentous. [2:189]

So much has never ridden on the turn of a head, so much has never "glimmered out" of a look, so grandiose a moral exchange has never been wrested from so little. The text of muteness is elaborate, fully charged and fully significant. Yet the whole mode of the late fiction, as we shall see in more detail, its tone, language, image, its refusal of literalness and its insistently metaphorical evocation of melodramatic states of consciousness, so operates that such a passage becomes both legible and effective.

It is certain that the discrepancy between motive and result, between indication and what is postulated on it, contributes to what Winters calls "obscurity," Wilson "ambiguity," Leavis simply "unsatisfactoriness." Yet we must also see that this very discrepancy attracted the novelist's own attention, and that it is very much a subject, sometimes the central subject, of much of the late fiction. The apparent blankness of referential meaning repeatedly becomes a central issue in the drama, the unspecifiable source of its most potent extrapolated and metaphorical meanings. James comes closest to a justification of the procedure in the preface to *The Princess Casamassima*, where he considers that he may from lack of knowledge not properly have rendered Hyacinth Robinson's "subterraneous politics and occult affiliations." The justification takes the form of saying that he need not have dealt with the thing itself so much as with the obscure appearances that it put forth, for "the value I wished most to render and the effect I wished most to produce were precisely those of our not knowing, of society's not knowing, but only guessing and suspecting and trying to ignore, what 'goes on' irreconcileably, subversively, beneath the vast smug surface" (p. xxii). He must deal rather with the "gust of the hot breath" emerging from the depths. "What it all came back to was, no doubt, something like *this* wisdom—that if you haven't, for fiction, the root of the matter in you, haven't the sense of life and the penetrating imagination, you are a fool in the very presence of the revealed and assured; but that if you *are* so armed you are not really helpless, not without your resource, even before mysteries abysmal" (p. xxiii). The terms here image a process similar to that we found at work in Balzac's novels, a penetration beneath and behind the surface of things to what is "subterraneous," "occult," to "mysteries abysmal." What lies behind surface and facade in this novel is notably Balzacian: secret societies comparable to "Les Treize," the mysterious superman Hoffendahl, a shadowy struggle in the depths. James's decision not to treat the content of the depths directly, to present it only through the charge it gives to the surface, the way it is reflected in the individual consciousness, determines the metaphorical quality of the novel's melodrama. Hyacinth, the princess, Paul Muniment, even Mr. Vetch, do not live out their lives simply on the plane of interpersonal relations. The motor of their acts and their imaginings lies in the depths; they are driven by something occult, mostly hidden even to themselves. When the content of the abyss surfaces, it is in the form of the letter from Hoffendahl to Hyacinth, taken from its first envelope and delivered, unopened, by Schinkel, who has himself received it from an unnamed intermediary. The letter is a blank, we can never know its content directly but must piece it together from Paul Muniment's and Schinkel's deductions and from its deflected result, Hyacinth's suicide.

"Abyss" is a word that recurs with insistent frequency in James's writing and holds a particularly significant place, as we shall see, in *The Wings of the Dove*. It may be taken to stand for all the evacuated centers of meaning in his fiction that nonetheless animate lives, determine quests for meaning, and which confer on life, particularly on consciousness, the urgency and dramatics of melodrama. There are parabolic instances of these pregnant voids in some of the late tales and novellas, *The Figure in the Carpet*, for instance, and *The Jolly Corner*, perhaps most notably *The Beast in the Jungle*. John Marcher's life is determined by his feeling of a looming menace, of something appalling and grandiose that is to befall him, of a beast lurking in the jungle in wait to spring at him. The lack of specificity of the image is total: all Marcher "knows" is that it is nothing he is to do, but rather something that is to happen to him. The very indeterminacy of the thing, the beast, confers its force, gives the result that Marcher's existence is completely determined by his "waiting." His wait is joined by May Bartram, and together they warily probe the central darkness, "sound the depths": "These depths, constantly bridged over by a structure firm enough in spite of its lightness and of its occasional oscillation in the somewhat vertiginous air, invited on occasion, in the interest of their nerves, a dropping of the plummet and a measurement of the abyss" (p. 92). The "abyss" here is many layered: it is the abyss of Marcher's unspecified menace and also the abyss of the unspoken between him and May Bartram, who has begun to see that his menace is to be precisely nothingness, the sterility of his solitary egotism. The abyss is hence also the void of their relationship, the depths of which she alone has partially sounded. The sentence figures as well the very composition of the tale itself, built as a bridgelike structure over its central void, gaining meaning precisely as the fragile structure of articulation over an abyss of the unspeakable that charges language with the meanings that the characters cannot consciously read out of the void. By the end of the tale, Marcher, revisiting May Bartram's grave and perceiving in the "deeply stricken" face of a mourner at another tomb what passion could mean, at last comes to the realization that his menace, his beast, is simply nothingness itself. He has missed the possibility of passion, of May Bartram's love; "he had been the man of his time, *the* man, to whom nothing on earth was to have happened" (p. 125). This lack of event—of passion, of relationship—makes of his whole life now, not a pregnant abyss, but an empty one: "what he presently stood there gazing at was the sounded void of his life" (p. 125). It is significant that with Marcher's recognition of the void comes, not a quiet falling-away, but one of the most highly wrought melodramatic endings in all James's fiction. "He saw the Jungle of his life and saw the lurking Beast; then, while he looked, perceived it, as by a stir of the air, rise, huge and hideous, for the leap that was to settle him. His eyes darkened—it was close; and, instinctively turning, in his hallucination, to avoid it, he flung himself, face down, on the tomb" (pp. 126–27).

What elicits this lurid and impressive ending is the very void over which the story has been constructed, the final emergence into the light of what Marcher has referred to as "the lost stuff of consciousness" (p. 117). As in *The Princess Casamassima*, the abyss, fully in the manner of the Freudian unconscious, throws up its flotsam, the indices of what has been lost to consciousness, repressed, become unusable. Marcher's void figures perfectly one aspect of the moral occult, the realm from which we are cut off in quotidian existence, but which we must sound and explore to discover the animating imperatives of our ethical life. That the moral occult remains a void for Marcher suggests his illegitimate exploitation of May Bartram and his incapacity to "live" in the only sense that mattered to James, as a full "vessel of consciousness." That Marcher's void and menace are imaged as a Beast in the Jungle of course makes the relation of the moral occult to the unconscious compelling. And when there is, as here at the end, a piercing of repression—a return of the repressed—the result is the melodrama of hysteria and hallucination.

The Beast in the Jungle is one of the best examples of James's virtually epistemological explorations of the abyss, and of the relation of melodrama to this exploration. Epistemological because Marcher's efforts, misguidedly, and May Bartram's, more pertinently, are all directed toward scrutinizing a blank at the center of existence that evidently contains the key to existence if one only knew how to read its message. The tale is that fragile, threatened structure over the abyss, and the reader must drop the plummet into a central meaning which is unarticulated and which finally signifies as the very absence of meaning. *The Beast in the Jungle* in this manner demonstrates how James transcends the problem of discrepancy between motive and result, the excess of emotion in respect to its vehicle, through a thematization of the problem itself, through a metaphorical construction where the vehicle evokes a tenor that is both "meaninglessness" and the core meaning of life. The tale is analogous in structure to such works as Melville's *Moby-Dick*, Conrad's *Heart of Darkness*, Faulkner's *Absalom, Absalom!* as they have been described by James Guetti in *The Limits of Metaphor*: works which, he maintains, demonstrate ever more audacious and desperate attempts to understand and to speak of a central "darkness" that is finally inexpressible, that can only be alluded to, can never be the achieved goal or objective of the teller's tale that it claims to be.[35] Like Marlow's discovery in the heart of darkness, it is "unspeakable," and the whole narrative construction is a metaphor whose tenor is ineffable, a tenuous "as-if" structure that can never say its meaning and its goal. If Marcher, like Marlow, does at the last penetrate to the heart of darkness, he is blinded and struck dumb by "the horrors"—we are reminded of Kurtz's dying line: "The horror! The horror!"—which then are figured, as in *The Turn of the Screw*, through the overt but deflected melodrama of the story's close.

The supreme example in James's work of a similar metaphorical construction over the void that refuses any sort of conclusion is *The Sacred Fount*, a fiction so baffling that some critics have judged it a self-parody and some have simply dismissed it as trivial. Though the book is indeed impervious to explication, its mode makes perfect sense in our context. It is the most developed case of the melodrama of interpretive consciousness. As in *The Turn of the Screw*, both the perceiver and the perceptual field on which he operates are shifting and unreliable. What is evident is that the unnamed narrator must make sense of that field with the means that come to hand. He resembles the perfect *bricoleur* in the sense defined by Claude Lévi-Strauss: he does not seek beyond the boundaries of the closed system—the party at Newmarch—and the given cast of characters and properties for his explanatory arrangements.[36] He rather establishes a set of ratios based on the observable phenomena—those people who have bloomed and those who have shriveled—and seeks an overall hermeneutic principle: that of drinking at "the sacred fount," an image that is never precisely defined but has evident connotations (since what he is describing is a set of liaisons) of libidinal energy. Whether his structure and his principle are sound or not can never be discovered. When Mrs. Briss at the end tells him he is simply crazy, we, and even he, must accept this as a reasonable hypothesis. But it is no more provable than it is provable that a game of chess is crazy. The point is what can be done within the perfect closure and the rules of the game. The artist Ford Obert defines for the narrator the "honor" of playing the game right: "Resting on the *kind* of signs that the game takes account of when fairly played—resting on psychologic signs alone, it's a high application of intelligence. What's ignoble is the detective and the keyhole." [37] The narrator, we might say, has found or created the Jamesian ideal of a society that meets the high expectations of the investigatory consciousness, where signs are fully significant to the hypersensitive observer, where they speak of relations and mysteries abysmal. The melodrama of *The Sacred Fount* can hence never be overt, can never reach the plane of outer representation as it does at the end of *The Turn of the Screw* and *The Beast in the Jungle*. It is perfectly and purely the melodrama of a heightened and excited consciousness that must find the stuff of an impassioned drama in the field of observation set before it. In this case, the "lurid document" and the "baseless fabric of vision" have truly become indistinguishable; we, and perhaps even the narrator himself, have no means for discriminating between them. The high coloring of his report seems indeed to be a function of the lack of provability of his vision: the higher the melodramatic consciousness soars in flight, the more ineffable becomes its tenor, the more its vehicle must be charged, strained, portentous.

The narrator is at the end, and the reader too, left alone with what he calls a "private and splendid . . . revel—that of the exclusive king with his Wagner opera" (p. 296). While Mrs. Briss's attack on his structure unnerves him, "I could only say to myself that this was the price—the price of the secret success, the lonely liberty and the intellectual joy" (p. 296). The terms used figure the sheer intellectual exaltation, excitement, drama that provide a reader's pleasure in *The Sacred Fount*. It is arguable that the story "fails" because its vehicles have been so overcharged and its tenor has become so hidden and absent that the reader feels duped. Yet if he is willing to play a game of unverifiable interpretations resting on uncertain epistemological foundations, he may find an inner melodrama of disturbing implications.

These explorations in the most ambiguous and baffling of James's fictions should make us aware of the extent to which the problem of the excess of feeling in respect to situation, the discrepancy between symbol and moral sentiment, the use of melodrama, and the problem of epistemology are all related. James from the very beginning was involved in an endeavor—presenting a dramatic account of the dilemmas of moral consciousness—that forced him to work with meanings that could not be grounded and justified, either in any known system of manners or in any visible and universally accepted code of moral imperatives. Hence he had on the one hand to work with concepts, states of being, decisions that could never be wholly justified by his representations, that were ever in excess of them, and on the other hand to heighten those representations so that they might deliver the terms of his higher, occult drama. If this meant at first, in such a novel as *The American*, using the literal devices of melodrama, he evolved toward a melodrama that was more and more in and of consciousness itself: where the perceptions and reactions of consciousness charge the terms of the ordinary with a higher drama. His theatrical experience helped him to sharpen the relation between the surface tokens of his drama and the tenor they were to convey. And, as if aware of the tenuousness of his constructions, the lack of clear reference of his terms—especially the polar concepts corresponding to "good" and "evil"—he undertook, mainly in the period of the 1890s and early 1900s, to write fiction that turns around the problem of the pregnant void or abyss, sounding its depths in the effort to know what is unknowable but which nonetheless confers upon the knowable its charge of meaning and affect.

The "abyss of meaning" may stand as the most elaborated version of James's preoccupation with the content of the moral occult, which, through its very unspeakability, determines the quest for ethical meaning and the gesture in enactment of meanings perceived or postulated. The existence of the abyss shows clearly why the Jamesian mode must be metaphorical, an approach from known to unknown, and why there must be an expressionistic heightening of the vehicle in order to approach and deliver the tenor. What James refers to in his prefaces as "going behind"—"behind the face of the subject"—is a technique itself largely metaphorical, an extrapolation of the depths of motive and causes from seized and identified appearances.[38] To the extent that "going behind" is psychological, the abyss is fully analogical to unconscious mind; and especially in the late novels, the metaphorical texture of the prose will constantly suggest surfacing of matter from the unconscious. To the extent that this "matter" is essentially ethical in its eventual reference, the abyss is correctly a moral occult. It is merely logical that the most "abysmal" meanings are figured through the trope of muteness—Eugenio's slight smile, Maggie's silent exchange with the Prince—for this provides the ultimate approach to recognitions that are so delicate, obscure, submerged that they cannot be embodied in direct statement but only gestured toward. Gesture indicates the locus and shapes the contours of the abyss. The very rhythm and punctuation of late Jamesian conversations—"he hung fire," "this fairly gave him an arrest," "she took it in," "she stared"—suggest the need to postulate meanings in the margins between words, a desire to make the reader strain toward making darkness visible.

We should now attempt to gather these perceptions into a workable critical application and address an example of James's most achieved fiction, from the major phase. In discussing *The Wings of the Dove*, we will by no means be attempting a full explication of the novel but will try to show the degree to which "melodrama" is both theme and method in it, and how this is used to establish and promote the terms of its issues and conflicts, and to figure the abysses of meaning in which the story abounds.

II

The first sketch of *The Wings of the Dove*, which James set down in his Notebook in 1894, has many elements of overt melodrama and is also conceived (he was in the midst of his theatrical years) as a three-act play. The kind of villainy associated with the character who was to become Kate Croy is heartless and scheming; she is both rival and enemy of the Milly Theale figure, whose brother she has jilted. She is imagined as saying to her fiancé, in regard to the dying heiress, "Play a certain game—and you'll have money from her. But if she knows the money is to help you marry me, you won't have it; never in the world!" [39] Milly Theale is herself presented as a figure of excruciating agony: "She learns that she has but a short time to live, and she rebels, she is terrified, she cries out in her anguish, her tragic young despair . . . She is equally pathetic in her doom and in her horror of it. If she only could live just a little; just a little more—just a little longer. She is like a creature dragged shrieking to the guillotine—to the shambles." [40] The image of revolutionary execution recurs to James to suggest the panic terror and revolt of a person condemned to untimely death. It forcibly suggests the unmitigatedly manichaean terms of the story. As James would write in his preface, it is by the "act of living" that Milly must appeal to the reader (1:vi), by the primal force of the will for life that he attributed to Minny Temple in the last lines of *Notes of a Son and Brother*: "Death, at the last, was dreadful to her; she would have given anything to live." [41] It is this Eros that must struggle with blackness, extinction. Milly's will to live is itself an analogue of the melodramatist's desire to intensify experience, to make "life" a heightened drama.

The finished novel, while evidently shading and complicating these

initial elements, maintains a certain fidelity to its underlying melodrama. Kate Croy's situation, aspirations, and motives are rendered at
length; she is a character of exceptional intelligence, wit, loyalty, and
attractiveness; yet her willpower, her acts, even her statements retain
a whiff of sulphur, a tinge of the cold-blooded assassin. "We've
succeeded," she is able to say even in book 10. "She won't have loved
you for nothing. . . . And you won't have loved *me*" (2:333). The
novel's plot, more than any of the others in the late phase, is informed
by plotting, by a Balzacian intrigue of deceit, deception, and
betrayal.[42] Milly Theale, whatever her fortune, whatever her definition as "heiress of all the ages," remains consistently associated with
the sign of innocence. Her physical flaw—like those of the mutes and
cripples of melodrama—is a sure sign of her status as victim.[43] The
novel turns on the remarkably melodramatic either/or of Milly's life
and death. "She'll really live or she'll really not," Kate says (2:54).
Milly herself has been told by Sir Luke Strett that "one could live if
one would"; she reverses the terms: "one would live if one could"
(1:254). The would and the could become practically synonymous:
living is a physical struggle and a moral combat. When the crisis
arrives, with the knowledge of betrayal, she "turns her face to the
wall." She lives and dies, then, by an act of will that is a moral choice.
The situation is possibly more melodramatic than death from the
traditional broken heart: Milly chooses to die because the sign of
innocence has been morally betrayed. Like all James's late novels, and
perhaps with the greatest intensity of them all, *The Wings of the Dove*
constantly refers us to a grim struggle of good and evil and creates the
excitement of its drama from essential moral conflict.

   The Wings of the Dove is indeed very much about how one can
subtilize and complicate the terms of melodrama, their relation to
individual character and their conflict, while at the same time
preserving their underlying identity and nourishing the drama from
their substratum. The long preparations of the first two books—preliminary to the appearance of Milly Theale—serve both to explain, to
justify Kate Croy's ambitions for herself and Merton Densher, and to
put these ambitions in the most hyperbolic light. Kate carries Densher
forward in subtle debate that exposes with analytic clarity the
constraints of their situation, the need for temporizing and for an
indirect approach to conciliating Aunt Maud Lowder. Her lucidity
dictates not only a cold appraisal of their assigned roles, but also a
clear-sighted confrontation of her totalistic goals: "that's just my

situation, that I want and that I shall try for everything," she tells Densher in book 2, and "if we avoid stupidity, we may do *all*" (1:73). Through all the seeming meanders of her exposition and argument with Densher, Kate has the capacity (which will also by the end be the novelist's capacity) to come forward with the essential terms of their choice and their passion. She can deliver the fully expressive gesture and phrase, as when she turns to Densher and says to him, with "extraordinary beauty," "I engage myself to you forever" (1:95). Yet these conversations with Densher arrive, by the end of book 2, at the evocation of their "secret," by which they are "made deeper and closer" (1:96), and at the evocation of the possibility that lying may be necessary—an evocation that is "a shade too candid" (1:99). For it is a measure of their situation and ambition that the most lucid analysis and unflinching courage can only arrive at a certain opacity, at certain central possibilities that must be veiled, left unsaid, covered over by Kate's appeals to "imagination." When Kate concludes that men are "too stupid," too unimaginative about the more refined possibilities of sentiment and motive, Densher concludes the chapter with the line, "Then that's exactly why we've such an abysmal need of you!" (1:99).

"Abysmal" here suggests all the possibilities for motive and action that Kate senses but that cannot be directly articulated, in part because they are insufficiently known as yet, in part because Densher has not yet been prepared to face them, in part because any vulgar name that one might give to them—"lying," for instance—seems inadequate to the complexity of motive and intent involved. Their silences are a measure of the fact that they are necessarily if not willfully preparing what James calls in the preface an "abysmal trap," a trap "for the great innocence to come" (1:ix, xix–xx). The image of the abyss ramifies throughout the novel. Our first direct perception of Milly Theale, in the chapter following, shows her seated on a slab of rock overhanging "gulfs of air" (1:123). Susan Stringham's first reaction grasps at the possibility of "some betrayed accordance of Milly's caprice with a horrible hidden obsession": the possibility of a plunge into the gulf. She quickly reverses her judgment and sees that Milly is much rather "looking down on the kingdoms of the earth, and though indeed that of itself might well go to the brain, it wouldn't be with a view of renouncing them" (1:124). The two possibilities of the gulf at whose perimeter Milly is seated subsist, for her potential domination of the kingdoms of earth, which ought by right to belong to her wealth, her intelligence, her goodness, her status as "princess" of the new world, is ever menaced by the gulf of extinction, of nothingness. It is precisely this combination of enormous po⁀ntial power with the menace of extinction that makes her the prey of Kate Croy. The "dove," the bearer of the sign of innocence and of the potential power of innocence, she is herself victim of a hyperbolic logic of the excluded middle. She can live if she will, she will live if she can.

"I want abysses," Milly declares to Mrs. Stringham in book 4 (1:186), by which she means that she wants to have to deal with complication and indirection of motive and action, which she detects in the situation of Kate Croy, a situation obscure but offering the potential of lurid illumination: "when the light should come it would greatly deepen the colour" (1:173). But it is specifically the abyss of nothingness that she first faces, in her confrontation, at Matcham, of the Bronzino portrait that is thought so to resemble her. For this wonderful and magnificent woman is "a very great personage—only unaccompanied by a joy. And she was dead, dead, dead" (1:221). The scene of the Bronzino portrait marks the irruption of mortality into her consciousness at the moment of her greatest social "success," when Lord Mark and the others gathered at Matcham are most being "kind." She looks ill, and in a moment we hear her ask Kate to accompany her the next day on her visit to the doctor, Sir Luke. Concurrent with the evocation of this abyss is something else, "something that was perversely *there*" (1:225): the reminder of Kate's acquaintance with Merton Densher combined with her absolute lack of mention of him; the possibility of a profound dissimulation. This reminder comes through Milly's perception of Kate as reflected in Densher's vision of her: " 'Is it the way [Kate] looks to *him?*' [Milly] asked herself." There is hence a double process of mirroring: Milly mirrored in the portrait of "her painted sister," who returns her image as grand but dead; Kate mirrored in Densher's eyes, which show her living identity as object of desire. The mirrors reveal two abysses, the one mortal and empty, the other erotic, full of vitality—which is why it generates seductive traps, and why it must be hidden from view. The scene is itself a subtle play of mirrors, juxtaposing vital and destructive abysses through Milly's occult self-recognition in Bronzino's woman, heritage of the ages that can only bring her tears.

It is following this scene that her mortal abyss is given more literal contours by her consultation with Sir Luke. The great passage that follows her visit to the doctor describes her wandering into Regent's

Park, seeking refuge with those sharing in the "great common anxiety . . . the practical question of life" (1:250). Plumbing the depths of Sir Luke's attitude, his lack of specific diagnosis and his injunction "to live," she can find clarity finally in the distinction of his compassion, sign, she deduces, of her condemnation. So that she must feel his compassion as "divesting, denuding, exposing. It reduced her to her ultimate state, which was that of a poor girl—with her rent to pay for example—staring before her in a great city" (1:253). As in the case of Mme de Vionnet, following Strether's discovery of the full meaning of her liaison with Chad, a plumbing of the depths leads to the uncovery of primal conditions, to a baring of Milly's "ultimate state," her role as melodramatic menaced innocence, her stripped and exposed fragility in the struggle of life. Milly comes face to face with what James in a famous passage of the Notebooks called the "cold, Medusa-face of life," [44] the blank at the center of existence, figured as the excluded middle in the proposition Milly now considers: "It was perhaps superficially more striking that one could live if one would; but it was more appealing, insinuating, irresistible, in short, that one would live if one could" (1:254). The oxymoron at the center of the novel—"that of a young person conscious of a great capacity for life, but early stricken and doomed, condemned to die under short respite, while also enamoured of the world," James states it in his preface (1:v)—is here confronted directly, and the result of the confrontation is to reduce Milly's situation and her struggle to the barest possible terms, the fight to survive.

The interesting conclusion to Milly's drama of consciousness in Regent's Park (so comparable to Isabel Archer's at the core of *The Portrait of a Lady*) is her lie to Kate about her condition. There is here a notable symmetry with the conclusion of Kate's and Densher's plumbing of their abysses. The nearer approach to the truth, it appears, produces a decision to mask its dark content, to shroud it. We begin to understand that the content of the abyss must, in terms of social intercourse and the public language, be unspoken, presented as a semantic void. This is of course literally true of Milly's illness, which is never named, which is perfectly desemanticized, though it dominates and determines the course of the plot. Its very desemanticization is what allows it to operate with such effect: its lack of specification permits presentation of Milly's case as purely volitional, a pure struggle of the will to live, Eros, as in Freud's final formulations of his manichaeism, in struggle with Thanatos. To see this is to become aware immediately of how many other crucial issues, gestures, and scenes are unarticulated in the novel, including the critical interview of Milly and Lord Mark in Venice, Densher's ultimate visit to Milly there, and the content of Milly's testamentary letter to him.

These we will explore in a moment. What we must notice first is how Milly's confrontation of the abyss at the center of her life and destiny is at once conjoined to the epistemology of the abyss in her relation to Kate and in the Kate-Densher relation. By the end of the chapter following her meditation in Regent's Park, she can become aware, without a word being uttered, that Densher has returned to London. "Kate had positively but to be there just as she was to tell her he had come back" (1:272). The bases of this perception cannot be specified; it proceeds from a kind of "astronomical observation" frequent in James's late fiction, where the invisible presence of a new planetary body is deduced from its influence, its "pull," on the observable bodies and their interrelations. Plumbing the abysses hence comes to mean almost literally positing the mass and contours of the unseen from the gestures of the observed. It is in this manner that the evening of desultory talk between Milly and Kate, marked by silences and pauses, will unfold. "What was behind showed but in gleams and glimpses; what was in front never at all confessed to not holding the stage" (1:274). A central "gleam and glimpse" is Kate's near approach to articulation of the abyss-as-trap: she speaks her "honest advice," which is for Milly "to drop us while you can" (1:281). The result is an image of terror risen from the abyss, as Milly feels herself "alone with a creature who paced like a panther. That was a violent image, but it made her a little less ashamed of having been scared" (1:282). The approach to the violent content of the void is then conjured away as Kate responsively calls Milly "a dove" and embraces her (in what must inevitably evoke the kiss of Judas); when Aunt Maud returns, Milly is once again prepared to lie and to assert that Densher is not in London.

The novel moves from here to its climax in a series of more and more penetrating approaches to these abysses, to Milly's illness and Kate's dissimulated plot, sounding the possible depths of meaning in these seemingly desemanticized blanks, searching epistemological clues to their signification. It is in the second chapter of the second volume that Kate begins to sketch for Densher the relation of Milly to their own problem. What precisely her vision and plan consist in she does not say. Her silence about future courses of action corresponds to her silence to Milly about her relationship with Densher. Densher is in both cases forced to fill in her silences as best he can, and as much as he dares. He at moments attempts articulation of the most brutal and definitive meanings extrapolated from her silences. He asks if Kate wishes him to be "a brute of a humbug" to Milly (2:25), and, further on, "What you want of me then is to make up to a sick girl" (2:56). Yet the approach to meaning is matched by a concomitant withdrawal from it. When Kate urges Densher to consider the difference it will make if Milly does know of their union, neither she nor he is willing to specify what this may entail: "But here in truth Kate faltered. It was his silence alone that, for the moment, took up her apparent meaning" (2:29). Kate indeed manages Densher's continued loyalty to her plans by equating his situation with Milly's, imaging them both as her "victims" who must passively play out the roles she has assigned to them and will continue to direct. When Densher says of Milly, "She's just such another victim?" Kate replies, "Just such another. You're a pair" (2:63). The melodramatic terms serve to excuse Densher, for the moment, from looking further into the abyss of her meanings, and to imitate, in his own behavior, her own silences. In his subsequent call upon Milly, he judges the only fully truthful behavior would be to speak "the particular word," that Kate "likes" him; yet there are "but too palpably" "difficulties" about uttering it (2:76–77). The darkness of the abyss is maintained, the central intentions remain unarticulated, and the crises of Venice—a Venice of appearances "rich and obscure and portentous" (1:xvii)—are prepared as Milly and Kate, like figures of "some dim scene in a Maeterlinck play," live out, along with Susan Stringham, "the logic of their common duplicity," all the while fearing "to bring down the avalanche" (2:139–41).

For crisis to arrive, the abysses must begin to yield their latent meanings. There must be a beginning of explicitation, and the clash of explicitated meanings. And these must come in what James in the preface calls "the discriminated occasion . . . which is apt, I think, to show its fullest worth in the Scene" (1:xvi). The first such scene, and the beginning of revelation, is Lord Mark's proposal to Milly. The proposal brings a first semantic crystallization of both the principal abysses. Milly for the first time in the novel is brought to a declaration of her physical condition: "I'm very badly ill" (2:155). And her refusal of his proposal brings in turn Lord Mark's enunciation of Kate and Densher's relation. Yet this articulation elicits Milly's denegation—

not, this time, a lie to enshroud the truth, but a denial of the truth from a well-implanted error: "You're wholly mistaken" (2:164). The denial is of course a measure of Milly's interpretive failure and of the extent to which her complex and sophisticated "innocence" is still marked by a fatal ignorance. When Lord Mark suggests that she might question the validity of the authority on which she bases her denial—Kate's word, which we know in fact to be largely Kate's silence—she can only "stare." She and Lord Mark stand on the brink of frightening statement. Their eyes meet "as for their each seeing in the other more than either said" (2:165). But full articulation is suspended. Lord Mark's speech is finally reduced to a series of "oh's," virtually presemantic utterances. And then Merton Densher is announced, himself an ambiguous signifier that conveniently meets either interpretation of the situation, Milly's or Lord Mark's.

The exchange with Lord Mark occurs at the end of book 7. In book 8, all is brought to the verge of climax, to the moment of inevitable crisis and outburst. The movement of the book is largely one of semanticizing the abysses of meaning. The fact and consequence of Milly's illness begins to be felt as a clear and immediate impediment to her living. She is for the first time unable to "come down," leaving the members of the assembled group to look at one another in a consciousness too dark for speech: "It was lurid—lurid, in all probability, for each of them privately—that they had uttered no common regrets" (2:191). The lack of utterance is "lurid"—James's preferred word of sinister emotional coloring—in that silence figures the extent of the unutterable abyss. It is on this same day that Densher presses Kate for an end to their waiting game, asking that she take him as he is. In reply, Kate is obliged to designate areas of meaning that she has previously avoided: she suggests that Densher's breaking off at this point might kill Milly; she puts before him the fact that "We've told too many lies" (2:199). She then will tell him, "If you want things named you must name them" (2:225). This challenge sets off the central passage of "naming" in the novel, as she and Densher finally confront and articulate what has up to now been lodged in the abyss of Kate's unspoken meanings. The two stand in the foreground as Milly's soirée unfolds behind them, like stage conspirators making confidences "aside." The scene takes the form of Densher's assignment of names, followed by Kate's confirmation of names:

> "Since she's to die I'm to marry her?"
> It struck him even at the moment as fine in her that she met it

with no wincing nor mincing. She might for the grace of silence,
for favour to their conditions, have only answered him with her
eyes. But her lips bravely moved. "To marry her."

"So that when her death has taken place I shall in the natural
course have money?" . . .

"You'll in the natural course have money. We shall in the
natural course be free." [2:225]

The refusal of "the grace of silence" here is our indication that the
manners and conventions, the reticences that have masked the central
meanings, have been breached, permitting the "brave" articulation of
the intent and extent of Kate's "villainy." The moment is, for Densher
at least—who turns "considerably cold"—comparable to the melodramatic moment at which the villain breaks forth in statement of his
evil. It is a measure of James's moral transmutations that Kate has so
arranged the terms of the "plot" that for Densher to abandon it at this
point would be to commit another sort of villainy, to fail in the central
imperative of being "kind" to Milly. So that Densher's response shifts
the ground from his relation to Milly to the degree of his confederacy
with Kate. He now poses the equation by which his acceptance of his
role in the plot must be paid for by her "coming to him," their
becoming lovers physically, giving carnal meaning to that abyss,
bringing incarnation to the exchanged word of their engagement. If he
is to be cast in the role of "villain," he will at least enjoy the villain's
prerogative: power, constraint exercised over others. If, as James
argued in the preface to *The American*, a sure indicator of "the
romantic" is the way in which it images people getting into others'
power, here we have a clear if momentary instance of such a
relationship: "He had never, he then knew, tasted, in all his relation
with her, of anything so sharp—too sharp for mere sweetness—as the
vividness with which he saw himself master in the conflict" (2:231).
And it is most significant that this relationship of constraint is figured
in terms of an exchange about the meaning of the not wholly
articulated, an exchange that poses the question of whether or not
they are to semanticize the remaining areas of tacit void in their
relationship: "If you decline to understand me," Densher says, "I
wholly decline to understand you. I'll do nothing" (2:230–31). The
constraint and the power finally have to do with meaning, with the
impossibility of avoiding meaning. One could finally (at some critical
risk) suggest that the abyss or void is here ultimately given a sexual

dimension similar to King Lear's "sulphurous pit," the ultimate place where the search for meaning, for the missing letter of the signifier, must be sought.[45] The novel represents this pit in the blank between books 8 and 9, the space in which Kate comes to Densher's rooms.

When, following this blank, Densher remains alone in Venice, daily calling at Milly's palazzo, it is with a situation stripped to the barest essentials, a situation where he holds in his hands her life and death. "Anything he should do or shouldn't would have close reference to her life, which was thus absolutely in his hands—and ought never to have reference to anything else. It was on the cards for him that he might kill her" (2:251–52). The realization of this either/or comes to Densher as a "terror." The only form of action that he can construct on its basis is perfect inaction: he must be "kind," and this must mean doing nothing. He maintains the medium of tacit relationship, avoiding names—though Milly indeed wants "some name" for their relationship (2:240)—preserving the void. It is into this situation that action will violently intrude, but by way of another agent, Lord Mark. Densher's first perception of the action is through its effect as blockage of communication: he is refused entry to the palazzo (in the passage discussed in chapter 1) in a gesture which can by this point in the novel be charged with such significance that "a Venice all of evil" is unleashed by it. As he faces Eugenio's denial of him, Densher finds that "the air had made itself felt as a non-conductor of messages" (2:260). The void has become a dead medium no longer animating, rather a black hole of disaster.

The revelation of the cause of this effect comes as a fully melodramatic recognition, a mute scene of encounter with the villain on a half-darkened stage, a flashing vision of disaster and innocence undone. As Densher circles restlessly in the storm-lashed Piazza San Marco, "the drawing-room of Europe, profaned and bewildered by some reverse of fortune," he is brought to a halt "with the force of his sharpest impression" (2:261). He has caught sight of Lord Mark, seated in Florian's. The instantaneous recognition of his identity at once has "all the effect of establishing connexions—connexions startling and direct" (2:262). As Lord Mark turns and their eyes briefly meet, Densher catches "his answer to the riddle of the day." The mere appearance of Lord Mark provides the missing link of plot; his presence in Venice has "already made the difference"; "it explained" (2:263). The atmosphere of crisis is fully personalized, assigned to the stroke of the villain: "The vice in the air, otherwise, was too much like the breath of fate. The weather had changed, the rain was ugly, the wind wicked, the sea impossible, *because* of Lord Mark" (2:263). Without a word of recognition being exchanged between the two, things are "as plain to Densher as if he had had them in words" (2:264). He can conclude that Lord Mark's return is "sinister," is "evil." With articulation of these defining and polarizing terms, our consciousness, with Densher's, has reached the full measure of melodramatic intensity.

It is striking that such a figure as Lord Mark should be pressed into service as the melodramatic villain. If there has all along been something slightly sinister in his very lack of specification, in Aunt Maud's postulation of a "genius" that no one ever directly perceives, he has largely appeared a man of impeccable taste lacking in the higher imagination. That his lack of imagination should make his "genius" that for evil is a contrapuntal irony in relation to the immense and dangerous imaginative constructions that Kate has elaborated. Brutality is a product of unconsciousness. Unconsciousness kills. It is also evident that in some measure Lord Mark stands in for Densher, assuming the role of villain precisely so that Densher may do nothing. The latent violence that has more and more permeated relationships in the novel has in Densher's case pierced through to the surface in his erotic constraint upon Kate. It is left to Lord Mark to do violence to Milly, to bring about the irremediable catastrophe. That Densher is nonetheless capable of feeling his latent identity with the bringer of evil is suggested in his reflection, "There recurred moments when in spite of everything he felt no straighter than another man" (2:267).

What now confronts Densher, now that Milly "has turned her face to the wall" (2:270), is the question of directly lying, lying to save Milly's life. This is the choice put to him by Mrs. Stringham in their long conversation, punctuated by his pauses, his "hanging fire," his lapses from speech, in which his reticences about central meanings, about what he "knows," are progressively violated, forced into articulation. Yet Densher stops short of full avowal of his engagement to Kate, as he will stop short of a denial to Milly when pushed toward that "abyss"—the word stands in the last sentence of book 9 (2:309)—first by Mrs. Stringham and then by Sir Luke. His sense of his only refuge lies in the refusal to articulate, and through this refusal he tries to distinguish himself from the overt, the "speaking" villain, Lord Mark, to whom he assigns names: "the horrid little beast," "the

hound" (2:240), "the scoundrel" (2:321). Had he denied his engagement to Kate, he tells her, he would then have felt obliged to act
upon the denial, to leave Kate for Milly. To this self-canceling
balancing of avowal and denial, Kate replies with a bolder, more
passional, and possibly, at the last, more effective morality:

> "She never wanted the truth"—Kate had a high headshake. "She
> wanted *you*. She would have taken from you what you could give
> her and been glad of it, even if she had known it false. You might
> have lied to her from pity, and she have seen you and felt you lie,
> and yet—since it was all for tenderness—she would have thanked
> you and blessed you and clung to you but the more." [2:326–27]

Kate's position in respect to articulation and dissimulation finally
stands in direct opposition to Densher's: she will name names to
herself and draw the consequence that they call for public lying, the
active effort to shroud the abysses of meaning that may be perceptible
but are best protected from the violation of words. To refuse the logic
of Kate's position is to enter Densher's strange bind at the end, where
on the one hand he stands in "horror, almost, of [Kate's] lucidity,"
and where on the other hand he feels he must refuse to break the seal
of Milly's final letter to him as sign of a "sacrifice" to Kate (2:385).
The status of this letter as a perfect blank of meaning, a meaning
"protected" with a vengeance, is assured when Kate, in a heroic
gesture, throws it in the fire.

The heroism of the gesture may be ironized by Kate's awareness
that the meaning that matters to her—the terms of the bequest—will
be known by way of Milly's bankers. There is, however, a true loss of
"the stuff of consciousness" (to use the phrase of *The Beast in the Jungle*)
for Densher in the erasure of Milly's final words of benediction and
understanding. It is comparable to the reader's loss from consciousness
of the words of Densher's last meeting with Milly, the meeting from
which he felt himself "forgiven, dedicated, blessed" (2:343). The point
is that "loss of consciousness" is the only attitude in which Densher
can now seek refuge, for consciousness encompasses too much that is
melodramatic and terrible. "His honesty, as he viewed it with Kate,
was the very element of that menace: to the degree that he saw at
moments, as to their final impulse or their final remedy, the need to
bury in the dark blindness of each other's arms the knowledge of each
other that they couldn't undo" (2:391–92).

Yet this blindness cannot be; they cannot deny that they see too much and too fully. As they confront one another in their final interview, "It had come to the point really that they showed each other pale faces, and that all the unspoken between them looked out of their eyes in a dim terror of their further conflict" (2:401). It is from this terror that they back away, avoiding open melodramatic struggle. They nonetheless delineate the abyss that separates them. It is imaged as a temporal gulf. They have sought to "recover the clearness of their prime" (2:345). It is the impossibility of that recovery, the closing of the gap of knowledge, that the final lines record:

> "I'll marry you, mind you, in an hour."
> "As we were?"
> "As we were."
> But she turned to the door, and her headshake was now the end. "We shall never be again as we were!"

"As we were" figures specifically their state of being, back in book 2, "as we are," "so gone" (1:97), and more generally their state of relative innocence, purity at least in the commission of good and evil. It is now the knowledge of their knowledge that fixes them, free but fallen, on the opposite edges of the abyss.

What finally is the status, and the fate, of the sign of innocence in regard to the lovers' abyss? James notes in the preface that "Milly's situation ceases at a given moment to be 'renderable' in terms closer than those supplied by Kate's intelligence, or, in a richer degree, by Densher's, or, for one fond hour, by poor Mrs. Stringham's" (1:xvii). As mortal darkness rises to cover her, Milly becomes not directly representable. This situation is figured in the novel by Densher as a protection from violation of Milly's reality: as "an impenetrable ring fence, within which there reigned a kind of expensive vagueness made up of smiles and silences and beautiful fictions and priceless arrangements, all strained to breaking" (2:298). His metaphor suggests the necessity *of* metaphor in dealing with Milly's abyss: the impossibility of direct confrontation of it, the need to allude to it only through forms that, in their strain, figure its existence. He elaborates his view in another metaphor that images Milly's illness as simultaneously pervasive and lost to consciousness: "It was a conspiracy of silence, as the cliché went, to which no one had made an exception, the great smudge of mortality across the picture, the shadow of pain and horror, finding in no quarter a surface of spirit or of speech that consented to reflect it" (2:298–99). This complex figure suggests that Milly's abyss is known only through a "text of muteness" which yet records its pervasive presence as a "smudge" that spreads across the picture, visible to those who consent to see—as Milly did when facing the Bronzino portrait—filling the abyss with palpable darkness. The image is of melodrama pervasive but refused, carefully maintained within consciousness. Before the end, Densher's imagination will penetrate within the ring, find the surface of speech, and use terms specifically melodramatic, recalling James's original Notebook sketch: "Milly had held with passion to her dream of a future, and she was separated from it, not shrieking indeed, but grimly, awfully silent, as one might imagine some noble young victim of the scaffold, in the French Revolution, separated at the prison-door from some object clutched for resistance" (2:341–42). Through Densher's agency, James's imagination reaches (as in Strether's final vision of Mme de Vionnet) to an image of ultimate political and Gothic horror, to a world-historical struggle of torturers and victims. The story of Milly Theale is at the last faithful to its melodramatic premises.

Yet this is not all, for from the unrecorded blank of Milly's death other significances emanate. Densher and Kate piece it together that Milly has at last achieved what they could not: she has "squared" Aunt Maud by assuring Lord Mark—in the interview that was fatal to her—that Densher was indeed suing for her hand, not Kate's. Then she has died that this lie need not be acted upon, that Kate and Densher may be free. To discover this much is to become newly aware of how much Milly's consciousness finally embraced, the melodrama acted out in the consciousness of innocence itself. Kate understands: " 'She died for you that you might understand her. From that hour you *did*.' With which Kate slowly rose. 'And I do now. She did it *for* us.' Densher rose to face her, and she went on with her thought. 'I used to call her, in my stupidity—for want of anything better—a dove. Well she stretched out her wings, and it was to *that* they reached. They cover us' " (2:403–04). The terms of this final estimate of Milly are extraordinary. They imply that Milly has at the last lived her life, and has plumbed the depths of her mortal abyss, in order that she be understood, that her *sign* be legible and that it signify in the lives of others, including the "villain." In Kate's interpretation, we are made to feel that Milly has chosen the terms of her life and death in order for her sign to dominate the stage, to be read and recognized. Life has been dramatized, the abyss has been sounded, to produce finally the pure emblem of the dove. And the avoidance of overt melodrama, the circumambulation of the central abysses, has ultimately assured the assumption of melodrama into a consciousness so intense and self-reflective, on the part of Milly, Kate, even Densher, that it can best be described as the consciousness *of* the melodrama of consciousness. It is on the basis of their fully heightened consciousness of Milly's final consciousness that Kate and Densher act out, as if within Milly's consciousness, their final destinies.

The terminal image of Milly prompts Dorothea Krook to quote T. S. Eliot in "Little Gidding": "The dove descending breaks the air / With flame of incandescent terror / Of which the tongues declare / The one discharge from sin and error." More appropriate still might be Milton's invocation of the Holy Spirit in book 1 of *Paradise Lost*: "Thou from the first / Wast present, and with mighty wings outspread / Dove-like satst brooding on the vast Abyss / And mad'st it pregnant." The image of the dove and her action of grace, effected on Christmas Eve and producing in Densher what could be called a conversion (a suggestion furthered by his visit to Brompton Oratory on the day of Milly's death), inevitably evoke a register of Christian symbolism that makes one ask if the novel does not in fact image a true sacrifice in which the survivors partake, if there is not a true sharing of the Sacred body, if we are not in fact within a realm more properly described as tragedy than melodrama. F. W. Dupee considers that *The Wings of the Dove* constitutes James's nearest approach to tragedy, and other readers appear to agree.[46] It would seem to me most accurate to say that the intense innerness of the novel's moral melodrama and its complete spiritualization of Milly's consciousness create, by the end, the illusion of a sacred mantle—imaged in the dove's wings—that seems to "cover" the other characters. Yet its sacred status is an illusion, as the irreparable split between Kate and Densher at the end indicates: it brings no sacred community, it operates only through the individual consciousness, the individual interpretation of life's crises and their stakes. It is in its operation as in its source: the full attainment of the moral imagination, finding the terms to express and to act upon its individual judgments of ethical imperatives. When James in the preface refers us to the central importance of "what she [Milly] should have *known*," he suggests his desire to place the drama ultimately in personal ethical consciousness. It is the individual "sacrifice to the ideal" that redeems; and it redeems only in the individual imagination.

While *The Wings of the Dove* may be James's most accomplished melodrama of consciousness, a word yet needs to be said about *The Golden Bowl*, for this last work of the major phase is centrally about melodrama threatening, impending, and then avoided. Maggie's discovery of her husband's adultery with Charlotte Stant, her discovery of what Fanny Assingham calls "Evil—with a very big E" (1:385), gives a first scene of melodramatic encounter, as Fanny, performing an act precisely of the kind that Maggie strives to avoid, smashes the golden bowl. Fanny's act is a violent denial of a hidden truth, whereas Maggie needs rather to recognize it, protect it through silence, and conjure it away through the pressure of her ethical consciousness. The rest of the novel describes Maggie's effort to bring the Prince back into a true bond of marriage without any melodramatic outburst. The climactic scene of the novel, one of the most successful representations of the sinister that James ever wrote—the scene of the bridge game at Fawns—is about the threat of melodramatic outburst and its transcendence. As the Prince, Charlotte, Adam Verver, and Fanny Assingham sit at the card table, Maggie wonders at the good manners and control of appearances their figures present and feels the temptation of breaching this "high decorum." "There reigned for her absolutely during these vertiginous moments that fascination of the monstrous, that temptation of the horribly possible, which we so often trace by its breaking out suddenly, lest it should go further, in unexplained retreats and reactions" (2:233). She conceives that "springing up under her wrong and making them all start, stare and turn pale, she might sound out their doom in a single sentence, a sentence easy to choose from among several of the lurid." The full Jamesian vocabulary of melodramatic outburst is in place here, imaging melodrama as the breakthrough of the violent latent and suppressed content of the gathered persons' relations and consciousness, as the discovery of "the secret behind every face" in all its lurid and monstrous truth. The moment is specifically scenic, theatrical, with Maggie the stage manager ready with an arsenal of pyrotechnics and traps: "Spacious and splendid, like a stage again awaiting a drama, it was a scene she might people, by the press of her spring, either with serenities and dignities and decencies, or with terrors and shames and ruins, things as ugly as those formless fragments of her golden bowl she was trying so hard to pick up" (2:236).

Instead of outburst, what comes to consciousness is Maggie's judgment that melodrama has failed her and must fail her. She conceives the approach of the melodramatic reaction in an image from the exotic adventure tale or popular drama:

> a wild eastern caravan, looming into view with crude colours in the sun, fierce pipes in the air, high spears against the sky, all a thrill, a natural joy to mingle with, but turning off short before it reached her and plunging into other defiles. She saw at all events why horror itself had almost failed her; the horror that, foreshadowed in advance, would by her thought have made everything that was unaccustomed in her cry out with pain; the horror of finding evil seated all at its ease where she had only dreamed of good; the horror of the thing hideously *behind,* behind so much trusted, so much pretended, nobleness, cleverness, tenderness. [2:237]

Nowhere more effectively than in this renunciation of melodrama did James image the melodramatic tenor of his imagination, the attraction of melodrama, the continuing need for it as mode of consciousness and rhetorical stance, as well as the need to conquer it. The true horror is that of the thing hideously *behind,* the latent lurking horror, concealed by manners, yet just visible through them; unconscious horror, welling, as the nearly surrealistic imagery of the passage suggests, from the deepest recesses, the abysses of the soul. The metaphor stands for James's constant fictional technique: the pressure to reach through to the "behind," and then the pressure to keep it behind.

Melodrama in Maggie's terms is too easy, too simplifying, a satisfaction that misses the main point. To say exactly why horror has failed her, we need to read on:

> yes, amazingly, she had been able to look at terror and disgust only to know that she must put away from her the bitter-sweet of their freshness. . . . It was extraordinary: they [the four at bridge] positively brought home to her that to feel about them in any of the immediate, inevitable, assuaging ways, the ways usually open to innocence outraged and generosity betrayed, would have been to give them up, and that giving them up was, marvellously, not to be thought of. [2:237]

If "the ways usually open to innocence outraged" are to be rejected, it is because the possible ideal of human relationships suggests an imperative higher than the breakthrough of repression provided by theatrical outburst, a new form for realization of the bearer of the sign of innocence, which must probably be described as the active working toward salvation, conversion, or even redemption. What this role requires, here, is not Milly Theale's dying that she might be understood, but rather the refusal publicly to dramatize private truths, the assumption of the burden of consciousness, and the example, to the Prince, of what its ethical pressure can do. So that when Charlotte arises from the table and approaches Maggie on the terrace, bringing the very presence of terror—"The splendid shining supple creature was out of the cage, was at large" (2:239)—Maggie is able to lie and to accept the "conscious perjury" of Charlotte's kiss. The "high publicity" of the embrace, framed by the Prince and Mr. Verver as witnesses, ends the scene, brings a strong curtain, and leaves us to reflect how much the thematic refusal of melodrama has been doubled by a melodramatic presentation. The manners which are preserved through the refusal of melodrama yet bear the imprint of the melodrama refused, the melodrama evoked as possible and thus brought to bear on the scene. The abyss of "the thing hideously *behind*" remains behind, but it charges the gestures that both indicate and mask its hidden presence.

What determines Maggie's decision to work for salvation, and the stakes of her decision, comes out with supreme directness in her earlier conversation with Fanny Assingham, when she claims that she can "bear anything":

> "Oh, 'bear'!" Mrs. Assingham fluted.
> "For love," said the Princess.
> Fanny hesitated. "Of your father?"
> "For love," Maggie repeated.
> It kept her friend watching. "Of your husband?"
> "For love," Maggie said again. [2:116]

Through the meanders and subtleties of his drama of consciousness, his complex epistemological probings, James is nonetheless capable of such ringing nomination of the basic imperatives in which his imagination deals. The love of which Maggie speaks is not limited to love of her father or her husband—though it includes these and explicitly embraces an intense sexuality. It is more inclusive and elusive, the central imperative, indeed, that all James's fiction has gestured toward, its ideal of human relationship. One may again quote Eliot: "Who then devised the torment? Love. / Love is the unfamiliar Name / Behind the hands that wove / The intolerable shirt of flame."

If the "familiar name" would be charity, we must recognize at the last the fragments and shards of the Christian idea of the Sacred in James's imagination. This should not tempt us to recreate him as a Christian moralist—a temptation to which Dorothea Krook too much succumbs—but rather to recognize how much he shares, and recognizes that he shares, in the fragmentary elements of the mythology that had spent itself or been shattered in the century or two before the arrival, with Romanticism, of modern consciousness. James represents a late and significant development of that consciousness, an understanding that nothing so coherent as a unitary system of belief can be salvaged from modern society and the modern mind, yet that there are ethical imperatives and moral absolutes that the finely attuned sensibility can, through its metaphorical grasp, be in touch with, and ought to be in touch with. The way through to the ethical realm proceeds by way of the intensification of consciousness. This means that the representation of ethical conflict and choice must summon up the stuff of unconscious mind as it is congruent with the moral occult, and that the terms of the conflict can be imaged only in the polarized and heightened mode of melodrama, yet melodrama within the domain of consciousness itself, as a struggle for perception, for insight, for knowledge.

When we remember James's repeated critical strictures on the narrowness of Flaubert, and his unaltered allegiance to Balzac, we understand the justice of Jacques Barzun's observation that "James went back, over the realists' heads, to the romanticists whom he wished to purge and renovate." [47] James remains remarkably in touch with the wellsprings of the Romantic tradition, perhaps partly because of his admiration for Balzac, George Sand, and the French Romantic theatre, and partly because of his sense that the generation that preceded his own possessed a fuller, truer, more grandiose moral imagination. James was preëminently the novelist of "going behind"; and to go behind was eventually to discover the primal sources of being, for "bliss or bale," the moral emotions that in their absolute state, the state in which the melodramatic moral imagination discovers them, have the strong taste of the pure essence.[48] So that we might conclude (reading with the right, literal emphasis the word "terrible") by the Prince's remark to his wife: "Everything's terrible, cara—in the heart of man" (2:349).

Conclusion

Melodrama: A Central Poetry

"Transgression—punishment—bang! Pitiless, pitiless. That's the only way."
—Joseph Conrad, *Heart of Darkness*

"We work in the dark—we do what we can—we give what we have. Our doubt is our passion and our passion is our task. The rest is the madness of art."
—Henry James, *The Middle Years*

We have talked at some length of Victor Hugo, of Balzac and James. We could as well have discussed Dickens, Dostoevsky, Conrad, Lawrence, Faulkner, for instance, whose ambitions belong to the same mode. But we could not have extended the argument to Flaubert, Maupassant, Beckett, Robbe-Grillet, possibly Joyce and Kafka, and a number of others whose stance is radically ironic and anti-metaphorical. They indeed set against the ambitions of melodramatism an attitude of deconstructive and stoic materialism, and a language of deflationary suspicion. Flaubert appears the initiator of the modern tradition that most consciously holds out an alternative to melodrama, that discerns the void but refuses to read it as the abyss of occulted meanings, that rather lets it stand as the regulatory principle of aspiration. Such a work as *L'Education sentimentale* radically deconstructs the very forces and systems that function in the creation of meaning in the Balzacian or Jamesian novel. Plot and action are de-dramatized, voluntarily insignificant. Desire, the relation of intention to action, the coherence of subjectivity, ambition as the self's project are all stripped of significant status, shown to be inauthentic or illusory. Reading *L'Education sentimentale* superimposed upon *Le Père Goriot* or *Illusions perdues* (a reading the text invites), we realize that it is not so much a vision of life as it is a form of the novelistic that Flaubert has subverted. Meaning, he implies, cannot be manufactured in the Balzacian manner. From a search for the hidden signified and its metaphorical absent presence we are led rather to the play of the signifier: the reader's engagement with the plane of representation as

198

pure surface and with the process of narration—their ultimate coherence as systems radically severed from that which they pretend to record and recount, their status as pure fiction.

The counter-tradition of Flaubert stands in contrast to the expressionism of Balzac and James. They remain convinced that the surface of the world—the surfaces of manners, the signifiers of the text—are indices pointing to hidden forces and truths, latent signifieds. The energy and excess of their writing betrays an unwillingness to exclude occulted meanings from the systems operative in human life and its fictions. The gestures recorded in the text must be metaphoric of something else. Increasingly in James—and this is also true in Balzac's most ambitious moments—the direct articulation of central meanings is difficult, dangerous, and even impossible. But this is not viewed as reason to abandon the search for them. The novel comes indeed to be about the approach to meaning, about life lived with signifiers that are constantly tensed to deliver their overwhelming signifieds. The excess of Balzacian narrative rhetoric, and of late Jamesian mannerism, records the effort to suggest what would be the (impossible) incarnation of final meanings.

Flaubert is finally preoccupied with representation itself as a textual system, with the possibilities of significant surface, with the manufacture of form as itself the signifying act. For Balzac and James, there appears to be an irrecoverable gap between the plane of representation and the plane of signification: the former cannot necessarily be made perfectly to embody the latter. There is a constant effort to overcome the gap, which gives a straining, a distortion, a gesticulation of the vehicles of representation in order to deliver signification. This is the mode of excess: the postulation of a signified in excess of the possibilities of the signifier, which in turn produces an excessive signifier, making large but unsubstantiable claims on meaning.

It can be argued that James never understood what Flaubert was up to and censured his protagonists' limited capacity as "registers and reflectors" without an awareness of Flaubert's deconstructive stance. Yet James is lucid and coherent in the perception that the Flaubertian mode makes the Balzacian and Jamesian novel impossible. To renounce the metaphorical and expressionistic quest, James might claim, is to fall into true mannerism, the love of surfaces for their own sake: to be, ethically, in the condition of a Gilbert Osmond, or more genially, a Fanny Assingham. To push the quest, even if the goal appear uncertain and unstable, is to assume the ethical heroism of a

Maggie Verver. For the artist, acceptance of the Flaubertian premise means abandonment of Frenhofer's doomed but admirable ambition, or of what Dencombe, in the much-quoted lines of *The Middle Years*, calls "the madness of art." And we realize how much what we have been calling melodrama constitutes the very conditions of possibility of the novel, in Balzac and James's understanding of the form. Melodrama offered a complete set of theatrical signs, words, and gestures, corresponding to heightened meanings. It was thus a complete convention in the interpretation of life as inhabited by significant forms. Its theatricality constitutes the substratum of Balzac's and James's art: by referring us to "life" by way of the theatrical medium—through the reader's and the characters' own consciousness of their heightened enactments—they postulate significant form, read out meaning from the indifferences of reality. To state it bluntly (to overstate it): they could not have written their novels as direct interpretations of reality; they needed the model of reality made significant and interpretable furnished by theatricality, and particularly—given their particular ambitions—by what we have discussed as melodrama.

Those who stand in the Flaubertian tradition accept as the unfixed, unstable standpoint of their writing the very "decentering" of modern consciousness, its lack of a central plenitude.[1] It is arguable that melodrama represents a refusal of this vertiginous but possibly liberating decentering, a search for a new plenitude, an ethical recentering. Melodrama may in this manner have the characteristic of a "central poetry," in the definition of Wallace Stevens: a poetry "in the very center of consciousness," in that it responds to the common concern, in a search for the common ground.[2] Yet to the extent that the melodramatic imagination at its most lucid recognizes the provisionality of its created centers, the constant threat that its plenitude may be a void, the need with each new text and performance to relocate the center, it does not betray modern consciousness.

We suggested that melodrama may be born of the very anxiety created by the guilt experienced when the allegiance and ordering that pertained to a sacred system of things no longer obtain. In the radical freedom produced by this situation (in its most intense version, by revolution), all is potentially permitted, as Dostoevsky most explicitly recognized, as Balzac and James also clearly understood. For all not to be permitted, a new demonstration of the possibility of a moral order is required. At the moment of what Maurice Blanchot calls the "prodigious suspension" figured by the Revolution, when the law—social, moral, natural, rhetorical—falls silent, a new form of enactment and demonstration, a new creative rhetoric of moral law arises to demonstrate that it is still possible to find and to show the operation of basic ethical imperatives, to define, in conflictual opposition, the space of their play.[3] That they can be staged "proves" that they exist: the melodramatic mode not only uses these imperatives but consciously assumes the role of bringing them into dramatized and textual—provisional—existence. The anxiety of man's prodigious revolutionary freedom, his infraction of the law, is dealt with, not necessarily through the assurance of retribution for guilt (the case in literal melodrama), but through the promise of a morally legible universe to those willing to read and interpret properly its signs.

Through the nineteenth century and into the twentieth (if the terminus has been reached it is not yet discernible), the thought and culture of the Western world are dominated by systems of conflict that are systems of expressionistic clarification: most obviously, those of Hegel, Marx, and Freud. The last of these has clear relevance to melodrama. Psychoanalysis can be read as a systematic realization of the melodramatic aesthetic, applied to the structure and dynamics of the mind. Psychoanalysis is a version of melodrama first of all in its conception of the nature of conflict, which is stark and unremitting, possibly disabling, menacing to the ego, which must find ways to reduce or discharge it. The dynamics of repression and the return of the repressed figure the plot of melodrama. Enactment is necessarily excessive: the relation of symbol to symbolized (in hysteria, for instance) is not controllable or justifiable. The Evil of melodrama is reworked, only partly de-ethicalized, in the processes of repression and the status of repressed content; the unconscious is ever ready to act as *le traître*. The structure of ego, superego, and id suggests the subjacent manichaeism of melodramatic persons and indeed the specific characters most often put on the stage. Freud's thought is of course ever dualistic, and his later formulations of the struggle of Eros and Thanatos suggest an explanation for the fascination of both melodramatic virtue and evil, their necessary interdependence in eternal conflictual union. We have already noted the resemblance of melodrama's text of muteness to the rhetoric of dreams. Psychoanalysis as the "talking cure" further reveals its affinity with melodrama, the drama of articulation: cure and resolution in both cases come as the result of articulation which is clarification. For psychoanalysis, like melodrama, is the drama of a recognition. If psychoanalysis has become the nearest modern equivalent of religion in that it is a vehicle for the cure of souls, melodrama is a way station toward this status, a first indication of how conflict, enactment, and cure must be conceived in a secularized world.

That psychoanalysis has so many points of analogy to melodrama is of course not surprising, it is almost tautological in that our psychic lives are full of melodrama, and our study of melodrama immediately suggested that the form exteriorized a world within. At least from the moment that Diderot praised Richardson for carrying the torch into the cavern, there to discover "the hideous Moor" within us, it has been evident that the uncovering and exploitation of the latent content of mind would bring melodramatic enactments, and that melodramatic enactments would, in their breakthrough of repression, carry the message of our inner selves. What we have called "the moral occult," the locus of intense ethical forces from which man feels himself cut off, yet which he feels to have a real existence somewhere behind or beyond the facade of reality, and which exerts influence on his secular existence, stands as an abyss or gulf whose depths must, cautiously and with risk, be sounded. When this abyss is located within the structure of mind by Freud, it is as *das Unbewusste*, the unconscious and the unknown, which yet must be known through its effects. The signs of the world are symptoms, never interpretable in themselves, but only in terms of a behind. If melodrama can reach through to this abyss behind, bring its overt irruption into existence, it has accomplished part of the work of psychoanalysis.

To talk of psychoanalysis as a modern fulfillment and codification of melodrama is not frivolous. And the possibility of doing so suggests further confirmation of the claim that melodrama has become a necessary mode within modern consciousness. Melodrama and psychoanalysis represent the ambitious, Promethean sense-making systems which man has elaborated to recuperate meanings in the world. We continue to need expressionism, the possibility of acceding to the latent through the signs of the world.

We have in this study largely been concerned with "the melodramatic," a mode, a certain imaginative complex and set of dramatic conventions which can be seen at work both in the theatre and the novel. It is this literary aesthetic of excess—and the coherence and necessity of the excess—that has largely engaged our attention. In closing, it may be worth considering the value of "melodrama" as an analytical focus in the description of the forms of our culture. If our use of the term has been convincing, it may have suggested the value of perceiving the distinction between melodrama and other aesthetic forms that give related but significantly different versions of reality. The most important of these other forms are comedy and tragedy, which each possess structures, persons, outcomes, effects distinct from those of melodrama. It is particularly the distinction from tragedy that matters, because we are persistently surrounded by spurious claims for the tragic, by erroneous tragification of experience. The drama of virtue misprized and persecuted, of innocence wronged, is regularly presented as tragic. So is the drama of disaster, as Robert Heilman points out, the intrusion of natural cataclysm or absurd event, or the fall of public personages whose abrupt eclipse, or assassination, leads to their automatic classification as tragic figures.[4] The relevant aesthetic in most of these instances may be less tragedy than melodrama. What counts is clarification and recognition of the signs in conflict, and this may be true even when expulsion cannot be achieved and virtue succumbs.

This is notably true in the case of the drama of public and political figures. As the modern politics of created charisma—inevitably a politics of personality—and self-conscious enactments must imply, we are within a system of melodramatic struggle, where virtue and evil are fully personalized.[5] Rarely can there be the suggestion of illumination and reconciliation in terms of a higher order of synthesis. It is indeed struggle that alone matters: the modern political leader is obliged to posit continuous battle with an enemy. If it is not another suborning political power or leader, it may be a natural scourge on which "war" is declared, poverty or hunger or simply inflation. The leader must image himself in constant bipolar dynamism with the enemy, winning the war, gaining the upper hand, on the verge of achieving expulsion; or else succumbing, or cataclysmically struck down. The melodramatism of modern politics suggests again that Robespierre and Saint-Just are the ultimate models of reference, in their increasingly manichaeistic struggle of virtue, personalized in the Comité de Salut Public, eventually in themselves, against vice, the enemies of the Republic, the traitors, the uncitizens, the nonpersons.

When President Ford wanted to image the end to what journalism called the "tragedy of Watergate," he declared: "Our national nightmare is over." The terms chosen had the unconscious virtue of situating such an episode as Watergate in the proper aesthetic and cultural interpretive framework, identifying it as melodrama rather than tragedy. For melodrama regularly simulates the experience of nightmare, where virtue, representative of the ego, lies supine, helpless, while menace plays out its occult designs. The end of the nightmare is an awakening brought about by confrontation and expulsion of the villain, the person in whom all evil is seen to be concentrated, and a reaffirmation of the society of "decent people." Such an image was no doubt desired by most of America in the summer of 1974. One can then surmise that the subsequent pardon extended to the villain violated the cathartic effect of the melodramatic ending, indeed introduced a spurious and inappropriate reference to the world of tragedy, in which the Christian imperative of mercy could make sense in relation to a dominant emblem of sacrifice. It did not and could not make sense within the framework of strong justice demanded by melodrama. For in the absence of any more transcendent principles, melodrama must at the last sacralize Law itself, a perfect justice of punishment and reward, expulsion and recognition.

Political melodrama is fully homologous to the dramas played out every day on television screens, to soap opera (the name suggests the filiation to melodrama via grand opera) in its various form. If modern mass entertainment is so dominated by a limited number of fixed sub-genres—police story, western, hospital drama—it is because these offer the clearest possible repertories of melodramatic conflict. They provide an easy identification of villains and heroes (who can often be recognized simply by uniform), of menace and salvation. They give a set of situations in which virtue can be held prisoner, made supine and helpless, while evil goes on the rampage, and they offer highly exteriorized versions of its vindication and triumph. That all these forms have become increasingly "psychologized"—that cops must be experts in human relations and badmen are quasi-Dostoevskyan figures—in no sense violates the melodramatic context. It is not that melodramatic conflict has been interiorized and refined to the vanishing point, but on the contrary that psychology has been externalized, made accessible and immediate through a full realization of its melodramatic possibilities.

That we can go on entertaining ourselves day after day with the chase, the shoot-out, the open-heart operation is evidence of our need for fully externalized, personalized, and enacted conflict, and for its clarifying resolution. If much of the time we submit to the logic of prohibition and the necessity of repression, at other times we feel the need for a melodramatized reality, both within and without ourselves. For such conflict is our constant promise that life is truly inhabited by primal, intense, polarized forces—forces primal and intense because they are polarized—that can be made manifest. As Walter Benjamin argued, it is from the "flame" of fictional representations that we warm our "shivering lives," and this is nowhere more true than in the most enduringly popular fictions, which suggest over and over again that we do not live in a world completely drained of transcendence and significance, that the principles of a superdrama are to be found near to hand.[6] Such fictions are both frightening and enlivening, suggesting the overt presence in the world of forces we sense within ourselves. We both want to believe, and yet cannot wholly credit, that we live on the brink of the abyss, the domain of occult forces which, for "bliss or bale," infuse an intenser meaning into the life we lead in everyday reality. Popular melodrama daily makes the abyss yield some of its content, makes us feel we inhabit amidst those forces, and they amidst us.

It is valuable to distinguish between tragedy and melodrama and to avoid the spurious tragification of experience, partly because it is useful to be aware of the limits of melodrama as aesthetic and cultural form, of what it cannot accomplish as well as what it can. The fall of the tragic hero brings a superior illumination, the anagnorisis that is both self-recognition and recognition of one's place in the cosmos. Tragedy generates meaning ultimately in terms of orders higher than one man's experience, orders invested by the community with holy and synthesizing power. Its pity and terror derive from the sense of communal sacrifice and transformation. Melodrama offers us heroic confrontation, purgation, purification, recognition. But its recognition is essentially of the integers in combat and the need to choose sides. It produces panic terror and sympathetic pity, but not in regard to the same object, and without the higher illumination of their interpenetration. Melodrama cannot figure the birth of a new society—the role of comedy—but only the old society reformed. And it cannot, in distinction to tragedy, offer reconciliation under a sacred mantle, or in terms of a higher synthesis. A form for secularized times, it offers the nearest *approach* to sacred and cosmic values in a world where they no longer have any certain ontology or epistemology.

A clarity in regard to the use of such an aesthetic form as

melodrama can foster in us a greater clarity about our cultural history, an increased understanding of our historical position, of "where we are," the kinds of problems we have to deal with, and the means we have for undertaking their imaginative "solution." The use of a study of melodrama must at the last repose on a conviction that the study of aesthetic form—modes of expression and representation—can be useful in situating ourselves. Aesthetic forms are means for interpreting and making sense of experience. Any partial rewriting of cultural history must be a rethinking of how we make sense of our lives, of the successive episodes in the enterprise of *homo significans,* of man as the creator of sense-making sign-systems.

It may then be appropriate to conclude with the suggestion that, with the death of tragedy and the rise of melodrama, all has perhaps not been loss. For melodrama has the distinct value of being about recognition and clarification, about how to be clear what the stakes are and what their representative signs mean, and how to face them. Melodrama substitutes for the rite of sacrifice an urging toward combat in life, an active, lucid confrontation of evil. It works to steel man for resistance, it keeps him going in the face of threat. Even if we cannot believe in the easier forms of reward that melodrama traditionally offers, there is virtue in clarity of recognition of what is being fought for and against. The dissipation of the mythic orders that made true tragedy possible is an irreversible condition that is better accepted than masked with spurious appeals to synthetic mythologies. In a culture whose concerns have increasingly become secularized and existential, the stakes have increasingly become those of clear-sightedness and authenticity. Virtue has become the capacity to face the abyss even if its content may be nothingness, and to assume the burden of consciousness that results from this confrontation. To reintroduce a sense of tragedy in this encounter is surreptitiously to renounce radical freedom, to offer false hope of reconciliation. So it is that recognition of melodrama's pervasive presence in our representations and our thought may be useful in the recognition of what we have to deal with, and what—in all its limitations—we most often have at hand for dealing with it.

Notes

PREFACE

1 John Barth, "The Literature of Exhaustion," *Atlantic Monthly* 20, no. 2 (August 1967): 29–34. One could cite numerous novelists who fit this description: Nabokov, Robbe-Grillet, Vonnegut, Borges, Barthelme, Butor, etc.

2 Leslie A. Fiedler, "The Death and Rebirth of the Novel," in *The Theory of the Novel: New Essays*, ed. John Halperin (New York: Oxford University Press, 1974), pp. 189–209. Fiedler, however, creates too sharp a division between the popular novel and the "high art" novel. What is perhaps most interesting is the area of their interaction and the use of the former by the latter. Fiedler also seems to me in error in his identification of Henry James as exclusively committed to the high-art novel, without connections to popular forms.

3 Harold Bloom, *The Anxiety of Influence: A Theory of Poetry* (New York: Oxford University Press, 1973). The persuasive argument of Raymond Williams in *Culture and Society, 1780–1950* (London: Chatto and Windus, 1958)—that from the Industrial Revolution on, culture in England became progressively divorced from society and a popular audience—might need modification when talking of France: here the true divorce seems to have come later in the nineteenth century. In both countries the novel tends almost always to conceive of itself as *generically* popular, at least until the time of Symbolist and Modernist experiments in the genre.

4 Eric Bentley, "Melodrama," in *The Life of the Drama* (New York: Atheneum, 1964), pp. 195–218; James L. Rosenberg, "Melodrama," in *The Context and Craft of Drama*, ed. Robert W. Corrigan and James L. Rosenberg (San Francisco: Chandler, 1964), pp. 168–85; Robert B. Heilman, *Tragedy and Melodrama: Versions of Experience* (Seattle: University of Washington Press, 1968); Michael R. Booth, *English Melodrama* (London: Herbert Jenkins, 1965); David Grimsted, *Melodrama Unveiled: American Theater and Culture, 1800–1850* (Chicago: University of Chicago Press, 1968); James L. Smith, *Melodrama*, The Critical Idiom, no. 28 (London: Methuen, 1973).

5 On the social situation of the English theatres, see for example Smith, *Melodrama*, p. 16. Grimsted describes the social conditions of American melodrama. On drawing-room melodrama, see Booth, *English Melodrama*, and Maurice Willson Disher, *Melodrama: Plots That Thrilled* (London: Rockliff, 1954), p. 180. To my knowledge, the only book that attempts a comparative study of melodrama in France, England, and America is Frank Rahill's *The World of Melodrama* (Philadelphia: University of Pennsylvania Press, 1967), which confirms my sense of the superiority of the French productions. Rahill's book is informative and useful, but not entirely reliable: one has the impression that he has sometimes worked from summaries or reviews of plays rather than from the plays themselves.

6 Geoffrey H. Hartman, "Toward Literary History," in *Beyond Formalism* (New Haven: Yale University Press, 1970), p. 356.

1 Honoré de Balzac, *La Peau de chagrin*, in *La Comédie Humaine*, ed. Marcel Bouteron (Paris: Bibliothèque de la Pléiade, 1955–56), 9:11–12. All volume and page references to *La Comédie Humaine* are to the Pléiade edition and will henceforth be given in parentheses in the text. I refer to the Pléiade text for the sake of convenience, because it is relatively compact (11 volumes) and widely available. In some instances, its text needs emendation, and I have had recourse to the most reliable edition, the replica of the "Furne corrigé," published as Balzac's *Oeuvres complètes* (Paris: Les Bibliophiles de l'Originale, 1966–   ). All translations from the French are my own.

2 Martin Turnell, *The Novel in France* (New York: Vintage Books, 1958), p. 220.

3 Theodora Bosanquet, *Henry James at Work* (London: Hogarth Press, 1924), p. 32. This passage is also cited by Leo B. Levy, *Versions of Melodrama: A Study of the Fiction and Drama of Henry James, 1865–1897* (Berkeley and Los Angeles: University of California Press, 1957), a valuable study to which I shall refer in chapter 6.

4 See Jacques Barzun, "Henry James, Melodramatist," in *The Question of Henry James*, ed. F. W. Dupee (New York: Holt, 1945).

5 Henry James, *The Portrait of a Lady* (New York: Scribner's, 1908), 1:xxi. Following the original reference, page references to James's novels will be given in parentheses in the text.

6 Henry James, *The Ambassadors* (New York: Scribner's, 1909), 2:274.

7 Henry James, "Honoré de Balzac (1902)" in *Notes on Novelists* (New York: Scribner's, 1914), pp. 140–41.

8 I. A. Richards, *The Philosophy of Rhetoric* (New York: Oxford University Press, 1936), p. 94. We might note, in reference to the initial passage quoted from *La Peau de chagrin*, that *parable* has been defined as "teaching a moral by means of an extended metaphor" by Richard A. Lanham in *A Handlist of Rhetorical Terms* (Berkeley and Los Angeles: University of California Press, 1968), p. 70.

9 Henry James, *The Wings of the Dove* (New York: Scribner's, 1909), 2:259.

10 *Tragedy and Melodrama: Versions of Experience*, p. 85.

11 "Melodrama," in *The Life of the Drama*, pp. 195–218.

12 Denis Diderot, "Entretiens sur *Le Fils naturel*," in *Oeuvres esthétiques*, ed. Paul Vernière (Paris: Garnier, 1959), pp. 148–49. For Diderot's discussion of the "interest" specific to the *genre sérieux*, see p. 136. The same aesthetic category is discernible in his discussion of Richardson (in "Eloge de Richardson") and in his comments on the paintings of Greuze (in "Salons"). On the concept of the *intéressant*, see also chapter 2, note 11.

13 Diderot, "Entretiens," p. 148.

14 The play was *Pygmalion*, "Scène lyrique," first staged in Lyon in 1770; and the word *mélodrame*, characterizing *Pygmalion*, is mentioned in Rousseau's "Observations sur l'*Alceste* Italien de M. le Chevalier Glück" (probably written in 1774 or 1775), in Jean-Jacques Rousseau, *Oeuvres* (Paris, 1801), 10:319–20. See below, chapter 4, note 14.

15 Jean-Paul Sartre, *Les Mots* (Paris: Gallimard, 1964), pp. 101–02.

16 See Heilman, *Tragedy and Melodrama*, passim. This usage is continued by James L. Smith, who subdivides the genre into melodrama of triumph, of defeat, and of protest.

17 Louis de Saint-Just, "Institutions républicaines," in *Oeuvres choisies* (Paris: Gallimard, 1968), p. 327.

18 I take this definition of tragedy from Northrop Frye, *Anatomy of Criticism* (Princeton: Princeton University Press, 1957), pp. 214–15. I find confirmation of my view of desacralization and its aftermath in a similar argument urged by Leslie Fiedler; see, in particular, *Love and Death in the American Novel* (1963; reprinted ed., London: Paladin Books, 1970), p. 34.

19 See, in particular, the closing paragraph of book 4 of Rousseau's *Confessions*.

20 Devendra P. Varma, *The Gothic Flame* (London: A. Barker, 1957), p. 211. On this aspect of the Gothic novel, see also Lowry Nelson, Jr., "Night Thoughts on the Gothic Novel," *Yale Review* 52 (1963); Eino Railo, *The Haunted Castle* (London: G. Routledge, 1927); Robert D. Hume, "Gothic versus Romantic: A Revaluation of the Gothic Novel," *PMLA* 84 (1969).

21 Rudolf Otto, *The Idea of the Holy* [*Das Heilige*], trans. John W. Harvey (Oxford: Galaxy Books, 1958), chaps. 4, 5.

22 Matthew Gregory Lewis, *The Monk* (New York: Grove Press, Evergreen Books, 1959), p. 266. For a more detailed discussion of this passage, of *The Monk* and the problem of the Sacred, see my article "Virtue and Terror: *The Monk*," *ELH* 40, no. 2 (1973).

23 Clifford Geertz, "Ethos, World View, and the Analysis of Sacred Symbolism," in *The Interpretation of Cultures* (New York: Basic Books, 1973), p. 126.

24 Sigmund Freud, "The Uncanny" ["Das Unheimliche"], in Standard Edition (London: Hogarth), 17:218–56.

25 Diderot, "Eloge de Richardson," in *Oeuvres esthétiques*, p. 32.

26 A prime example of claustral literature is *Les Victimes cloîtrées* (1791), a play by Boutet de Monvel which Lewis saw in Paris shortly before beginning work on *The Monk*, and which he translated as *Venoni*, staged in London. Another celebrated example, which Lewis may also have known, is *Le Couvent, ou les Voeux forcés*, by Olympe de Gouges (1790). And there are many more, particularly of the revolutionary period. See my discussion of Pixerécourt's *Latude, ou Trente-cinq ans de captivité* in chapter 2. See also Robert Shackleton, "The Cloister Theme in French Preromanticism," in *The French Mind: Studies in Honor of Gustave Rudler*, ed. Will Moore, Rhoda Sutherland, Enid Starkie (Oxford: Clarendon, 1952). The importance of *The Monk* and its exploration of psychological depths, as well as the close relation of the Gothic novel to the Revolution, was lucidly recognized by the foremost expositor of the claustral and its repressed content, the Marquis de Sade, in his essay "Idée sur les romans," in *Oeuvres* (Paris: Cercle du Livre Précieux, 1964), 10:15.

27 Henry James, "The Art of Fiction," in *The Future of the Novel*, ed. Leon Edel (New York: Vintage Books, 1956), p. 13.

CHAPTER 2

1 On the Cornelian concept of *admiration*, see Octave Nadal, *Le Sentiment de l'amour dans l'oeuvre de Pierre Corneille* (Paris: Gallimard, 1948), p. 141. Nadal refers to Corneille's definition of the concept in the *Examen de Nicomède* and specifically distinguishes *admiration*, an intellectual reaction, from *étonnement* ("astonishment").

2 *Traité du mélodrame*. Par MM. A! A! A! (Abel Hugo, Armand Malitourne, J.-J. Ader) (Paris, 1817), p. 64.

3 These constitute an important and convenient triumvirate. Other major melodramatists referred to in this chapter are: J. G. A. Cuvelier de Trie, Hubert (Philippe Jacques de Laroche), and, of a slightly later generation, Auguste Anicet-Bourgeois, Joseph Bouchardy, and Adolphe Dennery.

4 See Northrop Frye, "Theory of Mythos," in *Anatomy of Criticism* (Princeton: Princeton University Press, 1957), pp. 158–239.

5 For a good discussion of the virgin-heroine in American melodrama, see David Grimsted, *Melodrama Unveiled: American Theater and Culture, 1800–1850* (Chicago: University of Chicago Press, 1968).

6 "Evil is on the earth." Voltaire, "Poème sur le désastre de Lisbonne."

7 The statistics of crime committed on the boards of the Boulevard are cited by Henri Beaulieu, *Les Théâtres du Boulevard du Crime* (Paris: H. Daragon, 1905), pp. 5–6: according to the *Almanach des spectacles* for 1823, the actor Tautin "has been stabbed 16,302 times, Marty has been poisoned, with variations, 11,000 times. Fresnoy has been done in by different methods 27,000 times, Mlle Adèle Dupuis has been 75,000 times innocent, seduced, abducted, or drowned, [etc.]." The imaginative total given is 132,902 crimes.

8 Bentley, *The Life of the Drama*, pp. 205, 217. See also Michael R. Booth, *English Melodrama* (London: Herbert Jenkins, 1965), p. 14.

9 Manichaeism has been recognized as the essence of melodrama by its best students. See, for example, Heilman, *Tragedy and Melodrama*, pp. 74–87; Barzun, "Henry James, Melodramatist," in *The Question of Henry James*; also, Jean Follain, "Le Mélodrame," in *Entretiens sur la paralittérature*, ed. Noel Arnaud, Francis Lacassin, Jean Tortel (Paris: Plon, 1970), and Jean Tortel, "Le Roman populaire," in the same volume.

10 Heilman, *Tragedy and Melodrama*, p. 85.

11 Jacques Truchet finds a touch of sadism in the way the word "intéressant," so often applied to beautiful victims, is used in later eighteenth-century theatre. See his introduction to *Théâtre du XVIIIe siècle* (Paris: Bibliothèque de la Pléïade, 1972), 1:LI. Victimization is surely part of the "interesting," the appealing and touching, offered by melodrama. However, the connotations of the word in Pixérécourt seem to belong to a more purely sentimental tradition, deriving from Rousseau: it concerns the process of recognition of one *belle âme* by another.

12 Willie G. Hartog, *Guilbert de Pixérécourt* (Paris: H. Champion, 1913), p. 208.

13 The *Traité du mélodrame* offers the following "essence and elixir" of the villain's last-act soliloquy, where "each exclamation point equals a sigh": "Oui!!... non!!! mais ... non, non!!!!! Se peut-il? Quoi! ... Oh grands dieux!!!!!! ... Malheureux, qu'ai-je fait????? ... Barbare!!!!!! ... Hélas!! ... O jour affreux! ... ô nuit épouvantable!! ... Ah! que je souffre!! ... Mourons!!!! ... Je me meurs ... je suis mort!!!!!!! ... aie, ay! aie!!!!!!!! ..." (p. 43).

14 *Traité du mélodrame*, p. 57.

15 What Théophile Gautier wrote of Joseph Bouchardy could be applied to all melodrama: "He loved to present the great and beautiful commonplaces which form the very basis of man's soul, and which bring an evil smile to the lips of the sceptic: paternal love, fidelity, devotion, chivalric loyalty, the defense of honor,

and all the noble motives that can determine action" (*Histoire du romantisme*, 2d ed. [Paris: Charpentier, 1874], p. 186). I can confirm the effectiveness of such unembarrassed naming of home truths, from the experience of seeing a revival of Anicet-Bourgeois' *La Vénitienne* (1834), retitled *Le Poignard masqué*, at the Théâtre Hébertot in Paris in 1974. The production had the great merit of playing the melodrama "straight," without irony; and if as spectator one divested oneself of irony, the result was remarkably effective, emotionally strong and pure.

16 Charles Nodier, Introduction to *Théâtre choisi*, by Pixerécourt, 4 vols. (Paris and Nancy, 1841–43), 1:ii–iii. Nodier is quoting from his own article of 1835 in the *Revue de Paris*.

17 There is also in melodrama a certain predilection for the unfettered life of wild, rural areas, and for democratic places, countries that represent more democratic and communal social structures, such as the Switzerland of Ducange's *Lisbeth* and *Thérèse*—both of which include protestant pastors (very different from corrupt Catholic clerics). "Jacques-le-Souffleur"—an anonymous and percipient commentator on the form—notes that Tautin and Frénoy (two pillars of melodramatic acting at the Gaîté and the Ambigu-Comique) "have saved Scotland eighteen times, Corsica forty-six times, and Switzerland two hundred and thirteen times, which makes this last, thanks to them, a very free state . . ." (Jacques-le-Souffleur, *Petit Dictionnaire des coulisses* [Paris, 1835], p. 47). Virtue is often acted out in a Rousseauian space.

18 See the very useful study by Marie-Antoinette Allévy, *La Mise-en-scène en France dans la Ière moitié du XIXe siècle* (Paris: E. Droz, 1938). See also Petr Bogatyrev, "Les Signes du théâtre," *Poétique* 8 (1971), pp. 517–30.

19 See Jacques-le-Souffleur, *Petit Dictionnaire des coulisses*, pp. 33–34.

20 Théophile Gautier, *Histoire de l'art dramatique en France depuis vingt-cinq ans* (Paris: Hetzel, 1858–59), 1:24–25. The play was *Le Corsaire noir* (1837).

21 "*Let's dissimulate* [*dissimulons*]. The sacramental word of old melodrama. It can always be found on the lips of the villain. 'Come, young maiden,' said M. Tautin, 'come let me take you to your cherished mother.' The villain accompanied this sweet phrase with a sweet look from his left eye, and in a hollow voice the hypocrite said, 'Let's dissimulate,' which meant that the young maiden was going to be abducted, poisoned, or strangled, according to the usages and customs of the place. 'Let's dissimulate,' said M. Frénoy, and at the moment of committing a murder, he would dance the barcarole to the sound of castanettes. Those were the good old days" (Jacques-le-Souffleur, *Petit Dictionnaire des coulisses*, p. 30).

22 Dickens' reactions to a revival of Ducange's *Trente ans, ou la Vie d'un joueur* at the Ambigu-Comique in 1855, with Frédérick Lemaître in the lead role, are reported by Robert Baldick, *The Life and Times of Frédérick Lemaître* (London: Hamish Hamilton, 1959), pp. 218–19. Baldick's source is John Foster, *The Life of Charles Dickens* (London, 1893). The best extended discussion of melodramatic acting styles is to be found in the appendix to Booth, *English Melodrama*. There are, of course, many contemporary comments on the styles of the famous actors, particularly Frédérick Lemaître, Bocage, Marie Dorval. One is impressed by the extent to which gestures and stage business that would strike us as utterly hyperbolic were considered the height of the "natural." A source of the success of Lemaître and Dorval indeed seems to have been their capacity to make the

hyperbolic natural. See, among many other examples, Gautier's remarks on Dorval in Dumas' *Antony*: "she possessed accents of nature, cries of the soul that overwhelmed the audience. . . . What truth in her gestures, in her postures, in her glances when, giving way, she leaned against a piece of furniture, wrung her hands, and lifted toward heaven her pale blue eyes bathed in tears" (*Histoire du romantisme*, p. 170). We can detect from such a passage that, while Lemaître and Dorval represent a more "naturalistic" style of acting than earlier Boulevard heroes like Tautin, Frénoy, Adèle Dupuis, it is a naturalism within a medium still radically heightened and hyperbolic.

23   Since the French tradition was to publish successful plays in regular commercial editions, rather than, as in England, "acting editions" destined for the trade, one usually lacks the music cues, often abundantly noted in the English melodramas. One can gain an impression of the places where music was used, however, from following the handwritten annotations preserved in directors' and actors' copies of the plays. In particular, there is the collection of the Amicale des Régisseurs de Théâtre, housed in the Bibliothèque Historique de la Ville de Paris. The importance of music to the plays is suggested by the fact that the name of the composer is always given on the title page, and by the contemporary fame of such composers (and conductors) as Piccini and Quaisain.

24   I take this label from Donald Fanger, *Dostoevsky and Romantic Realism: A Study of Dostoevsky in Relation to Balzac, Dickens, and Gogol* (Cambridge: Harvard University Press, 1965). Fanger's formulations of romantic realism are often close to my analysis of melodrama, though with considerable differences of emphasis. I have learned much from his fine study.

CHAPTER 3

1   Animals were in fact frequently used on the stage. The example was set by the Cirque Olympique of Astley and Franconi, which specialized in military and equestrian spectaculars. These could be such pieces of Napoleonic hagiography as *Le Mont Saint-Bernard*, melodramas, or pantomimes such as Cuvelier de Trie's *Martial et Angélique, ou le cheval accusateur*. The animal is often, as in this latter example, the mute witness and indicator of crime and innocence.

2   The *selam*—the mute, coded message put together from flowers, fruits, or ribbons—reappears frequently in early Romantic literature, testimony to an interest in non-verbal communication. Jean-Jacques Rousseau describes its possibilities in the *Essai sur l'origine des langues* (Paris: Bibliothèque du Graphe, 1970), p. 503. (This edition is a reprint from *Oeuvres* [Paris: A. Belin, 1817]); and Balzac alludes to it when Félix de Vandenesse composes his sensual bouquets for Madame de Mortsauf in *Le Lys dans la vallée* (8:855–59). For some comments on the mute messages of *Le Lys*, see my article, "Virtue-Tripping: Notes on *Le Lys dans la vallée*," Yale French Studies, no. 50 (1974), pp. 150–62.

3   A curious testimonial to the expressive power of pantomime deployed by a great actor can be found in a letter written to a theatre manager by a group of deaf-mutes who attended a performance of *Faust*, with Frédérick Lemaître in the role of Mephistopheles, and Marie Dorval in that of Gretchen. As observers used to following "every expression of the features and every movement of the heart,

down to the finest nuance of feeling," they pay homage to the intelligence and verity of the actor's and the actress's performance. Thus we have a confirming inverse mirror-image of the text of muteness. See Robert Baldick, *The Life and Times of Frédérick Lemaître* (London: Hamish Hamilton, 1959), p. 60.

4   See Baldick, *Frédérick Lemaître*, pp. 218–19. Dickens, along with Wilkie Collins, saw the revival of the play at the Ambigu-Comique in 1855.

5   This is related to the somewhat later vogue of *tableaux vivants*. F. Laloue, at the Cirque Olympique, specialized in doing tableaux vivants that imitated famous paintings, such as Gros' *Les Pestiférés de Jaffa* and Gericault's *Le Radeau de la Méduse*. See Allévy, *La Mise-en-scène en France*, p. 112.

6   *Traité du Mélodrame*, p. 47.

7   These questions of theatrical history are treated at greater length in chapter 4, pp. 84–88.

8   See the more detailed discussion in chapter 4, pp. 83–84.

9   On the novelistic model, see Denis Diderot, "De la poésie dramatique" (1758) in *Oeuvres esthétiques*, ed. Paul Vernière (Paris: Garnier, 1959), p. 277; and also the "Eloge de Richardson." On the writing out of pantomime, see "De la poésie dramatique," *Oeuvres esthétiques*, p. 270. On the rewrite of *Le Fils naturel*, see "Entretiens sur *le Fils naturel*" (1757), in *Oeuvres esthétiques*, pp. 143–47. It is interesting to note the reaction of Paul Vernière, who calls the revised version: "du mauvais mélodrame" (p. 147, note).

10   "De la poésie dramatique," *Oeuvres esthétiques*, p. 275.

11   See Roland Barthes, *S/Z* (Paris: Seuil, 1970), p. 62.

12   *Supplément* to the *Encyclopédie*, vol. 4, s.v. "Pantomime" (Paris and Amsterdam, 1777).

13   "Entretiens sur *Le Fils naturel*," *Oeuvres esthétiques*, pp. 101–02. I am aware that the view of spontaneous emotionalism suggested here could be complicated by reference to Diderot's "Paradoxe sur le comédien," where gesture, like all else in the actor's repertory, belongs to the realm of artifice. This considerably complicates questions about the referentiality of gesture, and attention to *Le Neveu de Rameau* would make it still more difficult to assign any unambiguous view to Diderot. Yet from the point of view of the spectator—essentially my standpoint here—inarticulate words and gestures must *appear* the product of uncontrollable passion.

14   *Encyclopédie;* s.v. "Geste" (Paris, 1757).

15   *Essai sur l'origine des langues*, p. 516.

16   Jacques Derrida, *De la grammatologie* (Paris: Editions de Minuit, 1967), p. 33.

17   Claude-Prosper-Jolyot Crébillon, *Les Egarements du coeur et de l'esprit* (Paris: Le Divan, 1929), p. 23. For a more extended treatment of the social code and its workings in Crébillon and other eighteenth-century novelists, see my study *The Novel of Worldliness* (Princeton: Princeton University Press, 1969).

18   On the necessity to "tout dire," see in particular the final paragraph of book 4 of Rousseau's *Confessions*. For Sade, see especially *La Philosophie dans le boudoir* and the remarkable essay by Maurice Blanchot "L'Incovenance majeure," printed as preface to the section of *La Philosophie dans le boudoir* known as *Français encore un effort si vous voulez être républicains* in the Collection Libertés (Paris: J.-J. Pauvert, 1965).

19   Roret, ed., *Nouveau Manuel théâtral* (Paris, 1854).

20 Ferdinand de Saussure writes: "quand la sémiologie sera organisée, elle devra se demander si les modes d'expression qui reposent sur des signes entièrement naturels—comme la pantomime—lui reviennent de droit" (*Cours de linguistique générale* [Paris: Payot, 1966], p. 100).

21 Charles Aubert, *L'Art mimique, suivi d'un traité de la pantomime et du ballet* (Paris: E. Meuriot, 1902), pp. 2, 11.

22 *L'Art mimique*, p. 197.

23 For a useful summary of the distinctions between language and other sign-systems, see Anthony Wilden, *The Language of the Self* (Baltimore: Johns Hopkins University Press, 1968), p. 221.

24 *Grande Encyclopédie Larousse*, supplement, s.v. "Langage gestuel," unsigned article by Christian Metz (Paris, 1968).

25 A. J. Greimas, "Conditions d'une sémiotique du monde naturel," in *Du sens* (Paris: Seuil, 1970), p. 86. This essay originally appeared—along with the essay by Julia Kristeva cited below and other valuable contributions by François Rastier, Claude Brémond, Claude Hutt, and a bibliography—in *Langages*, no. 10 (June 1968), an issue devoted to "Pratiques et langages gestuels." On the semiotics of gesture, see also Paul Bouissac, *La Mesure des gestes* (The Hague: Mouton, 1973). I have also considered the relevance to my analysis of the "Kinesics" established by Ray Birdwhistell, but I do not find this system of notation and analysis very useful.

26 Julia Kristeva, "Le geste, pratique ou communication?" in *Semiotikè: Recherches pour une sémanalyse* (Paris: Seuil, 1969), pp. 96–98. See Greimas, *Du sens*, p. 87.

27 Roman Jakobson, "Two Aspects of Language and Two Types of Aphasic Disturbances," in *Fundamentals of Language*, by Jakobson and Morris Halle (The Hague: Mouton, 1956).

28 *Essai sur l'origine des langues*, p. 502.

29 *S/Z*, p. 41.

30 Alfred de Vigny, *Chatterton* (Paris: Garnier/Flammarion, 1968), p. 107.

31 This relation is further considered in chapter 4, pp. 89–92.

32 *S/Z*, p. 87.

33 On the *trace*, see Derrida, *De la grammatologie*.

34 Charles Dickens, *Great Expectations* (New York: New American Library, Signet Classics, 1963), p. 89. Another notable example can be found in Michelangelo Antonioni's film *Blow-Up*, when the photographer, attempting to make sense of the scene he has witnessed in a London park, makes enlargements of portions of his photographs. He is first led, by the direction of the girl's glance, to enlarge a portion of the shrubbery; in the enlargement, he finds the outline of a pistol. Then, by following its line of direction, he finds what appears to be a corpse under a tree. Line of sight, directionality, is the principle for putting together the beginnings of a plot, hence structuring and making sense of reality.

35 On the arguments of Warburton and Condillac, see Derrida, *De la grammatologie*. To be sure, the situation is more complicated than this, for the "graph" of writing is not identical to the hieroglyph and is less "representative" of gesture. One would need—in the manner of Derrida—to interrogate here the whole notion of representation.

36 Honoré de Balzac, "Théorie de la démarche," in *Oeuvres complètes* (Paris: Les Bibliophiles de l'Originale, 1966–   ), 19:230.

37 Antonin Artaud, *Le Théâtre et son double*, Collection Idées (Paris: Gallimard, 1964), pp. 138, 81.
38 *Le Théâtre et son double*, pp. 116, 142.
39 See Sigmund Freud, *The Interpretation of Dreams*, in Standard Edition 4, 5. The fundamental procedures of the dream work—condensation, displacement, and recourse to plastic figurability—all have analogies in the functioning of mute signs: condensation represents the substitutive activity of metaphor; displacement can be read as that indication of meaning, that anaphora that signals the presence of meaning elsewhere; recourse to plastic figurability is basic to melodramatic mute expression. If we accept the corrective offered by Emile Benveniste, that dreams more accurately demonstrate a rhetoric than a language—in that the symbolism of dreams is both "infra- and supra-linguistic" —and the true correspondence between the dream work and other discourses is to be found in its repertory of tropes and figures, we may find further confirmation of our identification of mute gesture as a trope. Its status is rhetorical rather than linguistic. See Benveniste, "Remarques sur la fonction du langage dans la découverte freudienne," in *Essais de linguistique générale* (Paris: Gallimard, 1964), p. 86.
40 *Great Expectations*, p. 341.

CHAPTER 4

1 George Steiner, *The Death of Tragedy* (1961; reprint ed., New York: Hill and Wang, Dramabook, 1963), p. 108. Although I shall in the course of this chapter often have occasion to disagree with Steiner, it should be apparent that I admire *The Death of Tragedy*, a book that engages the vital issues.
2 Robert B. Heilman, in *Tragedy and Melodrama*, offers a convincing analysis of melodrama within the modern theatre. While he does not consider it an exclusively modern type, he does note its contemporary pervasiveness.
3 *Death of Tragedy*, p. 164. Steiner here echoes Irving Babbitt, who writes, "Nothing is easier than to establish the connection between emotional romanticism and the prodigious efflorescence of melodrama, the irresponsible quest for thrills, that has marked the last century," and who characterizes Victor Hugo's plays as "parvenu melodramas" (*Rousseau and Romanticism* [Boston: Houghton Mifflin, 1919], p. 189).
4 The argument concerning social comedy and its relation to the sensibility of the audience is pursued at greater length in my study *The Novel of Worldliness*.
5 The *bienséances* really derive from the classical idea of *vraisemblance:* they postulate rules of taste designed to insure that probability (and the true may sometimes be improbable) is not threatened by representations that might shock the public's sensibility. Hence kings must behave in a certain manner and use noble language; killings must not take place on stage; Christian miracles should not be represented, and so on.
6 See Diderot, "Entretiens sur *Le Fils naturel*," *Oeuvres esthétiques*, especially p. 128; also the "Eloge de Richardson," *Oeuvres esthétiques*, p. 30, where Diderot as novel reader acts in the manner of a spectator at a melodrama: "How many times have I not caught myself, in the manner of children taken to the theatre for the first

time, crying out: *Don't believe him, he is deceiving you... If you go there, you'll be lost.*" See also Louis Sébastien Mercier, *Essai sur l'art dramatique* (Paris, 1773), and Beaumarchais, "Essai sur le genre dramatique sérieux" (1767), particularly this definition of "interest" (*l'intérêt*): "What is interest? It is the involuntary sentiment by which we adopt an event for our own, the sentiment which puts us in the place of the person who is suffering, in the midst of his situation" (Beaumarchais, *Théâtre complet, Lettres,* ed. Maurice Allem [Paris: Bibliothèque de la Pléïade, 1949], p. 18). One should note the influence here of eighteenth-century English sentimental drama, especially the work of George Lillo.

7   "Essai sur le genre dramatique sérieux," *Théâtre complet,* p. 20. On the aesthetics of eighteenth-century *drame,* see also Félix Gaiffe, *Le Drame en France au XVIIIe siècle* (Paris: A. Colin, 1910) and Michel Lioure, *Le Drame, de Diderot à Ionesco* (Paris: A. Colin, 1973).

8   On these questions of literary and theatrical history, see Maurice Albert, *Les Théâtres des Boulevards, 1789–1848* (Paris: Societé française d'imprimerie et de librairie, 1902); Henri Beaulieu, *Les Théâtres du Boulevard du Crime* (Paris: H. Dragon, 1905); Gaiffe, *Le Drame en France au XVIIIe siècle*; Paul Ginisty, *Le Mélodrame* (Paris: L. Michaud, 1910); Michel Lioure, *Le Drame*; Alexis Pitou, "Les Origines du mélodrame à la fin du XVIIIe siècle," *Revue d'histoire littéraire de la France* 18 (1911), pp. 256–96; E. C. van Bellen, *Les Origines du mélodrame* (Utrecht: Kemink & Zoon, 1927).

9   This figure is given by Frank Rahill, *The World of Melodrama* (Philadelphia: University of Pennsylvania Press, 1967), but it may be subject to caution. The *Almanach général des théâtres* mentions fifteen for 1791 (and twenty-two for 1800), but this census may not include the most minor theatres. See Bellen, *Les Origines du mélodrame,* p. 68.

10 Rahill, *World of Melodrama,* p. 44. This figure is confirmed by Pixérécourt in his erudite and intelligent article "Le Mélodrame," in *Le Livre des Cent et un* (Paris, 1831), p. 347. On the theatre during the revolutionary period, see Marvin A. Carlson, *The Theatre of the French Revolution* (Ithaca: Cornell University Press, 1966), and Henri Welschinger, *Le Théâtre de la Révolution* (Paris: Charavay, 1880). I have also had the benefit of reading an excellent manuscript by Jean-Marc Blanchard, yet to be published, on the language of the Revolution.

11 Théophile Gautier in *Le Moniteur Universel,* 30 May 1864, quoted by Alice M. Killen, *Le Roman 'terrifiant' ou roman 'noir' de Walpole à Ann Radcliffe et son influence sur la littérature française jusqu'en 1840* (Paris: Champion, 1915), p. 201. *La Nonne sanglante,* adapted from Lewis' *The Monk,* is by Anicet-Bourgeois and J. Mallian.

12 Kotzbue enjoyed extraordinary popularity at the turn of the century and is often cited as a major influence on melodrama. Armand Charlemagne, in his caustic pamphlet *Le Mélodrame aux Boulevards* (Paris, 1809), calls him "the Pixérécourt of Germany, as M. Pixérécourt is the French Kotzbue" (p. 40). His most celebrated play was probably *Menschenhass und Reue,* translated into French as *Misanthropie et repentir,* and staged in 1798.

13 We have touched, in the Preface, on some of the differences in the social condition of melodrama in France and in England. Until well past the mid-century, melodrama in England is distinctly lower-middle-class and working-class fare. And it is on the whole cruder than French melodrama, as the many

butchered adaptations from the French demonstrate. The genre would also have a longer life in England and embrace more subjects and causes, including some notable protests against the aftermath of the Industrial Revolution. See Booth, *English Melodrama* and J. L. Smith, *Melodrama*.

14 *Pygmalion*, "Scène lyrique," was first presented in Lyon in 1770, published in the *Mercure de France* in 1771, then staged in Paris in 1775. Rousseau characterizes the play as "the kind of *mélodrame* most suited to the [French] language," in his "Observations sur l'*Alceste* Italien de M. le Chevalier Glück," probably written in 1774 or 1775. (The date of 1766 given by Smith in *Melodrama*, p. 1, is impossible.) See *Oeuvres* (Paris, 1801), 10:319–20. Rousseau evidently conceives of his *mélodrame* as a subspecies of opera, adapting the common Italian term for opera, *melodramma*. A *Traité du mélodrame*, probably by Laurent Garcin, published in Paris in 1772, praises *Pygmalion* (without labelling it *mélodrame*) as promising a revolution in operatic theatre. The history of opera does record some further examples of *mélodrame* in the manner of *Pygmalion*—as a subspecies of opera—especially in German. See Jan van der Veen, *Le Mélodrame musical, de Rousseau au romantisme* (The Hague: Martinus Nijhof, 1955). But by the start of the nineteenth century, common usage had applied the term rather to the popular genre that is our subject. See Smith, *Melodrama*, p. 2. Rousseau's use of the term, while belonging to a separate history, is not irrelevant to popular melodrama: since Rousseau believed French to be a language ill-suited to singing, in *Pygmalion* pantomime and mute gesture, rather than voice, accompany the musical line. *Pygmalion* indeed belongs to the problematics of language and gesture most fully argued in the *Essai sur l'origine des langues*.

15 The conflicting claims are summarized in Hartog, *Guilbert de Pixerécourt*, p. 48 ff. Pixerécourt's testimony is to be found in "Le Mélodrame," *Le Livre des Cent et un*, p. 325.

16 Nodier, Introduction to Pixerécourt's *Théâtre choisi*, 1:ii. Some ambiguity yet subsists: in the *Théâtre choisi*, *Rosa*, of 1798, is labeled a melodrama; but the first play of Pixerécourt's to bear that label on its title page, in the original edition, appears to have been *La Femme à deux maris*, of 1802.

17 On Eugène Sue, on the *roman-feuilleton*, and implicitly, on melodrama, see the excellent article by Jean-Louis Bory, "Premiers éléments pour une esthétique du roman-feuilleton," in *Tout Feu, tout flamme* (Paris: Juilliard, 1966). See also the same author's *Eugène Sue* (Paris: Hachette, 1962).

18 Théophile Gautier, *Histoire du romantisme*, 2d ed. (Paris: Charpentier, 1874), p. 185. The passage also appears in Gautier, *Histoire de l'art dramatique*, 2:239–40.

19 On the question of the theatre public, see Maurice Descotes, *Le Public du théâtre et son histoire* (Paris: Presses Universitaires de France, 1964).

20 Though recent work, such as Lioure's *Le Drame*, has begun to revaluate the continuities between the popular genres and the "higher" forms, French studies remain largely under the impression that little work of interest was produced in this period. In the case of an individual career, a parallel to the genesis of Romantic drama from earlier popular forms may be found in Balzac, who from his apprenticeship in popular Gothic fiction in the 1820s went on to the *Comédie Humaine* in the 1830s and 1840s.

21 Maurice Albert recognizes and clearly states this in *Les Théâtres des Boulevards*, p. 297.

22 Julien-Louis Geoffroy, article of 27 nivose an 11, *Cours de littérature dramatique* (Paris: Pierre Blanchard, 1820), 5:391.

23 *Racine et Shakespeare* was first published in 1823, then a second part, a reply to the anti-Romantic academician Auger, was added in 1825.

24 See especially Georges Lote, *En préface à Hernani* (Paris: J. Gamber, 1930); Hippolyte Parigot, *Alexandre Dumas père* (Paris: Hachette, 1902). In antithetical recognition, see the comments by Irving Babbitt on the use of antithesis in Hugo: "A study of this one figure as it appears in his work and ideas, in his characters and situations, would show that he is the most melodramatic genius for whom high rank has ever been claimed in literature." (*Rousseau and Romanticism*, p. 59).

25 The prime example is Alfred de Musset. After the failure of *La Nuit vénitienne*, he wrote cabinet drama with no regard for the exigencies of the stage. Although his comedies have long since successfully been adapted for the stage, and his historical drama *Lorenzaccio* has (cut and rearranged) been effectively staged in our century, his work remains, to my mind, non-theatrical. *Lorenzaccio*, despite its poetic moments, is at least as hollow intellectually as Hugo's plays, and it does not offer Hugo's compensating sense of dramatic enactment.

26 Victor Hugo, "Préface de *Cromwell*," *Théâtre complet* (Paris: Bibliothèque de la Pléiade, 1967), 1:425.

27 Hugo, "Préface de *Lucrèce Borgia*," *Théâtre complet*, 2:287–88.

28 The "battle of *Hernani*" was a self-conscious, well-prepared, prepublicized symbolic event and has frequently been recounted, notably by Théophile Gautier in his *Histoire du romantisme*. Part of the struggle to impose a new drama at the Comédie-Française involved the incomprehension of the actors, who found Hugo's style and situations excessive: the author's conflicts with the famous tragedienne, Mlle Mars, who played Doña Sol, are well-documented (see in particular Alexandre Dumas, *Mes Mémoires* [Paris: Calmann-Lévy, 1883], 5:269–83). The triumph of *drame romantique* at the Comédie-Française was in fact short-lived, and Hugo would find greater sympathy for his work elsewhere. *Marion Delorme* (written before *Hernani*, accepted at the Comédie-Française, then held up by the censor) was produced at the Théâtre de la Porte Saint-Martin, with Marie Dorval and Bocage in the roles of Marion and Didier. *Lucrèce Borgia* played, with great success, at the same theatre; the role of Lucrèce was played by Mlle Georges, that of Gennaro by Frédérick Lemaître. *Ruy Blas* inaugurated the brief life of Hugo's own theatre, La Renaissance; the principal role was interpreted by Frédérick Lemaître. On the relation of the *drame romantique* to the actors and theatres, see Maurice Descotes, *Le Drame romantique et ses grands créateurs* (Paris: Presses Universitaires de France, 1955).

29 *The Death of Tragedy*, p. 163.

30 That is, the wordplay derives from the verb *être* (to be), which gives *je suis;* and from the verb *suivre* (to follow), which gives *je te suis,* and from which the noun *suite* is derived.

31 Jean Gaudon, *Victor Hugo, dramaturge* (Paris: l'Arche, 1955), p. 100.

32 Pierre Corneille, *Cinna*, V, iii; 1696–97.

33 The figure of the father could, with some critical ingenuity, be interpreted as a dominant though repressed imperative in all of Hernani's actions. Everything "positive" in his life—including his passion for Doña Sol—appears to him a

"betrayal" of the father; and Don Ruy, representative of the paternal generation, thus at the end brings into play a deeper level of culpability. Such is suggested by Hernani's nearly hysteric reaction to Don Ruy's arrival, and his characterization of Don Ruy as "le Vieillard qui rit dans les ténèbres" ("the old man who laughs in the shadows")—a phrase that suggests the punishment meted out by the Father. Thus *Hernani* also may contain a "second drama," one of primary psychic instances. But this second drama is not coherently plotted nor consistently alluded to. Finally, one could speculate that the final victory of the Father represents Hugo's own atonement, compensation for the Oedipal triumph represented by the "battle of *Hernani*," the victory of the younger generation and the overthrow of the literary patriarchs.

34 Steiner, *The Death of Tragedy*, p. 161.

35 T. S. Eliot, "Hamlet and His Problems," in *Selected Essays, 1917–1932* (New York: Harcourt Brace, 1932), pp. 124–25.

36 See Hugo, "Préface des *Burgraves*," *Théâtre complet*, 2:15–16.

37 "Le seul théâtre de notre esprit"—that is, a drama become interior monologue. See Stéphane Mallarmé, "Hamlet," *Oeuvres complètes* (Paris: Bibliothèque de la Pléiade, 1956), p. 300.

38 In *William Shakespeare*, Hugo defines the aesthetic of epic as *grandeur*, that of drama as *immensité*, and comments: "L'immense diffère du grand, en ce qu'il exclut, si bon lui semble, la dimension, en ce qu' 'il passe la mesure,' comme on dit vulgairement, en ce qu'il peut, sans perdre la beauté, perdre la proportion" (Paris: Hetzel, 188?), pp. 103–104.

39 Lote, *En préface à Hernani*, p. 168, note.

40 One might say as much of the ending of Shakespeare's *Antony and Cleopatra*, which may in fact be the most dubiously tragic of Shakespeare's tragedies. But the difference from *Hernani* is illuminating: in *Antony*, one has the overwhelming impression of a world lost through love, a fall of imperial and cosmic proportions.

41 Steiner, *The Death of Tragedy*, pp. 128–29.

42 Steiner, *The Death of Tragedy*, p. 133.

43 Much of Shelley's critical disrepute in our time (a disrepute from which his reputation is once again emerging) may be explained by his melodramatism. For instance, F. R. Leavis, a leader of the anti-Shelleyans, has noted his tendency to present "emotion in itself, unattached, in the void." He comments of a passage from *The Cenci*: "It does not grasp and present anything, but merely makes large gestures toward the kind of effect deemed appropriate." ("Shelley," in *English Romantic Poets: Modern Essays in Criticism*, ed. M. H. Abrams [New York: Oxford University Press, Galaxy Books, 1960], pp. 275, 283). These characteristics are typical of Romantic melodramatism and are inherent to Shelley's effort to be prophetic, a poet of the spiritual, without reference to a traditional theology.

44 *Antony* contains a manifesto concerning the *drame*, articulated by the playwright-within-the-play, Eugène d'Hervilly, in act IV, scene six. He argues (as Balzac will) that comedy has become impossible since the Revolution because manners have lost their distinction and relief. *Drame*, the representation of the passions, remains possible, but has usually meant historical drama, where distance from actuality permits the development of grandiose and heroic passions. By introducing these into a contemporary milieu, the playwright risks the accusation

of exaggeration and melodrama. Yet "the heart beats as warmly under a frock coat as under a breastplate"—and Dumas implicitly recommends, and *Antony* demonstrates, the unfolding of high passion within the "real" social world. In the efforts of Dumas' successors, however, passion itself becomes more and more simply a social problem. The nearest realization of Dumas' recommendation may be in the Balzacian novel.

CHAPTER 5

1   See chapter 1 under the heading "Overture."
2   See chapter 3 under the heading "Gesture, Writing, Meaning."
3   "All there is myth and figure." Balzac to M. de Montalembert, 25 November 1831, quoted by Maurice Allem in Introduction to *La Peau de Chagrin* (Paris: Garnier, 1967), p. vi.
4   See the excellent Introduction and Répertoire by René Guise in *Théâtre*, vols. 21–23 of *Oeuvres complètes*, by Honoré de Balzac (Paris: Les Bibliophiles de l'Originale, 1969). (The mention *Oeuvres complètes*, without further qualification, will refer to this edition, which currently includes 25 volumes.)
5   See Pierre Descaves, *Balzac dramatiste* (Paris: La Table Ronde, 1960). Guise, however, offers some thoughtful revaluations of the plays and demonstrates how adverse circumstances of staging, and censorship, contributed to Balzac's insuccess.
6   Guise, Introduction to *Théâtre, Oeuvres complètes*, 21:xxix.
7   The title role of *Vautrin* was played by Frédérick Lemaître. The principal roles of *Paméla Giraud* and *La Marâtre* were conceived for Marie Dorval, who indeed accepted the latter but withdrew while the play was in rehearsal.
8   Guise in *Oeuvres complètes*, 21:xxix.
9   "Homo duplex": see Dédicace of *La Cousine Bette* (6:134); "play of polar principles": see *Une Fille d'Eve* (2:80). Or, as the journalist Emile Blondet explains to Lucien de Rubempré in *Illusions perdues*, "Ideas are binary" (4:789). On the importance of contrast in Balzac's aesthetics, see Pierre Laubriet, *L'Intelligence de l'art chez Balzac* (Paris: Didier, 1961).
10 "Desire sets us afire and Power destroys us; but Knowledge. . . ." Page references given in parentheses in the text here, as in earlier chapters, are to the Pléïade edition of *La Comédie Humaine*.
11 Balzac, "Lettre à Hippolyte Castille," (1846), in *Oeuvres complètes* (Société des Etudes Balzaciennes. Paris: Guy Le Prat, 1963), 28:494.
12 "Flibustiers en gants jaunes et en carrosses": Préface to *Histoire des Treize* (1st ed.), 11:194.
13 On *Gobseck*, see Jean-Luc Seylaz, "Réflexions sur Gobseck," *Etudes de Lettres* (Lausanne), 3d ser., vol. 1, no. 4 (1968), pp. 295–310. On desire and its field of operation, see in particular André Allemand, *Unité et structure de l'univers balzacien* (Paris: Plon, 1965); also Ernst Robert Curtius, *Balzac*, French translation by Henri Jourdan (Paris: Grasset, 1933); Albert Béguin, *Balzac visionnaire* (1946; reprinted in Béguin, *Balzac lu et relu*. Paris: Seuil, 1965). Béguin's excellent book touches on many of the issues that concern us in this chapter.
14 See the interesting article by Martin Kanes, "Balzac and the Problem of

Expression," *Symposium* 23, no. 3–4 (1969), pp. 284–93. I think Kanes errs in considering the problem to be one of mimesis.

15 Préface to *Romans et Contes philosophiques* (1831), 11:184. The Préface was certainly "inspired" by Balzac, and perhaps in part written by him. The "law of disorganization" is treated at length by Harry Levin in *The Gates of Horn* (New York: Oxford University Press, 1963), pp. 150–66.

16 This is Emile Blondet speaking in *Autre Etude de femme*. On the loss of social distinctions in post-revolutionary society, and the difficulties of representation that this presents, see also the Préface to *Une Fille d'Eve*, 11:372–73. On Balzac's politics, see Bernard Guyon, *La Pensée politique et sociale de Balzac* (Paris: A. Colin, 1947).

17 Balzac, "Traité de la vie élégante" (1830), *Oeuvres complètes*, 19:182.

18 "Lettre à Hippolyte Castille," *Oeuvres complètes* (Société des Etudes Balzaciennes), 18:492.

19 Marcel Proust, *Contre Sainte-Beuve, précédé de Pastiches et mélanges, et suivi de Essais et articles*, ed. Pierre Clarac (Paris: Bibliothèque de la Pléiade, 1971), p. 277.

20 See "Etudes de moeurs par les gants" (1830) in *Oeuvres complètes*, 25:345–48. The Countess examines the gloves of her assembled friends and deduces, from the minutest details, what each has been doing: one has gambled, one has spent the evening dancing with the same lady, etc.

21 On the underworld, the world of shadowy manipulators and thrilling crime, see Jean-Louis Bory, "Balzac et les ténèbres," in *Pour Balzac et quelques autres* (Paris: Juilliard, 1960), pp. 11–101. Also relevant is Bory, "Premiers éléments d'une esthétique du roman feuilleton," in *Tout Feu, tout flamme*. There is evidence that Balzac at the time of *Splendeurs et misères* felt himself to be in competition with the immensely successful Eugène Sue, whose *Mystères de Paris* offer the most elaborate exploration of the underworld, its arch-criminals and regal redeemers, its hideous crime and redemptive purity of heart. See also Christopher Prendergast, "Melodrama and Totality in *Splendeurs et misères des courtisanes*," *Novel* 6, no. 2 (1973).

22 See the comment of Maurice Bardèche: "emotion is produced in *Illusions perdues*, as it may be produced in melodrama, from the opposition between two equally erroneous presentations of good and evil in the literary milieu. And I wonder if one could not say as much of many of Balzac's novels" (*Une Lecture de Balzac* [Paris: Les Sept Couleurs, 1964], p. 129).

23 Albert Béguin, *Balzac lu et relu* (Paris: Seuil, 1965), p. 49. A modern philosophical tradition (represented by the work of Jacques Derrida) would lead one to put into question Balzac's implicit theory of meaning, to see meaning as already present in the process of representation itself. Clearly, however, the melodramatic imagination needs to believe in the surface/depth distinction.

24 Balzac, "Théorie de la démarche" (1833), *Oeuvres complètes*, 9:230.

25 The process is described by Béguin, *Balzac lu et relu*, pp. 47–48.

26 This is an example of what caused Proust to characterize Balzac's style as preliterary in effect, marked by an irredeemable crudity—which is a result of the effort to block out, reorganize, and represent the essential hidden in the real. Proust notes the constant recourse to excessive, incongruous metaphors in order to deliver the essential: for instance, M. de Bargeton's smile goes off "like buried

cannon balls coming to life." See Proust, *Contre Sainte-Beuve* . . . , pp. 268–70.

27 This kind of solicitation in its developed form is admirably rendered in Proust's loving parody: "Is it not in fact one of the grandeurs of the mistress of the house—that Carmelite of worldly success—that she should immolate her coquetry, her pride, even her love to the necessity of creating a salon whose rivalries often constitute its most exciting ornament? Is she not in this the equal of the saint? Does she not merit her place, so dearly bought, in the social paradise?" (*Contre Sainte-Beuve* . . . , p. 8).

28 Gérard Genette, "Vraisemblance et motivation," in *Figures II* (Paris: Seuil, 1969), especially pp. 78–86.

29 "La Femme de province," in *Les Français peints par eux-mêmes* (1841), *Oeuvres complètes* (Société des Etudes Balzaciennes), 28:65.

30 Proust, *Contre Sainte-Beuve* . . . , pp. 8–9.

31 One could apply here the formulation of A. J. Greimas: "The visible world, instead of being projected before us like a homogeneous screen of forms, appears to us as constituted of several *layers of signifiers*, superimposed or sometimes even juxtaposed" ("Conditions d'une sémiotique du monde naturel," *Du sens*, p. 52).

32 On the importance of failure in the *Comédie Humaine*, see Charles Affron, *Patterns of Failure in La Comédie Humaine* (New Haven: Yale University Press, 1966); and the less rewarding study by Bernard Schilling, *The Hero as Failure* (Chicago: University of Chicago Press, 1968).

33 Balzac comments on the use of the word *drame* in "Des Mots à la mode" (1830): much more potent than the phrase "Il y a de la poésie" is "*Il y a du drame. Avec ce mot-là, vous égorgez sans pitié une dispute critique. —Vous jetez là tout un siècle et sa pensée, à la tête de vos auditeurs. —Ainsi: Bonaparte, Quel drame! —Quel drame que ce livre! —Que voulez-vous qu'on dise après vous?*" (*Oeuvres complètes*, 19:162–63).

34 See the classic analysis of the description of the Pension Vauquer in Erich Auerbach, *Mimesis*, trans. Willard Trask (1953; reprint ed. Garden City, N.Y.: Doubleday, Anchor Books, 1957), p. 413 ff.

35 A summary expression of the relation of substructure to superstructure appears in the phrase from *Gobseck* describing the adventurer Maxime de Trailles as a "shining ring which could join the penitentiary to high society" (2:643).

36 This, like Ducange's *Elodie* referred to in chapter 3, was an adaptation of the very popular novel by the Vicomte d'Arlincourt, *Le Solitaire*. Pixerécourt's play, like Ducange's, has a spectacular ending explicitly dramatizing heaven and hell; it is fully pertinent to Balzac's own climactic drama.

37 It is interesting that the description of Mme de Beauséant's ball originally included a brief scene where Rastignac comes upon Lady Brandon in conversation with Colonel Franchessini, the assassin of young Taillefer. When Rastignac has learned who this is, the narrator comments: "A cold sweat ran down his back. Vautrin appeared to him with his face of bronze. The hero of the prison offering his hand to the hero of the ball changed for Rastignac the aspect of society." This passage then led into Rastignac's perception of Goriot on his pallet beneath the diamonds. It offers a decisive, if somewhat crude, demonstration of the links of the upper and the lower world, and of Vautrin's haunting omnipresence as the metaphysician of these links. The passage was struck out by Balzac in the "Furne

corrigé" (the edition in which he made his last corrections), possibly because it seemed excessively crude to have Vautrin's agent, Franchessini, appear in the Faubourg Saint-Germain, or, more likely, because it distracted from the dramatic concentration of the ball scenes, which properly concern Rastignac's relationships to the Goriot daughters and to Mme de Beauséant. The conception of the passage nonetheless offers further confirmation of Balzac's metaphorical method. See *Oeuvres complètes*, 9:508.

38 See Béguin, *Balzac lu et relu*, pp. 65–77.

39 See the discussion of the "organizers" by Pierre Barbéris, *Le Monde de Balzac* (Paris: Arthaud, 1973), pp. 551–75. But Barbéris considers only the social reorganizers—Rabourdin is the most notable example—and neglects the more personal, cosmic, or metaphysical gestures.

40 The phrase "faire concurrence à l'Etat-Civil" is from the *Avant-Propos* of the *Comédie Humaine* (1:6).

41 See the comments on this scene by Harry Levin, *The Gates of Horn*, pp. 197–98.

42 *Oeuvres complètes*, 9:230.

43 I refer to the work of Erving Goffman and of Ray Birdwhistell. Balzac's own term is "Pathologie de la vie sociale," a rubric under which the editors of the *Oeuvres complètes* have, quite correctly to my mind, grouped such essays as "Théorie de la démarche," "Traité de la vie élégante," "Des Mots à la mode," "Etude de moeurs par les gants"—works that attempt to formulate the significant codes, the meaning systems, latent within social reality, apparent to the penetrating analyst who through their use can open new, systematic fields of understanding. I find irresistible the comparison to Freud's title *The Psychopathology of Everyday Life*. For Freud's study is equally about self-revelation, about decoding systems of latent meaning. The underlying postulate is the same for Balzac and for Freud: nothing in human behavior is meaningless.

44 For an attempt at such a deconstructive reading, see my article, "Virtue-Tripping: Notes on *Le Lys dans la vallée*," *Yale French Studies*, no. 50 (1974), pp. 150–62.

45 Balzac's self-consciousness as a novelist has often been contested or simply dismissed in favor of a view presenting him as a "force of nature," spontaneous, intuitive, occasionally brilliant, but essentially lacking in a sense of composition, style, and authorial self-awareness. The best criticism of Balzac (including that by Henry James) has always explicitly or implicitly contradicted this view, and recent studies have documented Balzac's sense of his craft. See, for example, André Allemand, *Unité et structure de l'univers balzacien*; Pierre Laubriet, *L'Intelligence de l'art chez Balzac*; François Bilodeau, *Balzac et le jeu des mots* (Montreal: Presses de l'Université de Montréal, 1971); Maurice Z. Shroder, "Balzac's Theory of the Novel," *L'Esprit Créateur* 8 (1967), pp. 3–10.

46 A recent dramatic adaptation of *Père Goriot*, in the BBC television Masterpiece Theatre series, suggested to me the antithesis of the stage Balzac conceived for his representations. The BBC version constantly underplayed the novel's melodrama, softened its manichaeism, reduced its stagy secondary characters to something closer to Dickensian satiric sketches. It struck me as another episode in the history of English misunderstandings of Balzac—who seems to create discomfort precisely in the measure that he is not assimilable to Dickens or to Thackeray. It should also be added that the essentially intimate space of the

television screen is not the ideal stage for Balzacian enactments, which demand a large volume of space and grandiose backdrops.

47 "Lettre à Hippolyte Castille," *Oeuvres complètes* (Société des Etudes Balzaciennes), 28:492.

48 See Barthes, *S/Z*, pp. 169–70, 218–19.

49 Walter Benjamin, "The Storyteller," in *Illuminations*, trans. Harry Zohn (New York: Schocken Books, 1969), pp. 86–87.

50 Much could be said here in exposition of Benjamin's insights and their application to Balzac. Benjamin notes that in traditional storytelling "traces of the storyteller cling to the story the way the handprints of the potter cling to the clay vessel" (*Illuminations*, p. 92), and we may detect in the presentation of the narrators of Balzac's tales a desire to give them the imprint of a personal voice and a lived experience. "Death is the sanction of everything that the storyteller has to tell," Benjamin also argues, in that the meaning of a man's life "first assumes transmissible form at the moment of his death" (ibid., p. 94). We are led to reflect on the number of deaths enacted in the *Comédie Humaine*, and the kind of significance they confer on life, the kind of reflection and judgment that they solicit.

51 "Henri IV conquered his kingdom city by city: M. de Balzac has conquered his morbid public infirmity by infirmity" (C. A. Sainte-Beuve, article of 1834, in *Portraits contemporains* [Paris: Didier, 1846], 1:462, note). Sainte-Beuve has in mind particularly Balzac's appeal to women, which he sees as operating through a knowledge of their secrets, which to Sainte-Beuve means especially their secret maladies, vices, desires.

52 Jules Janin, *Histoire de la littérature dramatique* (Paris: Michel Lévy, 1853–58), 4:309.

53 See Béguin, *Balzac lu et relu*, p. 125.

CHAPTER 6

1 Quoted in Percy Lubbock, ed., *The Letters of Henry James* (New York: Scribners, 1920), 1:8.

2 Henry James, *Letters to A. C. Benson and Auguste Monod*, ed. E. F. Benson (London: Elkins Matthews and Marrot, 1930), p. 35. The phrase returns in *The Spoils of Poynton*: in the last chapter, Fleda Vetch, setting out for the visit to a Poynton she will find consumed by fire, has "the sudden imagination of a disaster" ([New York: Scribners, 1908], p. 262).

3 Henry James, "The Lesson of Balzac" (1905), in *The Question of Our Speech*, reprinted in Henry James, *The Future of the Novel*, ed. Leon Edel (New York: Vintage, 1956), pp. 118, 102.

4 Henry James, *Notes on Novelists* (New York: Scribners, 1914), p. 132.

5 *Notes on Novelists*, p. 141.

6 Henry James, *The American* (New York: Scribners, 1907), p. xvi. I shall as much as possible refer to James's novels in the New York Edition (1907–1909) and give page references in parentheses in the text. When quoting from works not included in the New York Edition, or from the original (unrevised) versions, I shall give the reference in a footnote.

7 Jacques Barzun, "Henry James, Melodramatist," in *The Question of Henry James*, ed. F. W. Dupee (New York: Holt, 1945), pp. 255–56.

8   Leo B. Levy, *Versions of Melodrama: A Study of the Fiction and Drama of Henry James, 1865–1897* (Berkeley and Los Angeles: University of California Press, 1957), pp. 3, 30, 116.

9   "Indirect presentation": see Preface to *The Wings of the Dove*, I:xxii.

10 *The American*, in the text of 1881 (reprint ed., New York: Signet Classics, 1963), p. 278.

11 This has affinities with "drawing-room melodrama" as defined by Maurice Willson Disher: "It is the kind of melodrama on which the curtain does not rise until deeds of blood and violence are past." *Melodrama: Plots That Thrilled* (London: Rockcliff, 1954), p. 80.

12 *Versions of Melodrama*, pp. 51–52.

13 Yvor Winters, "Maule's Well, or Henry James and the Relation of Morals to Manners," in *Maule's Curse* (Norfolk, Conn.: New Directions, 1938), p. 210.

14 See in particular James's principal essay on Flaubert, "Gustave Flaubert" (1902) in *Notes on Novelists*, pp. 65–108.

15 *The Notebooks of Henry James*, ed. F. O. Matthiessen and Kenneth Murdock (New York: Oxford University Press, 1947), p. 263. See also *The Complete Plays of Henry James*, ed. Leon Edel (Philadelphia and New York: Lippincott, 1949).

16 Henry James, "The Théâtre-Français," in *French Poets and Novelists* (Boston: Houghton Mifflin, 1878), p. 323.

17 James, *Notebooks*, p. 100.

18 See Henry James, "Notes on the Theatres: New York," in *The Scenic Art*, ed. Allan Wade (1948; reprint ed., New York: Hill and Wang, Dramabook, 1957), pp. 24–25.

19 Henry James, *Parisian Sketches*, ed. Leon Edel and Ilse Dusoir Lind (New York: New York University Press, 1957), p. 82.

20 See Edel, Foreword to *The Other House* in *The Complete Plays of Henry James*, pp. 677–79.

21 James, *Notebooks*, p. 348.

22 Levy, *Versions of Melodrama*, p. 96. Levy's subtle and useful argument is possibly flawed by an excessively loose definition of stage melodrama, which seems to include Scribe, Sardou, Dumas *fils*, and other writers of "well-made plays." This leads to a lack of precision in discussing what James learned from the technique of such master craftsmen, and his adherence to the ethos and imagination of melodrama. Both are important in James, and they are interrelated, but they are not identical.

23 On the theatre as the realm of signs for signs, see Petr Bogatyrev, "Les Signes du théâtre," *Poétique* 8 (1971), pp. 517–30.

24 James refers to what Nanda learns by the end of *The Awkward Age* as "horrors": *Notebooks*, p. 192.

25 Edmund Wilson, "The Ambiguity of Henry James," in *The Triple Thinkers* (New York: Harcourt, 1938), pp. 122–64.

26 See Dorothea Krook, *The Ordeal of Consciousness in Henry James* (Cambridge: Cambridge University Press, 1962), pp. 106–34.

27 Graham Greene, *The Lost Childhood and Other Essays* (London: Eyre and Spottiswoode, 1951), pp. 26, 38.

28 The letters are to Howard Sturgis (2 and 5 August 1914) and Rhoda Broughton (10 August 1914). See James, *Letters*, 2:384, 389.

29 Greene, *The Lost Childhood*, p. 44; J. A. Ward, *The Imagination of Disaster* (Lincoln: University of Nebraska Press, 1961), p. 13.

30 Winters, *Maule's Curse*, p. 175.

31 Henry James, *The Bostonians* (1886; reprint ed., Harmondsworth, Middlesex, England: Penguin, 1966), pp. 75–76.

32 Winters, *Maule's Curse*, p. 203.

33 Laurence Bedwell Holland, *The Expense of Vision* (Princeton: Princeton University Press, 1964), p. 76. Holland has in mind the mannerist distortion of forms in James, a distortion that results from expressionism.

34 F. R. Leavis, *The Great Tradition* (1948; reprint ed., New York: New York University Press, 1963), p. 11.

35 See James Guetti, *The Limits of Metaphor* (Ithaca: Cornell University Press, 1967). See also Tzvetan Todorov's interesting treatment of the void of meaning as structuring principle in many of James's stories, in "Le Secret du récit," in *Poétique de la prose* (Paris: Seuil, 1971), pp. 151–85. The image of the abyss has also been discussed by Jean Kimball, "The Abyss and *The Wings of the Dove*," *Nineteenth-Century Fiction* 10 (March 1956), pp. 281–300, but with little attention to its nature or its status in the narrative.

36 See Claude Lévi-Strauss, *La Pensée sauvage* (Paris: Plon, 1962), p. 26 ff.

37 Henry James, *The Sacred Fount* (1901; reprint ed., New York: Grove Press, 1953), p. 66.

38 "Going behind": Preface to *The Awkward Age*, p. xvii; "behind the face of the subject": Preface to *The Wings of the Dove*, 1:xi.

39 James, *Notebooks*, p. 172. R. P. Blackmur comments that Kate, according to the Notebook sketch, "was meant originally to be the villainess in a standard social melodrama, and she never entirely loses that role." See "The Loose and Baggy Monsters of Henry James," in *The Lion and the Honeycomb* (New York: Harcourt Brace, 1955), p. 277.

40 James, *Notebooks*, p. 169.

41 Henry James, *Notes of a Son and Brother* (New York: Scribners, 1914), p. 515.

42 In his early essay on Balzac, James suggests that the faculty Balzac regarded most highly was "dissimulation" and "duplicity." See "Honoré de Balzac," in *French Poets and Novelists*, p. 91.

43 One might adduce here James's comment about his sister Alice's chronic invalid condition: he writes to William James that Alice's "disastrous, her tragic health was in a manner the only solution for her of the practical problem of life." (*Letters*, I, 215) The statement implies that illness, in life as in melodrama, can be a stance toward life, sign of the assumption of a certain role in life's drama.

44 James, *Notebooks*, p. 321.

45 See Jacques Lacan, "Le Séminaire sur la Lettre volée," in *Ecrits* (Paris: Seuil, 1966), pp. 36–39.

46 See F. W. Dupee, *Henry James* (1951; 2nd ed., reprint, Garden City, N.Y.: Anchor Books, 1956), p. 216. Dupee quotes the concurring opinion of F. O. Matthiessen and Kenneth Murdock. See also Dorothea Krook on the "irruption of the divine order into the natural" through Milly's act of "loving kindness" (*The Ordeal of Consciousness in Henry James*, p. 229).

47 Barzun, "Henry James, Melodramatist," in *The Question of Henry James*, p. 272.

48 "Bliss and bale": the phrase is from the preface to *What Maisie Knew*, p. viii.

CONCLUSION

1   On "decentering" see Jacques Derrida, "La Structure, le signe, et le jeu," in *L'Ecriture et la différence* (Paris: Seuil, 1967); English version in *The Languages of Criticism and the Sciences of Man: The Structuralist Controversy*, ed. R. Macksey and E. Donato (Baltimore: Johns Hopkins University Press, 1970).

2   Wallace Stevens, "The Effects of Analogy," in *The Necessary Angel* (1951; reprint ed., New York: Vintage Books, n.d.), p. 115.

3   Maurice Blanchot, "L'Inconvenance majeure," in Sade, *Français encore un effort si vous voulez être républicains*, Collection Libertés (Paris: J.-J. Pauvert, 1965), p. 40.

4   See Heilman, *Tragedy and Melodrama*, chap. 1. See also James L. Smith's distinction between melodrama of "triumph" and melodrama of "defeat," in *Melodrama*.

5   My thinking about the modern politics of personality has been stimulated by the study by Richard Sennett, *The Fall of Public Man*, to be published by Alfred A. Knopf in 1976.

6   Benjamin, "The Storyteller," *Illuminations*, p. 107.

Index